Religion and Genocide

Religion and Genocide: Changing the Conversation is a cutting-edge introduction to the complex and controversial relationship between religion and genocide. This book aims to widen the reader's understanding of religion and those who practice it, the nexus of religion and violence, and those who legitimate their violence by framing it in religious terms by looking at notions of holy wars, religious wars, and genocide and the practitioners of such.

This book delves into our current thinking of ourselves as biological entities, our relationship to genocide, and the impact of geography (including climate change) and diseases on our humanity and our ability to commit genocide. Tying together all these seemingly disparate threads, this text concludes with the significant and still largely unanswered question: "Where do we go from here?".

Highlighting the complex relationship between religion and genocide, this is an essential read for students and academics studying religion and violence, Judaism, Judaic studies, and holocaust and genocide studies. *Religion and Genocide* will also be of interest to researchers in related subjects such as history, politics, sociology, and anthropology.

Steven Leonard Jacobs is Professor of Religious Studies and Emeritus Aaron Aronov Chair of Judaic Studies at The University of Alabama, USA.

Religion and Genocide

Changing the Conversation

Steven Leonard Jacobs

LONDON AND NEW YORK

Cover image: Getty Images

First published 2023
by Routledge
4 Park Square, Milton Park, Abingdon, Oxon OX14 4RN

and by Routledge
605 Third Avenue, New York, NY 10158

Routledge is an imprint of the Taylor & Francis Group, an informa business

© 2023 Steven Leonard Jacobs

The right of Steven Leonard Jacobs to be identified as author of this work has been asserted in accordance with sections 77 and 78 of the Copyright, Designs and Patents Act 1988.

All rights reserved. No part of this book may be reprinted or reproduced or utilised in any form or by any electronic, mechanical, or other means, now known or hereafter invented, including photocopying and recording, or in any information storage or retrieval system, without permission in writing from the publishers.

Trademark notice: Product or corporate names may be trademarks or registered trademarks, and are used only for identification and explanation without intent to infringe.

British Library Cataloguing-in-Publication Data
A catalogue record for this book is available from the British Library

ISBN: 978-0-367-76886-7 (hbk)
ISBN: 978-0-367-76885-0 (pbk)
ISBN: 978-1-003-16879-9 (ebk)

DOI: 10.4324/9781003168799

Typeset in Bembo
by codeMantra

Contents

List of Charts	vii
Acknowledgments	ix
1 Introduction: Why This Book?	1
2 What Is This Thing Called "Religion"?	12
3 Who Are These Human Beings Who *Do* Religion—the Rise of Religion?	29
4 What about Religion and Violence?	36
5 What Is This Thing Called "Genocide"?	46
6 Who Are These Human Beings Who *Do* Genocide—the Perpetrators?	77
7 "Holy" Wars and "Religious" Wars: Is There a Connection?	96
8 Antisemitism as Genocide	109
9 Why Should Biology Matter?	117
10 Why Geography, Climate Change, and Disease Matter	131

11 Changing the Conversation: What Is to Be Done?   147

12 Conclusion
    Bringing It All Together: Religion, Violence, and Genocide   171

    Bibliography   175
    *Appendix: Convention on the Prevention and Punishment
    of the Crime of Genocide*   193
    About the Author   199
    Index   201

Charts

1	"Geno-cides"	47
2	A summary of Stanton's ten stages of genocide (for a fuller presentation of Stanton's model, see https://www.genocidewatch.com/tenstages)	67
3	A model of how ordinary people commit genocide and mass killing	90
4	Just War Theory	100
5	"The Crusades"	101

Acknowledgments

To the reviewers whose critically positive comments and recommendations have strengthened this work.

To Professor Gregory Stanton, president, and founder of www.genocide-watch.org for the inclusion of his "10 Stages of Genocide" in Chapter 5.

To my students over the years in my advanced undergraduate seminar "Religion and Genocide" at The University of Alabama who have not only made me a better teacher and professor but also whose insights and questions have continually sharpened by own thinking vis-a-vis the nexus between religion and genocide.

To the unnamed copyeditor whose careful editing and eye for detail has significantly enriched this text and made it a better overall book.

To my family—my wife Louanne; our children Hannah, Naomi, and Shea; their spouses Adam, Chris, and Suzanne; and our grandchildren Laun, Jacob, Greer, Drew, Liam, Molly, and Dorothy—who have allowed me to wade into the dark side of humanity but who have always brought me back into the light.

Chapter 1

Introduction
Why This Book?

"Of making many books there is no end, and much study wearies the body". So wrote the unknown author of Ecclesiastes—traditionally thought by religious Jews and Christians to have been King Solomon in his old age—in the Hebrew Bible/Old Testament (12:12; NIV). Perhaps the same might be said today of the veritable flood of texts now regularly appearing, addressing the concept of genocide in the aftermath of Raphael Lemkin (1900–1945) giving voice to the term in Chapter 9 of his 1944 magnum opus *Axis Rule in Occupied Europe: Laws of Occupation, Analysis of Government, Proposals for Redress*. In that all-too-brief chapter titled "Genocide—A New Term and New Conception for Destruction of Nations", pages 79–95 out of 644 pages, he wrote:

> New conceptions require new terms. By "genocide" we mean the destruction of a nation or of an ethnic group. This new word, coined by the author to denote an old practice in its modern development, is made from the ancient Greek word *genos* (race, tribe) and the Latin *cide* (killing), thus corresponding in its formation to such words as tyrannicide, homicide, infanticide, etc. Generally speaking, genocide does not necessarily mean the immediate destruction of a nation, except when accomplished by mass killings of all members of a nation. It is intended rather to signify a coordinated plan of different actions aiming at the destruction of essential foundations of the life of national groups, with the aim of annihilating the groups themselves. The objectives of such a plan would be disintegration of the political and social institutions, of culture, language, national feelings, religion, and the economic existence of national groups, and the destruction of the personal security, liberty, health, dignity, and even the lives of the individuals belonging to such groups. Genocide is directed against the national group as an entity, and the actions involved are directed against individuals, not in their individual capacity, but as members of the national group.
> (79; emphasis added)[1]

Here, initially at least, his concern appears to be the fate of either national or ethnic groups. However, in Section II—"Techniques of Genocide in Various Fields", he further briefly describes the following: political, social, cultural, economic, biological, physical (racial discrimination in feeding, endangering of health, mass killing), *religious*, and *moral*. Regarding the religious aspects of genocide, he further writes but does not further elaborate beyond the specific cases of both Luxemburg and Poland:

> In Luxemburg, where the population is predominantly Catholic and religion plays an important role in national life, especially in the field of education, the occupant has tried to disrupt these national and religious influences. Children over fourteen years of age were permitted by legislation to renounce their religious affiliations, for the occupant was eager to enroll such children exclusively in pro-Nazi youth organizations. Moreover, in order to protect such children from public criticism, another law was issued at the same time imposing penalties ranging up to 15,000 Reichsmarks for any publication of names or any general announcement as to resignations from religious congregations. Likewise, in Poland, through the systematic pillage and destruction of church property and persecution of the clergy, the German occupying authorities have sought to destroy the religious leadership of the Polish nation.
>
> (89)

Under his inspired and obsessive initial leadership, the United Nations would, ultimately, pass the "Convention on the Prevention and Punishment of the Crime of Genocide" in December of 1948, ratified into international law three years later, 1951, of which he was the preliminary and primary drafter of the "Genocide Convention" as it has come to be called, and defined the victim groups in Article 2 as follows:

> In the present Convention, genocide means any of the following acts committed with intent to destroy, in whole or in part, a national, ethnical, racial or *religious* group, as such: (a) Killing members of the group; (b) Causing serious bodily or mental harm to members of the group; (c) Deliberately inflicting on the group conditions of life calculated to bring about its physical destruction in whole or in part^2; (d) Imposing measures intended to prevent births within the group; (e) Forcibly transferring children of the group to another group.
>
> (Emphasis added)

Thus, religious groups, however defined and understood though unclear, were evidently part of Lemkin's and others' original thinking as potential genocidal victim groups even if not their primary focus. Yet if one were to quantitatively assess this increasingly vast and ever-growing literature, the overwhelming bulk of those authors—scholars, journalists, popularizers—would be historians, political scientists, psychologists, sociologists, and legalists whose overriding concerns would be the history of various genocides and the groups impacted (sometimes, but not always, addressing religious groups); the mindsets of those who perpetrate such acts—the *genocidaires*—the group identities of both perpetrators and victims focusing on ethnic and other seemingly obvious discriminations and distinctions (again, not always including religious groups); the expanding text of the Genocide Convention and introducing both international and nation-state laws and statutes; and the like. Far less attention has been paid to religious groups of both perpetrators and victims, especially their religious upbringings and the role such may very well have played in their present encounters, coupled with the concomitant reality that scholars of religion are few and far between in the overall community of those addressing genocide.

And therein lies the rub! Why this omission of both the literature vis-à-vis the religion and religiosity of both victims and perpetrators and what role, purpose, function, religion itself may have played, if any, in the unfolding of these horrors? Why have religious studies scholars, who themselves have already built up their own vast literature addressing the nexus between religion and violence—a topic with which I have long been interested and concerned, and addressed in a later chapter—been so seemingly reluctant to confront this ultimate expression of violence? And, even more broadly, does religion itself in its very construction, both institutionally/organizationally and intellectually/theologically/philosophically, bear any responsibility whatsoever as a *participating factor* in genocide? These questions and others constitute the raison d'etre of this text and are explored forthwith.

Well-known psychologist, genocide scholar, and executive director of the Institute on the Holocaust and Genocide in Jerusalem, Israel Charny (b. 1931) suggests a possible answer to these difficult questions:

> A second section [of the 1994 work *The Widening Circle of Genocide*[3]] was devoted to religion and genocide by Leonard Glick. There is quite a story to be told about how many years it took before we succeeded in getting this important open treatment of the subject of religion as both setting the expressed moral direction of Thou Shalt Not Kill[4], while in itself being responsible for so many genocidal killings over the centuries. Before Leonard Glick's fine contribution, there had been several well-known scholars in the field of religion who had agreed to do the project and then dropped it at a very late stage, almost without explanation. To me, it seemed that what happened was that they were unable to tell the truth about the religious establishment with which they were variously connected.[5]

Responding to Charny's comments in the same Introduction to *Confronting Genocide*, I wrote:

> If truth be told, the reason for such difficulty is far more significant than that of "religious discomfort". Those whose field is religious studies come late to the study of genocide, and, thus, that which is commonly identified in the popular mind as "religion" is all-too-often overlooked as an important factor in contributing to either the implementation and perpetuation of genocide, or as a foundational underpinning and rationalization for such collective acts...
>
> Then, too, many of those who study religion, like many of their colleagues in the academy, are themselves distanced from parochial religious commitments or heretofore have not chosen to address this intersection of religion and genocide.[6]

*

The impetus for this text then, if you will, is an expansion of and a far fuller exploration of an earlier article I published in the *Journal of Hate Studies* titled "Genocidal Religion" in 2010, and originally an earlier paper presented at the International Conference on Hate at Gonzaga University, Spokane, WA.[7] In that 2010 piece, after first defining both "religion" and "genocide", I attempted to draw what I now even more firmly believe are the *parallels* between these two social constructs.[8]

Summarily, then, as "operating definitions", I continue to define "religion" as "a system of communal beliefs and practices encouraging moral/ethical and ritual/ceremonial behaviors for the betterment of both the individual and the community and addressing questions of profound meaning and possibly including those of deity or deities". And "genocide" as "a systematic physical and/or cultural destruction *including religion* of a victim group or groups in war or peace, defined as such by a perpetrator group or groups and sanctioned by the state". Expanding and broadening these definitions are the substance of Chapters 2 and 5, while their practitioners are the substance of Chapters 3 and 6. Common to both definitions as further explained below are (1) systematization, (2) behaviors, (3) definitions, and (4) identities.

Before doing so, however, as I have suggested elsewhere, are four *precipitating factors* common to all religious communities that are, in and of themselves, all-too-easily adapted by and expanded upon and reformulated/modified, if necessary, by genocidal perpetrator communities as well: (1) tribalism, (2) religious exclusivism, (3) privileged access to the divine, and (4) particularistic and parochial readings of sacred texts.

1 **Tribalism**: All groups, religious and other, tend at times to function as if the world itself was conceived as a binary place—"us versus them"—and

too often coupled with a negative view of that same other—the "them"—and thus requiring some form of balancing act to bring the world back into some kind of equilibrium, harmony, or homeostasis. Added to that understanding is a self-perceived sense of group *superiority* and a concomitant sense of the *inferiority* of the other group, necessitating, if the group holds or desires to hold the reins of power, action on its behalf. Some actions are relatively benign, for example, convening a so-called "prayer circle" to "right the wrongs" of the larger secular nation-state and its governing officials. Others are far more ominous as practiced by those in power: diminishing minorities of whatever legal status they possess, depriving them of economic sources of survival, rounding up and ghettoizing members of a minority group as defined by the majority, and/or once collected, setting up and implementing structures of ghettoization, extermination and/or annihilation.

2 **Exclusivism**: Further expanding upon this concept of tribalism is this idea of exclusivism. All groups, sociologically speaking, present themselves to present and future adherents as special, privileged, unique, and worthy of commitment. Why else to either retain or join such a group if there is no discernible difference between it and others that appear at first glance to be of similar composition? Such a commitment to exclusivism requires continuous affirmation by both leaders and followers of the group's distinctive identity and ofttimes accompanied by denigration of other groups, from verbal abuse to physical destruction of others' institutions, organizations, and agencies.

3 **Privileged Access to the Divine**: Religious groups, through whatever ritual behaviors they have evolved over the course of their histories, undergirded by whatever sacred texts they affirm, understand themselves as uniquely privileged to accessibility to their God or gods while denying similar access to other groups (e.g., "No one goes to the Father, *except through me*", NT, John 14:6). And that understanding as well is likewise accompanied by notions of superiority versus inferiority. Thus,

> *their* prayers, *their* rituals, *their* sacred texts, *their* moral-ethical behaviors are the sanctified superior ways in which to affirm their relationship to God or gods, and, while others outside their communities may also have opportunities to engage the divine, theirs is a poorer or lesser second.[9]

4 **Particularistic and Parochial Readings of Sacred Texts**: "All religious traditions have sacred texts by which they connect themselves to their God or gods, connect themselves to each other, disconnect themselves from others, and provide the foundational bases, both for their ritual-ceremonial and their moral-ethical behaviors".[10] Such perceived "correct" readings, interpretations, and understandings of those texts likewise bespeak both an exclusivity of both texts and access to the divine

and a superiority of that same understanding. (The most obvious example would be a 2,000-year history of Jewish failures to see in their own Hebrew Bible/Old Testament the very real presence of the Christ in those same texts and ofttimes viewed as hardhearted reluctance or blindness.)

> Thus, these four participating factors—(1) tribalism, (2) religious exclusivism, (3) privileged access to the divine, and (4) a particularistic and parochial reading of sacred texts—by their very nature—contain within themselves seeds of genocidal potentiality all too easily and readily adaptable to the work of genocide by those who would trade upon them and use them for the extermination and annihilation of others.[11]

★

Thus, as I understand it, "religion" is:

1. A **system**, that is, an organized progression/evolution of thoughts and behaviors that continue to "make sense" on intellectual, emotional, physical, and spiritual levels to their adherents, no matter how much or little they are understood by outsiders.
2. A **communal multi-generational enterprise** for its very survival, and, therefore, characterized quite easily as either "historical" (i.e., that which has survived the lives of its founder or founders) or "new" (i.e., that whose founder or founders are still alive).
3. A **set of behaviors**—moral/ethical and ritual/ceremonial—consists of a series of guidelines in three areas: (a) how the members are to behave toward each other (almost always positively); (b) how the members are to behave toward those who are not (or not) yet members of the community (usually a mix of positive and negative); and (c) how the members are to behave toward their God or gods, and, if appropriate, toward other heavenly entities (almost always positive), not to mention how they are also to behave toward other non-group members (almost always negative).
4. An **attempt to make meaningful sense** of the human journey with all its twists and turns, peaks and valleys, and joys and sorrows.
5. A **system of communications** usually achieved through authoritative spokespersons—more often males than females—understood to have a much closer relationship to the divine than most of the membership.

Equally so, therefore:

1. Genocides are **systematic behaviors**, rational and organized, the result of careful planning to achieve specific ends and that fully make sense to their perpetrators, though often far less so to their victims.

2 Genocides are not only the **physical destruction**—murder—of all or some of the members of a victim group; they are, concomitantly, **the destruction of the cultural output** of the group as well—that is, everything the group has created by and through which it identifies itself to itself and by which others also identify its members.[12]
3 Central to genocidal behaviors, then, is the necessity of **defining** the victim group, that is, "Who is the enemy who is to be destroyed?", as well as who constitutes members of the "in-group" who will be tasked with this genocidal mandate.
4 Genocides are most often **state-sanctioned exercises**, that is, to achieve their desired ends, they go through a process of conversation by all those responsible for such decision-making and decision-implementing, sometimes secretive sometimes not, before they can be carried out.

In addition to these various factors, and without too much difficulty in extrapolating their commonalities, there are certain what I have chosen to call *core elements* usually associated with religions, but equally applicable to genocidal perpetrator groups as well. These now include, in addition to those already addressed: (1) community, (2) doctrine & texts, (3) ethics, (4) myths, (5) relevance, (6) rituals, (7) sacrality, and (8) symbolization.

1 **Community**: Both religionists and *genocidaires* strive to re-affirm to those who are already their members and equally strive to convince others with whom they choose to identify and who choose to identify with them that, together, they constitute *a community of like-minded persons*, and others—outside their circle for whatever are perceived to be valid reasons (racial, religious, ethnic, linguistic, intellectual, economic, etc.)—are objects of derision, and, taken to extreme, objects of *necessary* violence.
2 **Doctrines & Texts**: Central to both *religionists* and *genocidaires* are texts, both those written by their present leaders to inspire their followers and/or those sources of inspiration written prior to their group's founding to provide a certain historical and contemporary legitimacy if needed. As both groups develop, they expand their literature to include other texts that often tend to solidify which behaviors are permitted and which are not.
3 **Ethics**: Within their own groups, both religionists and *genocidaires* develop *behavioral standards* that tend to segregate their communities, bolster their visions and understandings, and internalize their own senses of superiority, while, equally, all-too-often, denigrating the behaviors of those outside their groups as immoral, unethical, corruptible, and, worst of all, threatening to the very society and/or nation-state wherein they reside, or, taken to conclusion, assaulting the very civilization of which they see themselves as the *only* hope for salvation, either religious *or* secular. Peter Haas' 1988 book *Morality After Auschwitz: The Radical Challenge of the Nazi Ethic* (Philadelphia: Fortress Press), for example, rightly

reminds us that the Nazis operated within an internal system of ethical norms and behaviors, e.g., "good" residing within the will of *Der Führer*; evil existing as contrary to that will, but ones which we consistently reject today as uncontestably immoral. His provocative insight is equally applicable to other cases and instances of genocide.

4 **Myths**: In the study of religion, myths are of two primary types: (a) stories told about God, gods, and/or ancillary divine beings and/or human heroes; and (b) stories told about the origins of the group. Both are regarded as "true" for the group and serve to bolster their own understandings of themselves and their group, regardless of how such stories are perceived by others, and usually disregarded and discarded as potentially irrelevant by so-called outsiders and therefore potentially subject to seriously negative and defamatory critique. *Genocidaires* likewise tell stories about their own group's founding and superiority—sometimes affirmed as divinely-inspired—recipients of a rich history even if presently and momentarily at a low point, and the overarching need to "right the wrongs" presently inflicted by often supposedly lesser and inferior groups and thus return the group to its former greatness and their leaders to positions of power.

5 **Relevance**: Both religious and perpetrator communities share a common desire to "make sense" of the world, to explain to their adherents causes for celebratory success and, even more importantly, how their failures were caused by others who operated insidiously, underhandedly, and dishonestly. The staying power of those in leadership is, thus, directly contingent on their continuing ability to explain the past, present, and future to those who are their members and potential members. The most infamous, but certainly not the only example of perverse relevance was the *Dolchstoßlegende*, the stab-in-the-back myth, or notion, widely believed in right-wing circles in Germany after 1918, that the German Army did *not* lose World War I on the battlefield, but was, instead, betrayed by the civilians on the home front, especially the Republicans, but, more importantly, the Jews, who overthrew the monarchy in the German Revolution of 1918–1919.

6 **Rituals**: Outside of the moral/ethical realm, the other core set of behaviors in which religious communities engage is rituals, that is, repetitive behaviors which draw their adherents, or so they believe, closer to their God or gods and to each other. Perpetrator communities, whether they are formal military groups or militia groups and/or the like, also engage in such ongoing rituals regularly (e.g., the "Horst Wessel" Lied of the Nazis; the hierarchical system of officers and enlisted leaders and followers, and their "correct" behaviors in each other's presence, etc.). All such repetitive behaviors by both groups serve to further strengthen affiliation and commitment. In some instances, such practices tend to be *secretive*, away from the "prying eyes" of outsiders, or expressed in coded languages known only to the in-group after initiating rituals, which bring welcomed outsiders into the groups.

7 **Sacrality**: The very notion of the sacred is part and parcel of what German theologian, philosopher, and comparative religionist Rudolf Otto (1869–1937) characterized as *das Heilige* ("The Holy"), that sense of awe and awesomeness, a profound emotional experience and which he termed the "numinous". It is this very sense of the emotionality of this awesomeness, which is foundational to both religious groups and perpetrator groups—one is part of something far greater than oneself—which inspires ongoing commitment, wonder, mystery, excitement, and the willingness to engage in behaviors, which, under other or ordinary circumstances, would be neither conceivable nor doable. So-called religious wars and acts of genocide fall into this category.

8 **Symbolization**: Scholars of religion have long recognized the *power* of the symbol used to mobilize communities of faith; scholars of political science have long recognized the *power* of nation-state symbols to mobilize their citizenry, especially their militaries. Genocidaires, too, have adopted and appropriated symbols positively in the formation of their own groups, and negatively in their depictions of their enemies through whatever media are at hand—TV, radio, newspapers, the Internet, and now Facebook and/or Twitter, Instagram, and other social media. Additionally, the *wearing* of such symbols—Crucifix, Magen David, various medallions and/or military patches and insignias, including flags—ultimately serves to strengthen commitment and bind adherents to their communities for good or evil.

To summarize, historically and contemporarily, both communities—religious and perpetrator—in their own evolving trajectories of development as humanly crafted constructions drawn upon these same flawed human systems out of our basic, biological need for socialization. In their development over time, religious communities have engaged in the very same violent and self-justified behaviors as genocidal perpetrator communities. Having thus laid out these somewhat paralleling and uneven intersections, even recognizing their inherent uncomfortability in many quarters of human endeavor, this relatively newer perspective further opens doors to newer and different directions in genocide research, and further points to one equally uncomfortable initial conclusion: *That "religion" may well very be a* participating factor *in all genocides, both historical and contemporary, one further legitimating source upon which perpetrators of genocide have drawn in the past, are drawing upon in the present, and may very well do so in the future.*[13]

*

Finally, I conclude this introductory chapter not solely with this focus on the involvement of religions in the destructive ways of genocide as an underexamined factor, but also with the ever-present question of what, therefore, can be done to break the world cycle of genocidal violence while fully acknowledging and addressing the upside of religion, religious communities, and religious leaderships to bring comfort, healing, and reconciliation to victim groups, consistent with their own historic missions and involving such persons to view the horizon as far more expansively than the next discovered mass gravesite or the next confrontation between the implementing power of those who have it and those who do not.

Theoretical perspectives, including this one, are important as are historical and contemporary contexts. Genocides are collective human tragedies whose aftereffects can consume generations for years to come, keeping alive memories of both events and victims. The roles of scholars, journalists, researchers, and popularizers are significant and important as well. The work of criminal and governmental investigators and the various nation-state judicial systems, including those now present in the aftermath of World War II and the International Military Tribunal at Nuremberg in 1945 (specifically the International Criminal Court [ICC], International Criminal Tribunal for Rwanda [ICTR], International Criminal Tribunal for [the former] Yugoslavia [ICTY], and others) takes all of that hard, difficult, and painful work and translates into a very real world with very real actions and consequences.

Thus, if religion is part of the problem of genocide, then it is equally and likewise part of the solution, most especially of future genocides, and even part of the solution in bringing to rapid conclusion genocides already happening.

Notes

1 Washington: Carnegie Endowment for International Peace, 1944. All-too-often, however, his first footnote has been overlooked: "Another term could be used for the same idea, namely, *ethnocide*, consisting of the Greek word '*ethnos*' -nation- and the Latin word 'cide'". Significant as well is Lemkin's assessment that genocide is both (1) a "coordinated plan aimed at destruction" and the (2) "destruction of the political and social instructions", thus enlarging his—and our—understanding beyond that of physical death only.

2 One can thus interpret this understanding to mean that of the cultural production of a given group, including religion as well, that is the "lifeblood" of the group.

3 Israel Charny, ed. *The Widening Circle of Genocide: A Critical Bibliographical Review* (New Brunswick and London: Transaction Publishers, 1994).

4 A more correct understanding of the original Hebrew would be "Thou Shalt Not Murder" and thus addressing unsanctioned life-taking, by the nation-state and/or nongovernmental groups.

5 Cited in my Introduction, "Genocide in the Name of God: Thoughts on Religion and Genocide" (2009), *Confronting Genocide: Judaism, Christianity, Islam* (Lanham: Lexington Books), ix. Leonard Glick's essay "Religion and Genocide" is also republished there, pages 95–118.

6 Jacobs, *Confronting Genocide: Judaism, Christianity, Islam* (Lanham: Lexington Books, 2009), ix & x.

7 Steven Leonard Jacobs (2010), "Genocidal Religion", *Journal of Hate Studies*, 9(1): 221–235.
   Even earlier, in that same journal in 2005, I published "The Last Uncomfortable 'Religious' Question: Monotheistic Exclusivism and Textual Superiority in Judaism, Christianity, and Islam as Sources of Hate and Genocide", 4(1): 133–143.
8 Since then, I have also contributed two forthcoming pieces relevant here: (2022) "Holy Wars, Judaism, Violence, and Genocide: An Unholy Quadrinity" to Stephen Smith and Sara Brown, eds., *Routledge Handbook of Religion, Mass Atrocity, and Genocide* (New York and London: Routledge), 37–43; and "The Religion Genocide Nexus" to Ben Kiernan, Tracy Lemos, and Tristan Taylor, eds., *The Cambridge World History of Genocide* (Cambridge: Cambridge University Press), forthcoming.
9 Steven Leonard Jacobs, "Genocidal Religion", 227.
10 Ibid., 228.
11 Ibid., 229.
12 While the notion of "cultural genocide", as such, does not appear in the UN Genocide Convention, and remains somewhat controversial among scholars, Lemkin himself, as early as 1933 in his failed attempt to encourage such a discussion at a legal conference in Madrid, Spain, which he himself was prevented from attending, saw them of a piece, drawing a distinction between "barbarism" (the destruction of a people) and "vandalism" (the destruction of a people's culture).
13 My use of this term "participating factor" is an attempt to arrive at a somewhat neutral term with no implication whatsoever or rank ordering or evaluative judgment that religion is (or is not) a primary, secondary, or even tertiary factor in the perpetration of genocide, but one—along with historical, social, economic, political, military, psychological, social, and sociological factors—which has informed and shaped the various perpetrator groups and enabled them to accomplish whatever goals they themselves have deemed central to realizing their destructive missions.

Chapter 2

What Is This Thing Called "Religion"?

The academic study of religion, requiring dispassionate objectivity, is a product of and consequence of the European Enlightenment of the 17th through the 19th centuries and has itself gone through several iterations in the ongoing attempt of scholars and others—journalists and researchers, for example—to understand this sociocultural construct we call "religion", its different manifestations, and the various components of its own self-presentation. Thus, foundational to the argument of the nexus between religion and genocide, this chapter lays out, however briefly, what religion is, how it manifests itself, as well as its constituent parts. Crucial to this examination becomes the necessary willingness to examine not only its positivities but its negativities as well—the so-called "dark side" of religion. As anthropologist Henry Munson in his review article vis-à-vis several books on "Religion and violence" writes:

> Religion kills. Throughout human history, people have killed in the name of their gods. Emile Durkheim rightly stressed that religion serves to strengthen the bonds of solidarity among those who worship the same god, in the same way. But the flip side of this solidarity is enmity towards those who worship other gods or worship the same god differently. Religious boundaries separate the pure and virtuous 'us' from the impure and evil 'them'. We who worship our god are truly human. The Other, who worships other gods, or the same god differently, is less than human and thus killable. Yet while the hostility towards the Other is found in most sacred scriptures has often had lethal consequences, one cannot assume that these texts dictate the actual behavior of believers for all time. *Scriptures are constantly being reinterpreted as historical circumstances change.* And some conflicts in which sacred texts get involved may have secular causes.[1]

Be that as it may, the purpose of this chapter is to "set the stage" by introducing to those concerned about genocide and its relationship to religion, what religion is, what constitutes its definition(s), and what constitutes its so-called "core elements". In turn, this summary of what has been studied and addressed, primarily within the last two hundred years of scholarship, then turns, in the next chapter, to further our understanding of those persons and groups who *do* religion, all the while determining whether there are similarities and commonalities vis-à-vis genocide and those who *do* genocide.

First off, though here, too, there is no common consensus or agreement as to the etymological origins of the word itself: ancient Latin possesses three words: *religio*—restraint; *relegere*—to repeat or read again (i.e., ritual behaviors as repetitive exercises?); and *religionem*—to show respect for that which is regarded as sacred, reverence for the gods, moral obligation, including the bond between humanity and the gods, and/or sanctity. Old French, however, has the word *religion*, referencing a "religious community". Quite possibly our modern thinkers, armed with their understandings of ancient languages, combined all of these insights into the late creation of the word "religion". The jury is still out.

Before, however, illustrating by way of examples various definitions of "religion" that have been proffered over time, a certain caveat is required vis-à-vis what we mean when we use this word definition itself. W. Richard Comstock, in an article "Toward Open Definitions of Religion" in the *Journal of the American Academy of Religion* (JAAR) makes the following substantive points, and, in so doing, presents a compelling case that such definitions are far richer when they open doors to more expansive thinking rather than attempting to understand a given entity by, somehow, ascertaining its "essence", itself a dubious enterprise.[2] Comstock himself is likewise fully aware that there is no one universally accepted definition or understanding of what we mean when we use the word "religion".

> A definition is nothing more than a brief text initiating an open set of interconnected texts providing the linguistic context through which the sense of the word to be defined receives specification and clarification.
>
> (509)

> Definitions always begin in the middle of things. They not only initiate a succession of further texts, but they are also themselves the products of texts that have preceded and initiated them. Every definition is not only a signifier of what follows, but also the signified of what has preceded.
>
> (510)

Thus, at least for Comstock, definitional brevity is important as is taking into consideration others who, in the past, have attempted the same resolution.

Furthermore, and more importantly:

> An open definition is a process of continuous interrogation rather than a definitive answer provided in advance of the empirical investigation that it initiates. It is a point of departure, not a conclusion. Each text leads to other texts where other aspects of religion besides that indicated by the initiating definition are encountered.
>
> (510)

> The function of open definitions of religion is to produce a rich flow of metonymic [a naming figure of speech for another thing] connections between texts. In doing so, definitions are specific enough to establish a definite field of discourse that is the province of religious studies. It is, to be sure, a territory without strict boundaries, but that is a strength rather than a weakness…An open definition resolves the issue by insisting that there are no absolute limits to the texts that a scholar will use in the process of clarification initiated by his [sic] proposal.
>
> (512–513)

Hence, Comstock, and those others who would agree with him, challenges us as readers and thinkers *not* to regard any such definitions as definitive ("closed") but, rather, as starting points on a quest for clarification of the very thing we are attempting to examine ("open").

With that rethought perspective in mind, we turn to various definitions of "religion", which have become part of the very arsenal of scholars and other writers who have attempted to examine this very thing, which in popular and common conversation is apparently far more easily understood by persons and groups outside the academy than within it. Furthermore, the definitions that follow fall into two categories: (1) *substantive* or *philosophical*, attempting to determine what a thing is by directing us to what are perceived to be its distinguishing characteristics; and (2) *functional* or *phenomenological*, looking at the impact(s) such a thing has on both the individual and the group, that is, what needs are met by the thing being defined.

Finally, it should also be noted that this "definitional exercise" is an initial reflection of a Euro-American bias, begun in the West to originally establish the superiority of a *Christian* religious orientation and worldview to other non-Western non-Christian groups. Over time, scholars have continued to challenge and reject that orientation while at the same time rejecting notions of so-called essential characteristics (i.e., "essentialism", a dubious category) in favor of comparative examinations of similarities and differences of groups, which they and others have labeled "religious",[3] all the while equally rejecting notions of superiority versus inferiority and evolutionary movements from so-called primitive religions to more complex religious systems.

Two of the most oft-quoted definitions of religion follow.

For the "father of sociology", Frenchman (David) Émile Durkheim (1858–1917), in his 1912 book *Les formes élementaires de la vie religieuse* (*The Elementary Forms of Religious Life*), religion was

> a unified system and practices relative to sacred things—things set apart—and beliefs and practices which unite in one single moral community called a Church [sic], all those who adhere to them.[4]

Durkheim also addressed the function of rituals as well, writing:

> The function of rituals, which are more fundamental than beliefs, is to provide occasions where individuals renew their commitment to community, reminding themselves in the most solemn fashion that they depend on the clan, just as it depends on them.
>
> Originally, there were no gods to command a ritual; there was only the ritual, which over time itself created the gods…Whatever the mood of society, the rites of religion will invariably reflect and reinforce it.
>
> *Religion's true purpose is not intellectual but social.* It serves as the carrier of social sentiments, providing symbols and rituals that enable people to express the deep emotions which anchor them to their community.[5]

For American anthropologist Clifford (James) Geertz [1926–2006], in his 1966 "Religion as a Cultural System" in Michael Banton's *Anthropological Approaches to the Study of Religion*,[6] religion was

> a system of symbols which acts to establish powerful, pervasive, and long-lasting moods and motivations in men [sic] by formulating conceptions of a general order of existence and clothing these conceptions with such an aura of factuality that the moods and motivations seem uniquely realistic.[7]

Importantly noted here by both is the lack of an appeal to the supernatural, God or gods.

Representative examples of various academic disciplinary investigators have also weighed in with their own definitions of religion, to wit:

- Robert N. Bellah (1927–2013), American sociologist:
    a set of symbolic forms and acts that relate man [sic] to the ultimate conditions of his [sic] existence.
- Frans de Waal (b. 1948), Dutch primatologist and ethologist:
    the shared reference for the supernatural, sacred, or spiritual as well as the symbols, rituals and worship that are associated with it.

- Ludwig Feuerbach (1804–1872), German philosopher and anthropologist:
    a dream in which our own conceptions and emotions appear to us as separate existences, being out of ourselves.
- James George Frazer (1854–1941), Scottish social anthropologist and folklorist:
    a propitiation or conciliation of powers superior to man [sic] which are believed to direct and control the course of Nature and of human life.
- William James (1842–1910), American philosopher and psychologist:
    the feelings, acts, and experiences of individual men [sic] in their solitude so far as they apprehend themselves to stand in relation to whatever they may consider the divine.
- Immanuel Kant (1724–1804), German philosopher:
    the recognition of all our duties as divine commands.
- Peter Mandaville, American academic, and Paul James (b. 1958), Australian academic:
    a relatively bounded system of beliefs, symbols, and practices that addresses the nature of existence, and in which communion with others and Otherness is *lived* as if it both takes in and spiritually transcends socially grounded ontologies of time, space, embodiment and knowing. [Emphasis in original.]
- Harriet Martineau (1802–1876), British social theorist and sociologist:
    the belief in an ever-living God, that is, in a Divine Mind and Will ruling the Universe and holding moral relations with mankind. [sic]
- Rudolf Otto (1869–1937), German theologian, philosopher, and comparative religionist:
    that which grows out of, and gives expression to, experiences of the holy in its various aspects.
- Friedrich Schleiermacher (1768–1834), German theologian, philosopher and biblical scholar:
    the feeling of absolute dependence; a sense and taste for the infinite.
- Max Lynn Stackhouse (1935–2016), American theologian and ethicist:
    a comprehensive worldview or 'metaphysical moral vision' that is accepted as binding because it is held to be basically true and just even if all dimensions of it cannot be either fully confirmed or refuted.
- Paul Tillich (1886–1965), German American Lutheran Christian philosopher and theologian:
    the state of being grasped by an ultimate concern, a concern which qualifies all other concerns as preliminary and which itself contains the answer to the question of the meaning of life.
- Antoine Vergote (1921–2013), Belgian Roman Catholic priest, theologian, philosopher, psychologist, and psychoanalyst:
    the entirety of the linguistic expressions, emotions, and actions and signs that refer to a supernatural being or supernatural beings.

Finally, here too my own definition of religion, cognizant of all of the above and attempting to incorporate these insights to a greater or lesser degree, falls within this overall discussion of both what it is and what it does:

> a system of communal beliefs and practices encouraging moral/ethical and ritual/ceremonial behaviors for the betterment of both the individual and the community and addressing questions of profound meaning and possibly including those of deity or deities.[8]

Nicholas Wade in *The Faith Instinct: How Religion Evolved & Why It Endures* defined religion somewhat problematically as

> a system of emotionally binding beliefs and practices in which a society implicitly negotiates [?] through prayer and sacrifice with supernatural agents, securing from them commands that compel members, through fear of divine punishment [?], to subordinate their interests to the common good.[9]

All of these and other attempts at definitional clarity as well are fully worthy of being unpacked and addressed. However, doing so would take us far afield of the focus of the nexus between religion and genocide, but is intended, instead, to illustrate the difficulties in defining religion but providing us nonetheless with a baseline framework, somewhat complex to be sure with which to understand its relationship to genocide.

Finally, two often-used American undergraduate textbooks—*America: Religions and Religion* authored by Catherine L. Albanese[10] and *Introduction to the Study of Religion*[11] authored by Nancy C. Ring, Kathleen S. Nash, Mary N. MacDonald, Fred Glennon, and Jennifer S. Glancy—translate and simplify such complexity and difficulty and attempt to provide undergraduates with a starting point for their own thinking and reflecting.

Albanese, Professor and Chair of the Department of Religious Studies at the University of California, Santa Barbara, writes that religion is

> a system of symbols (creed, code, cultus) by means of which people (a community) orient themselves in the world with reference to both ordinary and extraordinary powers, meanings, and values.

Ring et al., members of the Department of Religious Studies, Le Moyne College, Syracuse, NY, write:

> As an abstract noun, 'religion' signifies a human propensity to seek order and meaning within the mystery of life. By 'religion' or 'religions' we mean particular traditions...which in their constellations of ideas and

practices provide order and meaning for their followers, connecting them to what are considered the ultimate powers of life.

(2–3)

Religions, we could say, are systems of symbols in which the ideals, the aspirations, and the experiences of a community is represented…Religions express the human desire to understand and to engage the power of life…Religions suggest that this world of the senses, with all its unsatisfactory aspects, is not all that there is.

(13, 32–34)

Religion is a term that ordinary people use when they talk about gaining access to whatever it is they consider ultimately life-giving…'religion' is a term that scholars use when they study people's ideas and practices concerning whatever they consider life-giving.[12]

(58)

Religion is awareness expressed through symbols of relationship to, or participation in, the fundamental power of life…Religions are symbol systems which facilitate relationship to, or participation in, what the members understand to be the fundamental power of life.

(62)

Importantly, Daniel Pals—in his text *Seven Theories of Religion*[13]—addressing the work of E. B. Tylor (1832–1917); James Frazer, Sigmund Freud, Émile Durkheim, Karl Marx, Mircea Eliade (1907–1986); E. E. Evans-Pritchard (1902–1973); and Clifford Geertz—in his Conclusion posits five questions to be asked of any theory of religion. Replacing the word "theory" with the word "religion", his questions remain valid:

1 How does it [theory/religion] define the subject?
2 What type of theory [religion] is it?
3 What is the range of the theory [religion]?
4 What evidence does the theory [religion] appeal to?
5 What is the relationship between a theorist's [religionist's] personal religious belief (or disbelief) and the explanation he [sic] chooses to advance?[14]

No discussion, however, exploring the academic study of religion as it has developed over the last two hundred plus years would be complete without referencing its two foremost critics Sigmund Freud and Karl Marx, issues which arise out of its study, and what scholars have attempted to enumerate as the characteristics common to all religious communities but not necessarily equally a part of all of them, and the perspectives of the various disciplines which have weighed in on the study of religion—anthropology, history, philosophy, psychology, and sociology. In so doing, we will complete this all-too-brief survey of what we mean by this thing we call religion.

For Karl (Heinrich) Marx (1818–1883), German philosopher, economist, historian, sociologist, political theorist, journalist and socialist revolutionary—most well-known as the "father of socialism/communism" and the author of *Das Kapital: Critique of Political Economy* in 1867, and the second and third volumes published after his death by Fredrich Engels (1820–1895) in 1885 and 1894—religion was *not* central to his overall theory but understood rather as a tool used by an oppressive economic elite to both maintain its status and increase its wealth, coopting and corrupting the so-called "religious establishment" in the process while also attempting to maintain its own hold on the lower classes. Thus, his most well-known statement in this arena that religion was "the opium of the people"—a case of pure delusion and most definitely evil—remains fully consistent with his overall view of society as one of oppressors and oppressed and filtered through the lens of an economic reading of reality. As he expressed it:

> Religion is the sign of the oppressed creature...a protest against real suffering...it is the opium of the people...the illusory sun which revolves around man [sic] for as long as he [sic] does not evolve around himself [sic].

For Sigmund (Schlomo) Freud (1856–1939), Austrian neurologist and "father of psychoanalysis" (the so-called talking cure), religion was a delusional appeal to a neurotic, and at times infantile/child-like, desire to make sense of the world by appealing all-too-often to a father-figure (God) to make things right and meeting whatever psychological and emotional needs both the individual and the group have. Thus, his caustic comment, "religion is comparable to childhood neurosis":

> Religious teachings, therefore, are ideas whose main feature is that we dearly want them to be true...religious beliefs are in the end delusions... they cannot pass the test of the scientific method...the only way we have of reliably telling us what is true and what is not.
>
> Religion that persists into the present age of human history can only be a sign of illness; to begin to leave it behind is the first signal of health.[15]

Turning then to the problems or issues that almost immediately arise in the study of religion are the following: (1) *authority*: Whose viewpoint is to be understand and/or recognized as authorized and/or authentic—the "insider" who is a committed representative of a given religious community or the "outsider"—scholar, researcher, journalist, popularizer—who has done his/her homework and presents to a larger audience what he/she affirms is the very best description of which he/she is capable? A corollary question then becomes to whom is either presenter answerable—the community of the faithful and/or its leadership and followership or the scholarly and academic community who thus becomes the recipient of such endeavors? (2) *truth*: is a theological understanding and presentation of a given religious community to be understood as fully accurate by both its supporters and detractors? Or an objective (secular?) reading of that same material? To quote Stanley Fish *(b.* 1938), American literary theorist, legal scholar, author, and public intellectual:

> it is one thing to take religion as an object of study, and another to take religion seriously. To take religion seriously would be to regard it not as a phenomenon to be analyzed at arm's length, but as a candidate for truth. (2005)[16]

That same year, for example, the foremost American scholar of Judaic Studies, Jacob Neusner (1932–2016), in an opinion piece in the popular periodical *The National Jewish Post and Opinion* entitled "Faith and Scholarship" raised the following concerns:

1. How does the practitioner of a faith negotiate the conflicts between the affirmations of the tradition and the result of critical analysis?
2. How does one understand his/her position vis-à-vis one's readers and students?
3. How does one avoid that which is "unseemly"—apologetics [systematic defense of a religious position]—through suppressing what contradicts contemporary sensibility?
4. Is there no place in departments of religious studies for the representation of conviction, or should faith be left off campus?
5. What are the acute, not merely chronic, tensions between faith and scholarship? (12)

Pals' own conclusion in advance of the next chapter which addresses the question of those who *do* religion remains significant:

> Religion in the end seems to be a matter not of impersonal processes that can be known with certainty because they have been scripted by the laws of nature, but of personal beliefs and behaviors that can only be plausibly explained because they have arisen from complex, partly free and partly conditioned choices of human agents.[17]

To all of this, one should add the obvious complexities as evidenced by the various *definitions* enumerated above, as well as others, and the *theories* and *theorists* who have collectively attempted to understand religions and religious communities in the contexts of so-called "lived realities".

Before turning, finally, to the various disciplinary foci which have attempted to weigh in on religion, it is thus advantageous to, at least summarily, list what representative scholars/writers have attempted to enumerate as the "dimensions" or "characteristics" which appear to separate religious from other communities.

For Bryan Rennie, a British historian of philosophy and religion at Westminster College, New Wilmington, PA, they are as follows:

1. Experience (Revelation)
2. Response (Faith)
3. Knowledge
4. Ethics
5. Community
6. Expression (Witness)

For Ninian Smart (1927–2001), lastly, of the University of California, Santa Barbara, in his three texts *The Religious Experience of Mankind* (1969), *The Religious Experience* (1960), and *Dimensions of the Sacred* (1966), its dimensions are as follows:

1. Ritual
2. Mythical
3. Doctrinal
4. Ethical
5. Social
6. Experiential

For Frank Whaling (b. 1934) of the University of Edinburgh, Scotland, religion possesses these dimensions:

1. Community
2. Ritual and Worship
3. Ethics
4. Social and Political Involvement
5. Scripture/Myth
6. Concept
7. Aesthetics
8. Spirituality

For Mallory Nye, independent Scottish scholar, and author of the text *Religion: The Basics*,[18] its dimensions include the following:

1. Community
2. Doctrines and Texts

3   Ethics
4   Myth
5   Relevance
6   Ritual
7   Sacrality
8   Symbol

Here, too, we sense some agreed-upon similarities of understanding but not 100% universal agreement. (Similar to unpacking the various definitions, unpacking these enumerated dimensions would also take us far afield of our primary concern of the nexus between religion and genocide. Only Rennie, however, enumerating what he regards as "experience" (revelation) and "response" (faith) appears to focus on God/gods, the so-called "supernatural" dimension apparently common to many—but not all—of these communities (Buddhism and Confucianism being the obvious exceptions). The apparent reluctance of many in the scholarly/academic community to directly address/confront the Divine (with a capital "D") may say more about these authors than about religion itself or religions themselves.

Parenthetically, it is significant, perhaps that Rennie omits the idea of ritual in his list while Smart, Whaling, and Nye include it in theirs. Catherine Alcorda and Richard Sosis posit the intriguing idea that music—rhythmically repeated sounds either with the use of "instruments" or the human "voice"—may very well bear an important link to ritual behavior:

> The ability of music to abstract and codify ritual meaning over time and space may have been the critical first step toward symbolic thought. The introduction of such a symbolic ritual system introduced a new type of cognition in hominid evolution. The use of ritual to create associational neural networks linking symbolic, social, and affective systems provided social groups with a highly flexible tool for motivating individual behavior, forging inter-group alliances and discriminating between friends and enemies. Individuals within such groups would have realized fitness benefits resulting from inter-alliance sharing of patchily distributed resources, as well as enhanced cooperation for in-group ventures, including hunting and warfare.[19]

Lastly whether perceived as an aspect of the humanities or the social sciences, numerous academic disciplines have weighed in on looking at this humanly crafted social construct we call religion. For our purposes, however, let us all-too-briefly look at the foci of (1) anthropology, (2) history, (3) phenomenology, (4) philosophy, (5) psychology, and (6) sociology and what their differentiated perspectives must teach us about how to look at the phenomenon of religion.

Anthropology is that branch of the human sciences which deals with the origins, physical and cultural development, biological characteristics, and social customs, beliefs, and behaviors of humankind. In doing so, it looks at similarities and differences in those developments as well as their evolution across the globe. *Religion, as such, is thus understood to be an aspect of the ever-changing evolution of human culture, and the peoples who manifest it in their lived realities.* For now-retired Michael Dean Murphy, former Chair of Anthropology, in a presentation at The University of Alabama, Tuscaloosa, AL, several years back, defined religion is a set of "culturally constructed beliefs and practices concerned with supernatural forces and personalities", asking such questions as "What is it?", "Who are the people who do religion?", "What makes religion?", and "What does it do for us?" Murphy further suggested that so-called "classical anthropology" has four defined approaches to the study of religion: (1) *evolutionary,* focusing on change; (2) *functionalist,* focusing on social glue; (2) *psychodynamic,* focusing on human experience, and (4) *symbolic,* focusing on cultural context and code. Further, he also referenced the "father of anthropology" Lewis Henry Morgan (1818–1881) in his 1877 text *Ancient Society,* who wrote that "religion deals so largely with such uncertain elements of knowledge that all primitive [sic] religions are grotesque and to some extent unintelligible". He concluded his presentation by referencing John K. Nelson's 1990 "The Anthropology of Religion. A Field Statement for the Department of Anthropology, University of California, Berkeley, CA", and asking the following questions:

1. What is considered to be respected, disgusting, or taboo? What is held in awe?
2. What are the centers of "cityscape"?
3. What are the sources legitimating the authority of the religious and secular leaders?
4. Which persons or public positions are regarded as charismatically empowered?
5. What is the worldview of that society? Its symbolic universe? How do these support everyday life?
6. How do media news programs serve as regulatory agencies of this worldview?
7. What is the principal value-system?
8. Is the dominant reference group prescribed or selected?
9. How do the functional options of religious life or ritual life change within their structural contexts?
10. To what extent are the members of that society allowed to define for themselves a holist view of their ultimate concerns?

The questions which Murphy raised are far too easily applicable to genocidal perpetrator groups and those engaged in genocide, those who, using the French term, are the *genocidaires*. For example, activities of the perpetrator groups are validated by them and those of their victim groups are invalidated, especially when it comes to religious practices whereby the latter become objects of disgust and suitable as objects for violence. The fate of the Yazidi religious community by the Muslim ISIS (American ISIL) extremists comes readily to mind. The issue of charismatic leaderships of both religious and genocidal communities is addressed in Chapters 3 and 6. The *Weltanschauung* (German, "worldview" or "world-perspective") of both groups remains central to their overall existences and further defines and legitimates both them and their behaviors. The role of the media, both internally and externally—including the use of sacred texts—is a significant part of their abilities to create/recruit, sustain, and nourish their groups' cohesiveness, and is, equally, a useful tool in the denigration of other groups. Consider the case of Rwanda: The Roman Catholic Belgian Fathers who saw in the self-disregarded distinction between the Hutu and the Tutsi evidence of the false theological notion of the "Hamitic Hypothesis"—derived from the story of Noah in the Hebrew Bible/Old Testament—of the superiority of one group and the inferiority of the other. Its use in the genocide was exploited by the Hutu who then used the radio airwaves to their fullest advantage in locating their victims both before and during the genocide.

Historians are those who study, organize, and present the past of persons, events, and locales in as coherent a manner of which they are capable. Yet a more realistic and accurate view of the human sciences is that, when turning to all aspects of human behaviors which have preceded the present moment, all such scholars, whatever their particular discipline, are historians, and all such work is historical. In so doing, such persons as investigators make what for them are judicious selections of the data before them as they attempt to tell what more broadly and generally, we may refer to as "stories". Though much more a modern than earlier concept and understanding, dispassionate objectivity is considered a hallmark of good historical writing and presentation, leaving the "meaning" or conjectural consequences of such persons, events, and/or locales to that moment after what has been presented. Thus, the emphasis is on accurate description to the best of one's ability, gathering and organizing coherently the data one has at one's disposal at the moment, but fully recognizing that revisionism is mandatory as additional data/material becomes available.[20] As regards religious communities, the historical and contemporary literature describing them is vast as is the corollary literature vis-à-vis- their principal spokespersons, their sacred texts and interpretations, and their practices, both by insider-advocates and by outsider-scholars, journalists, researchers, and popularizers, and continues to grow ever larger exponentially. Thus, for so-called "historians of religion", the data themselves—in the plural rather than the singular—remains a veritable gold mine of study and pursuit. Equally so for those who remain engaged in the relatively newer field of Genocide Studies, an outgrowth of the earlier field of Holocaust Studies. Describing both victims and perpetrators, individuals, and groups; the genocides themselves, both precedents and what transpired (and reasoned speculating as to meanings and consequences); and the specific locales where they took place and how place itself remains important, including climatic conditions, may have also played a role, are now subject to investigation. Chapters 8 and 9 are attempts to sharpen and further expand our focus on their relationship to the religion-genocide nexus.

For the **phenomenologist** who studies the lived experience of those who *do* religion, its practitioners, ethnographic fieldwork is imperative as is a reasonable expectation of observational objectivity—as it is for those who study and investigate those who *do* genocide, both victims and perpetrators. Again, the subjects of Chapters 3 and 6. Broadening that scope somewhat, it must necessarily include not only the living but those who have died but who have previously shared those experiences vis-à-vis their own memoirs and autobiographies, as well as biographies about them using whatever evidence is momentarily available, testimonies (legal and other), and interviews when available. While the phenomenologist of religion may be on "safer" ground to do such fieldwork among living practitioners of a given religious community, such work during the time actual genocides are being experienced brings with it a degree of life-threatening behaviors only parallelingly encountered by journalists who accompany military troops engaged in war. Thus, many phenomenologists of genocide, realistically and of necessity, do their own work ex post facto/after the fact while initially, perhaps, able to rely on reporting when such horrors are taking place.[21]

Those **philosophers** who focus on religion do so by examining the idea-contents of religious communities—i.e., what they say about the world in which they find themselves, how they attempt to understand and make meaningful sense of the world, how they attempt to resolve its conflicts and contradictions (e.g., good vs. evil), as well as the language used in the construction of their worldviews, and how all of this intellectual work fits into the wider worlds of philosophical understandings of reality. Genocide Studies is still too new an investigative discipline to have brought to the table the richness of philosophical thinking and perspective, though the work of Berel Lang, Professor of Philosophy Emeritus at the State University of New York, Albany, NY[22]; Claudia Card (1940–2015), Professor of Philosophy at the University of Wisconsin–Madison, WI[23]; and John K. Roth (b. 1940), Professor Emeritus of Philosophy at Claremont McKenna College, Claremont, CA,[24] come to mind.

Despite Freud, perhaps, **psychology** remains a rich source of the examination of both religion and genocide. Studying the mental state of human beings who do religion, their characteristics and processes, their conscious and non-conscious awareness and motivations which propel their involvement in religion and religious communities, as well as assessing their own states of mental well-being have continually affirmed and reaffirmed the importance of religion in both individuals and groups. Among the areas of fruitful investigation have been (1) how religiously affirming persons have coped with traumas and tragedies—genocides included—in contradistinction to those who see themselves as "non-religious"; (2) how human beings have evolved and developed as religious persons; (3) what is mean by religious experience(s); (4) the impact of religious identity on both psychotherapy and psychopathology; (5) the "journey of conversion" (i.e., leaving one's faith community and embracing another—or not); and (6) religion as an enabling mechanism to confront the reality and inevitability of one's own demise. The same kinds of questions and investigations also have relevance in examining the psychological states of those for whom acts of genocide are their own experiences both as victims and perpetrators, most especially, how have religious persons confronted their own genocidal realities both as recipients and committers.

Lastly, **sociology**, the study of the origins, development, organization, and functioning of human groups, and here, particularly, religious groups, past and present, long-established, and newly constructed. For the "father of modern sociology", French philosopher, Auguste Comte (1798–1857), the development of human thought goes through three stages—*theological*, reliance on God or gods; *metaphysical*, more abstract understandings; and *positivistic*, turning to the scientific and practical, and ultimately abandoning religion altogether. He was, of course: ultimately wrong: humanity has not abandoned either its commitment to or practice of religion but, for many, has incorporated a scientific worldview into their own understanding. For the sociologist of religion, the tasks are threefold: (1) to further the understanding of the role of religion in society, (2) to analyze the significance of and its impact upon human history, and (3) to understand the social forces and influences that, in turn, shape religion.[25]

Again, and perhaps all-too-briefly, this chapter is intended to introduce readers unfamiliar with the academic study of religion, its origins in the European Enlightenment of the past two hundred plus years, what we have learned, what issues and concerns remain, and how one approaches its study today. Having thus laid it out in the broadest of brushstrokes, we now turn in the next chapter to the reality of "boots on the ground": what we have learned about those who *do* religion and how that knowledge may prove applicable not only to those who do genocide but also to the nexus between religion and genocide as well.

Notes

1 Henry Munson (2005), "Religion and Violence: Review Article", *Religions*, 35(4): 223. doi: 10.1016/j.religion.2005.10.006. Accessed 25 March 2021; emphasis added. Nancy C. Ring, Kathleen S. Nash, Mary N. MacDonald, Fred Glennon, and Jennifer A. Glancy, in their 1998 textbook *Introduction to the Study of Religion* (Maryknoll: Orbis Books), also note that "the modern study of religion looks not only to the positive contributions religion has made, but also to the suffering it has caused and the destruction it has wrought" (59).

2 W. Richard Comstock (1984), "Toward Open Definitions of Religion", *Journal of the American Academy of Religion*, 52(3): 499–517.
3 Scholar Wilfred Cantwell Smith (1916–2000) wrote in 1959 in an article entitled "Comparative Religion: Whither—and Why", "it is the business of comparative religion to construct statements about religion that are intelligible within at least two traditions simultaneously".
4 For Durkheim, the use of the word "Church" was understood in a more generic sense of a religious institution and/or organization rather than a specific reference to a Christian house of worship.
5 Daniel Pals, *Seven Theories of Religion*, 109–111; emphasis added.
6 London: Tavistock Publishers, 1–44.
7 Two important critiques of Geertz's definition, among others, are those of both Richard Comstock (pp. 501–503) and Henry Munson in his review article.
8 Paralleling somewhat is that proposed by John D. Carlson:

> Religion entails the practices, rituals, beliefs, discourses, myths, symbols, creeds, experiences, traditions, and institutions by which individuals and communities conceive, revere, assign meaning to, and order their lives around some account of ultimate reality generally understood in relation to God, gods, or a transcendent dimension deemed sacred or holy.

> John D. Carlson (2011), "Religion and Violence: Coming to Terms with Terms", in Andrew R. Murphy, ed., *The Blackwell Companion to Religion and Violence* (Malden and Oxford: Wiley-Blackwell), 8–9.

9 Nicholas Wade, *The Faith Instinct: How It Evolved & Why It Endures* (New York: The Penguin Press, 2009), 15.
10 Belmont: Wadsworth/Cengage Publishing, 2012; 5th Edition.
11 Maryknoll: Orbis Books, 2012.
12 Their comment calls to mind the oft-quoted statement by the late scholar of religion Jonathan Z. Smith (1938–2017) of the University of Chicago:

> while there is a staggering amount of data, phenomena, of human experiences and expressions that might be characterized in one culture or another, by one criterion or another, as religion — there is no data for religion. Religion is solely the creation of the scholar's study. It is created for the scholar's analytic purposes by his [sic] imaginative acts of comparison and generalization. Religion has no existence apart from the academy. For this reason, the student of religion, and most particularly the historian of religion, must be relentlessly self-conscious. Indeed, this self-consciousness constitutes his [sic] primary expertise, his [sic] foremost object of study.

> Jonathan Z. Smith, *Imagining Religion: From Babylon to Jonestown* (Chicago and London: The University of Chicago Press, 1982), xi; emphasis in original.

13 New York and Oxford: Oxford University Press, 1996.
14 Daniel Pals, *Seven Theories of Religion*, 269.
15 Ibid., 72.
16 As James K. Wellman, Jr., and Kyoko Tokuno remind us only too well:

> Truth claims, whether implicit or explicit, act as powerful motivators to individuals and groups in expressing beliefs about their religion. Implicit truth claims imply that one's rituals and one's behaviors are normal, that is real. Truth claims, however, do not always remain embedded in religious group behavior. They often become explicit and are discursively defended as to what is true about one's religion, the cosmos, and reality itself…*As the awareness and*

> *religious diversity increases in the modern period, the need to defend and articulate one's religious symbol system increases.*

James K. Wellman, Jr., and Kyoko Tokuno (2004), "Is Religious Violence Inevitable?", *Journal for the Scientific Study of Religion*, 43(1): 293; emphasis added. NB: Its ultimate articulation translated into ultimate defensive practice might very well legitimate genocide on the part of those who perceive themselves as "defending the faith" (e.g., the Crusaders whose march to Jerusalem was both a retaking of the holy land central to Christianity and a bulwark against the Islamization of the West.)

17 Daniel Pals, *Seven Theories of Religion*, 282–283.
18 London and New York: Routledge, 2008. 2nd Edition.
19 Catherine A. Alcorda and Richard Sosis (2005), "Ritual, Emotion, and Sacred Symbols: The Evolution of Religion as an Adaptive Complex", *Human Nature*, 16(4): 345.
20 The case of the so-called Holocaust revisionists is, in truth, a perversion of the historical enterprise, though they themselves would argue the contrary. Their collective and manipulative use of historical data—e.g., quoting a source out of context or incompletely when the fuller data would affirm the very opposite—is a case in point. The failed lawsuit in Great Britain of David Irving (b. 1938) against American academic Deborah Lipstadt (b. 1947) is an excellent example whereby the presiding judge at the trial found Irving not only a deeply flawed historian but an antisemite as well. Common today, therefore, is to label such persons not Holocaust revisionists but, rather, Holocaust denialists, or in French, Holocaust *négationnistes*.
21 For an interesting "look-see" into the minds of the perpetrators, see Jean Hatzfeld, *Machete Season: Killers in Rwanda Speak* (New York: Picador, 2006. Translated by Linda Coverdale), especially the section titled "And God in All this", 140–147; Guenter Lewy, *Perpetrators: The World of the Holocaust Killers* (New York and Oxford: Oxford University Press, 2017).
22 *Act and Idea in the Nazi Genocide* (Syracuse: Syracuse University Press, 2003); *Genocide: The Act as Idea* (Philadelphia: University of Pennsylvania Press, 2016).
23 *The Atrocity Paradigm: A Theory of Evil* (New York and Oxford: Oxford University Press, 2002); *Confronting Evil: Terrorism, Torture, Genocide* (Cambridge: Cambridge University Press, 2010).
24 *The Failure of Ethics: Confronting the Holocaust, Genocide, and Other Mass Atrocities* (Oxford and New York: Oxford University Press, 2015); *Teaching About Rape in War and Genocide* (New York: Palgrave McMillan, 2016; co-edited with Carol Rittner); and *Sources of Holocaust Insight: Learning and Teaching about the Genocide* (Cascade: Wipf and Stock, 2020).
25 Grace Davie (1998), "Sociology of Religion", in William H. Swatos, Jr., ed. *Encyclopedia of Religion and Society* (Walnut Creek: AltaMira Press), 483.

Chapter 3

Who Are These Human Beings Who *Do* Religion—the Rise of Religion?

Having now laid out in summary from what we mean by "religion" as an opening framework with which to address the religion-genocide nexus, this chapter will lay out our attempts to answer a series of intriguing questions, all subsumed by the title of this chapter, "Who are These Human Beings Who *Do* Religion?". Among these questions are the following: (1) When does "religion" enter the human evolutionary picture?[1] (2) What evidences, if any, exist early on for what we contemporaries would describe—and acknowledge—as "religion"? (3) When do we human beings become consciously aware that we are doing "religion"? (4) Are we pre-wired or hard-wired to engage in those activities and belief systems we call "religion"? (5) Are we genetically predisposed to do so?[2] And there are others to be sure. While we will expand our thinking somewhat in Chapter 8, these initial insights are intended to further our argument that *religion*—however defined and understood as well as its practitioners—bears an important and significant connection to genocide, just as those who are the practitioners of the various religious enterprises potentially become the same actors—state and/or non-state—who potentially engage in genocide and draw upon religion as a resource with which to perpetrate their genocidal agendas.

To begin: As an evolutionary species, hundreds of thousands more likely millions of years ago, paralleling our physical, biological, and genetic changes carried with them changes to our physical brains and thus a growing awareness (consciousness?) of ourselves, others with whom we came into contact, those with whom we mated to insure species survival (without necessarily knowing why), clustering with others of our own species to further insure that survival, recognizing ongoing threats by others apparently similar to us and other species different from us, and similar awarenesses. Increasingly with that growing sense of self and others came the ability to reason—thinking through and resolving whatever issues of survival presented themselves—and further development toward more abstract rather than concrete thinking, though perhaps not fully perceived as somewhat different but simply part of who and what we were (and are). Confronting our awareness of our physical reality as well—birth, growth, maturation, decay, and death as well as responding to climatic and geographical realities—we gathered together into whatever plural units we found advantageous to our survival and began not only to "mark the moments" of our lives' journeys by seemingly repetitive behaviors (rituals?) including carving out of our environment special places which proved not only advantageous but sources of physical and non-physical pleasure and marking them off as well—for want of a better term or phrase, a "territorial imperative". Corollary to our development of abstract thinking came the ability to *ask*, as communicative language developed, and we began to share our thinking with others who were part of our community, questions of *what* (*What* has happened? *Will* it happen again?) and *why* (*Why* did our 'family'/community member cease to exist? *Why* do those others, both human and animal, take our lives? *Why* is place a continuous source of conflict with other groups of species, again, both human and animal? *Why* do the climatic and other geographical elements—thunder, lightning, torrential rains, tsunamis, tornados, earthquakes, hurricanes—cause us so much pain and threaten our very existence?). Increasing awareness and articulation of these thoughts initiated not only repetitive responses to these realities—coping mechanisms to be sure (e.g., hiding from others and the elements)—but conceptions that other beings are similar yet different from us but unknown to us (gods?) controlled all such events even without our fully knowing or understanding why.[3] Thus, our first forays into explaining our physical universe and attributing to others more powerful than us our experienced realities provided necessary answers enabling us to continue the survival of our species. In microcosm, perhaps, the beginnings of religion, as we understand it today, may lie in as simple an answer as that which continues to sustain religious (and other) communities today: attempting to *make sense* of our existence with all of its difficulties and complexities which accompany us on our journeys from birth to death. And, in furthering this attempt, we continue to develop not only explanations but behaviors, which aid us in that sense-making enterprise.

Steven Clarke, Russell Powell, and Julian Savulescu, in the conclusion to their edited volume *Religion, Tolerance, and Conflict*, arrive at the same place:

> Religion promotes social cohesion and heightened tolerance within social groups, but also promotes intolerance and hostility between social groups. Plausibly, this is a result of religion's evolutionary history. For the vast majority of human history, people lived as members of small communities that banded together for protection against a range of environmental threats, predators, and other similarly small groups of humans. In this pre-Neolithic and pre-urban environment, before the conditions necessary to enable large communities to be established were put in place (which occurred about 10,000 years ago), it was strongly in the interest of individuals to be members of devout religious communities as these were the communities that were the most tightly bonded and which could be most relied upon to offer protection from the many threats that humans faced.[4]

Parallelingly, sociologically, the first groups of human beings we may, rather conveniently, label "families", that is, one or more males with birthing females and their offspring. Then, for reasons of safety, security, and survival, perhaps, clustering together with others perceived as non-threatening—"clans" or "tribes",[5] if one prefers—and then expanding out into even larger communities and moving from unsettled and migratory groups (ofttimes necessitated by food requirements for tamed/domesticated animals who were themselves sources of food) to settled groups where group protection was vital.[6] Along the way, stories were continuously told about the abovementioned God or gods and the worlds they inhabited similar perhaps to our own experiences. Commensurate with increasing language/communicative skills and memory/cognition development, one or more members of the group were tasked with or volunteered with both remembering the stories and telling and re-telling them. Furthermore, as the groups themselves solidified, hierarchies apparently developed, and so-called alpha males tended to predominate. That journey of group cohesions was thus reflected as well in the stories they told about their God or gods—resolving for them their confusions regarding natural phenomena—and hierarchically modeling the same group constellations. Accompanying these memories too was the development of symbol representations and cave art to remind the groups themselves of who they were and their "histories". All of this thus comes to argue, at least for this author, the origins of religious consciousness and awareness and accompanied by what continues to be the most dramatic event seemingly necessitating ritual behavior and repetitively demonstrated early on: death rites among early humanity and observed even among the animal kingdom (e.g., among the elephant population).[7] Attending to the death of group members—because of aging, disease (perhaps even attributed to divine disfavor), conflict with other humans or animals—early humanity would sometimes bury their dead, sometime accompanying them with foodstuffs or weapons of war or other implements to best prepare them for a life in the realm of the gods, i.e., somewhere else.[8]

If this theory of the origin of religion and religious behavior is at all correct, then it quite obviously answers other questions raised at the beginning of this chapter, i.e., that it is in our very physical/biological/genetic nature and makeup that we come to be *homo religiosus*/religious beings, that it is, in fact, part of who, what, when, where, and why we are what we are, part of the very warp and woof of our species. It does not, of course, address the question of the variations in beliefs and/or practices, which are, obviously, influenced by historical events, charismatic personages, geographical and climatic locales, and the like. But it does point us as well toward an even broader conclusion maintained in this book: *Given that if we are a "religious" species subject to a whole host of complicated and complicating factors, governed at least initially by our very physicality and its development, including our intellectual development, might not the same thing also be said of our predilection to engage in acts of genocide, influenced* by the very same or similar factors which mark our identity—factors of sense-making of our persons, communities and world; issues of safety, security, and survival and perceiving others as either hostile and/or threatening or safe and non-threatening; attributing to others and surrendering to others more powerful and knowledgeable than ourselves a willingness to engage in preservative behaviors—including ritualized repetitions—to further insure our survival by following their lead and directions, and the like? If we answer in the affirmative, then, can we at least not initially conclude that we are also *homo genocidosus*/species with the propensity and potentiality to engage in genocidal behaviors, given the right set of circumstances and contexts, but not necessarily mandated to do so?

Important to keep in mind, as well, is that, apparently over time, these "god(s) stories" acquired a measure of authority as did those who told them. Scholars of religion today use the word "myth" to identify both those stories of the past and those of the present without any evaluative judgments whatsoever vis-a-vis their "truth" or "falsity", and group them into three categories: (1) myths of origin, (2) myths of God or gods, and (3) myths of larger-than-life persons of importance, which we can label "superheroes" (e.g., Moses, Jesus, Mohammed, Buddha, and Confucius). With the acquisition and evolution of writing thousands of years ago, these stories further cemented their communal centrality and the importance of their storytellers. As repetitive communal behaviors exercised increasing significance and regularized their practice, the rites themselves (e.g., death rituals) also acquired a similar level of authority, and those who were tasked/designated to perform them were elevated in stature in those same population clusters. Thus, our word *sacrality* becomes appropriate for persons, texts, and rituals, and, equally over time, becomes above critique, not subject, at least initially once they become "fixed", to change. With regard to persons who both shared these texts and performed these rituals, sometimes they and their mantles of authority were passed down from parent to child (more often male than female, but not always), other times not. Sacred texts and rituals thus became "holy"; storytellers and practitioners thus became "priests", both above critiques, and coupled with a measure of authority and stature beyond question.

As we continued to evolve as a species and communities as well, the hierarchies continued to evolve similarly in all sorts of arenas: societally/politically, economically, militarily, and religiously. Ultimately, they would evolve into more broadly two categories of human entities: leaderships and followerships, the former maintaining their holds on power through various kinds of policing intimidations involving supportive others and the latter coercively accepting or submitting—or supporting and believing—this same power-powerless relationship.[9] Among the tools used, then, by those either interested in maintaining their power or those jealous of those already in power and desirous of taking it away from them and holding on to it for themselves, were manipulative uses of languages as authoritative and possessing airs of authority; access to sacred texts and god stories while denying them to others;

appointment of priestly officiants, themselves at times subject to coercion and/or threat; and even going so far as to re-shape, re-order, construct, and/or re-construct what we may term the "divine-human relationship" and its practical/ceremonial/ritual behaviors. Carried further, such power-powerless relationships as communities grew larger and larger would evidently result periodically in "othering", that is, labeling certain sub-communities within the larger societies as unworthy of continuation and propagation, perceived or misperceived or falsely perceived as threatening, physical destruction or confinement or relocation not out of the picture.[10]

All to the bad. Yet, in this same evolutionary journey, we see the upside of religious thinking and behavior as well, personally, familially, and communally/societally. Open-ended, however, is the further intriguing question of whether the rituals themselves as responses to the lived realities of those who created them preceded the thinking and conversations about them—*What* to do now that her/she/they have ceased to be? —or whether, non-consciously early on, we began to engage in these ritualistic repetitive behaviors as others began to be born, grew, were afflicted with all sorts of physical ailments and maladies, and died. Unsustained, however, would be the idea that both the rituals and the thoughts about them developed simultaneously. More likely and logically, the very presence of others—births and deaths—evoked even again non-consciously perhaps some sort of *doing*—bringing special foodstuffs to the birthing mother(s), evoking pleasurable sounds upon seeing the new lives created or sounds of pain acknowledging lives lost, moving/transporting the deceased outside the group domicile, and the like. As our thinking continued to evolve, so-called religious responses did so as well: Answering questions as to the *meaning* of our existence, acknowledging our presence as members of clustered groups, affirming the importance of our identities, comforting, and celebrating ourselves as members of our special and specific groups all come to the fore.

Yet these very same proclivities reconfigured and reconstrued have genocidal potential as well, most especially those of hierarchical leaderships, structures of the othering of vulnerable groups after first having them denied access to corridors of power, and the like. Thus, that which we drew/draw upon as *homo religious* are the very same things we draw up as *homo genocidosus*.

Furthermore, religious behavior fully expressed is part of but not the sum total of our cultural expression and creativity which itself makes up the fullness of our cultural productivity from the highest of highs (e.g., symphonic music and architecture; the plastic arts) to the lowest of the lows (e.g., ear-splitting heavy metal rock music—revealing something of this author's prejudice/bias here!)—the very domain of that which falls within the overall purview of anthropology. Taken together with our genetic endowments, they in toto make us who, when, where, and why we are what we are—human beings significantly distinguishable from other species, fully sense-making creatures with an ongoing awareness of our past, our present, and our future, and resolving the past nature versus nurture debate as realizing both are "partners in the crime" of our own existence. Or, as the Hebrew Bible/Old Testament would have it, "little lower than the angels and crowned with glory and honor" (Psalms 18:5), and yet, aware of our finitude, as the patriarch Abraham would have it "nothing but dust and ashes" (Genesis 18:27). And, perhaps tantalizingly, it is this overly complex mix of mind-body awareness that, more than we are willing to admit to ourselves, best positions us to engage in acts of genocidal behaviors as we falsely struggle to overcome our death-reality by inflicting it upon others further falsely believing we are, somehow, achieving a measure of immortality by lording over them their own demise.

Finally (but not really), in the next chapter, we turn to yet another contentious issue, that of the nexus between religion as a socio-cultural construction and its own translation into specific expressions of religion and the realities of violence in the human arena.

Notes

1 See, for example, E. Fuller Torrey, *Evolving Brains, Emerging Gods: Early Humans and the Origins of Religion* (New York: Columbia University Press, 2017); and Nicholas Wade, *The Faith Instinct: How Religion Evolved & Why It Endures* (New York: Penguin Books, 2009). Furthermore, I certainly would define myself religiously as an "evolutionist" rather than a "creationist" and thus understanding sacred texts in a non-literalist/metaphorical way rather than a literalist reading. (These latter two terms are far more preferable that the oppositional and too-often controversial "fundamental" versus "non-fundamentalist".)

2 Early on in his book *The God Gene*, Dean Hamer raises the following provocative questions:

> Why is spirituality such a powerful and universal force? Why do so many people believe in things they cannot see, smell, taste, hear, or touch? Why do people from all walks of life, around the globe, regardless of their religious backgrounds or the particular god they worship, value spirituality as much as, or more than, pleasure, power or wealth?

His answer: "Spirituality is one of our basic human inheritances. It is, in fact, an instinct", which he further defines as "a complex amalgamation in which certain genetically hardwired, biological patterns of response and states of consciousness are interwoven with social cultural, and historical threads".

Dean Hamer, *The God Gene: How Faith Is Hardwired into Our Genes* (New York and London: Doubleday, 2004), 6–7.

3 My own thinking has long been that, once we became *homo erectus*/upright humanity, we began to look *up* and wondered whether the realm beyond the clouds, which we could not see, was likewise inhabited by beings/entities similar to our own (including animals) who functioned as we functioned and lived lives as we lived lives. The populated multiple god-systems of the ancient Mediterranean world, Romans and Greeks included, and other locales as well, would appear to my mind to confirm such thinking. See, for example, Jeremy DeSilva, *First Steps: How Upright Walking Made Us Human* (New York: Harper, 2021) which, in many ways, furthers my own arguments.

4 Steven Clarke, Russell Powell, and Julian Savlescu, eds. (2013), "Religion, Intolerance, and Conflict: Practical Implications for Social Policy", in *Religion, Intolerance, and Conflict: A Scientific and Conceptual Investigation* (Oxford and New York: Oxford University Press), 271–272.
5 The use of the term "tribes" is itself, perhaps, somewhat problematic in that definitionally it sets up its own set of oppositional elements. See, for example, David Berreby, *Us and Them: Understanding Your Tribal Mind* (New York: Little, Brown and Company, 2005); Brian Fox, *The Tribal Imagination: Civilization and the Savage Mind* (Cambridge and London: Harvard University Press, 2011); Joshua Greene, *Moral Tribes: Emotion, Reason, and the Gap between Us and Them* (New York: Penguin Books, 2014).
6 Peoples, Duda, and Marlowe argue rather provocatively that the original hunter-gatherer societies were, in fact, the origin of religion: Hervey C. Peoples, Pavel Duda, and Frank W. Marlowe (2016), "Hunter-Gatherers and the Origin of Religion", *Human Nature*, 27: 261–282. doi:10.1007/s12110-016-9260-0
7 The late Professor of Philosophy and Theology Alvin J. Reines (1926–2004), Hebrew Union College-Jewish Institute of Religion, Cincinnati, Ohio, in a graduate class in philosophy once remarked that *"all* religion is a response to finitude".
8 A recent article by Maria Martinón-Torres and her colleagues would seem to support my conclusions. Maria Martinón-Torres, et al. (2021), "Earliest known human burial in Africa", *Nature*, 593: 99–117.
9 Michael Jerryson (2–21) reminds us that

> charismatic religious leaders have translated mundane problems into larger, more cosmic issues. Within the religious rhetoric, concerns are no longer simply a matter of money or physicality. The religion, sacred land, or the balance between good and evil is under attack. The charisma of religious leaders are abstracted more than ever in the digital age. One can become influenced by videos or websites online....

Michael Jerryson (2021), "Religious Violence as Emergency Mindset", *Journal of Religious Violence*, doi:10.5840/jrv20214684. Accessed 26 April 2021.

10 In a somewhat lengthy online essay writing about the French-Jewish poet-philosopher Benjamin Fondane (1898–1944), Blake Smith makes the following observation:

> Religions gather believers together around concepts, disguising the essential "powerlessness" of each efforts to think their life in their relationship to the absolute. Religious leaders give believers the impression that when concepts are uttered "someone is speaking and someone disappears", that our inexplicable, bewildered and utterly lonely existence can be made sense of together in a shared vocabulary.

Blake Smith (April 18, 2021), "Is Being Essentially Jewish? The poet Benjamin Fondane sought to hold God accountable for a confusing, alienating world", *Tablet Magazine*, www.tabletmag.com/sections/arts-letters/articles/is-being-essentially-jewish. Accessed 20 April 2021.

Chapter 4
What about Religion and Violence?

If, as the proverb would have it, "there are two sides to every coin", then, in truth, addressing the subject of the nexus between religion and violence, these two sides break down into two seemingly opposing camps: (1) those who regard the relationship between them as violating the very principles upon which the world's religions were and are constructed and remain present today ("positivists"), *versus* (2) those who argue that this "dark side" of religion and religious communities, historically and contemporarily, includes a violent component in their very construction ("negativists"?).[1] Most of humanity, however, obviously falls somewhere in between these two camps: Recognizing, on the one hand, that *their* religion is a "force for good" and those whom they tend to label as either extremists or violators are assaulting that which they hold sacred, and, on the other hand, that *their* religion—and others' religions—have, in both the past (e.g., the Christian Crusades) and the present (e.g., the tragedy of 9/11 in the United States by "radical Islamists"), both justified and legitimized such violence. This chapter lays out both sides of the argument and allows the reader to draw his/her own conclusions before turning to the ultimate expression of collective violence, genocide. As is the case with so much else, the literature of defense and critique is vast. (The texts included in the Bibliography are representative examples and only scratch the surface.) Two examples of positivists are British author and commentator Karen Armstrong and American academic William Cavanaugh; examples of negativists—many of whom are noted in the Bibliography as well—are legion, including the oft-cited "new atheists" Richard Dawkins (b. 1941),[2] Sam Harris (b. 1967),[3] and the late Christopher Hitchens (1949–2011).[4] Somewhere in between, perhaps, would be the "classicalists": French sociologist Emile Durkheim (1858–1917) and German sociologist Max Weber (1864–1920), as well as French historian and philosopher, the "modernist" René Girard (1923–2015).

Before addressing these seemingly seminal figures, two other issues are worth considering: (1) Is there an *inherent inevitability* to the nexus between religion and violence? and (2) What is the role of *charismatic religious leaders* in encouraging/fomenting violence on the part of their followers (almost always a method of retaining power)?

Etymologically, Vittorio Bufacchi writes:

> The word 'violence' is derived from the Latin *violentia*, meaning 'vehemence', a passionate and uncontrolled force. Yet because acts of excessive force frequently result in the violation of norms, rights or rules, the meaning of violence is often conflated with that of 'violation', from the Latin *violare*, meaning 'infringement'. Indeed, most attempts to define violence tend to combine the idea of an act of physical force with a violation.[5]

John R. Hall in a preliminary to publication article in 2001 and posted online raises an important caveat regarding defining violence:

> The twin difficulties of defining violence thus concern (1) the limitations of an understanding keyed to force resulting in physical injury, and (2) the difficulty of acknowledging the symbolic dimension without privileging the one or another ethnocentric or hegemonic definition. These challenges have led Mary Jackman[6] to formulate an expansive but culturally neutral definition. *Violence*, she argues, encompasses 'actions that inflict, threaten or cause injury'. Violent *actions*, she continues, may be 'corporal, written or verbal' and the *injuries* may be 'corporal, psychological, material, or social'.[7]

Definitionally, then, violence is thus as problematic and difficult to fully conceptualize as was religion in Chapter 2 and is genocide in Chapter 5. The following are two such examples of definition, both of which raise important and substantive concerns vis-à-vis how we define violence, and, most significantly, in its relationship to religion.

For Terence E. Fretheim, Professor of Old Testament, Luther Seminary, St. Paul, MN:

> violence may be defined as follows: any action, verbal or nonverbal, oral or written, physical or psychical, active or passive, public or private, individual or institutional/societal, human or divine, in whatever degree of intensity, that abuses, violates, injures, or kills. Some of the most pervasive and most dangerous forms of violence are those that are often hidden from view (against women and children, especially); just beneath the surface in many of our homes, churches, and communities is abuse enough to freeze the blood. Moreover, many forms of systemic violence often slip past our attention because they are so much a part of the infrastructure of life (e.g., racism, sexism, age-ism).[8]

38 What about Religion and Violence?

Even more expansively, the World Health Organization (WHO) defines violence as

> the intentional use of physical force or power; threatened or real, against oneself, another person, or against a group or community; that either results in or has a high likelihood of resulting in injury, death, psychological harm, maldevelopment, or deprivation.[9]

Both such definitions are thus contingent upon the recognition of the perpetrator-victim/powerful-powerless dyad, and thus, without stretching one's credulity overmuch, how those in positions of power—in our case religious leaders with a genocidal orientation or agenda against the other/outsider groups—can all-too-easily legitimate their authority before their followers. As Thomas Robbins writes:

> Authoritarian sects with messianic leadership are likely to have some sort of problematic "underside" (not necessarily violence) reflecting a lack of accountability and other factors...Bracketing the unduly polarizing debates about "brainwashing" and "mind control", intensive indoctrination plus the relatively isolated and close-knit nature of many authoritarian sects empower their leadership to cultivate and reinforce a "separate reality" for members that may diverge in some respects from the prevailing ethical codes in the broader society...
>
> Charismatic leadership, which predominates in small sects and NRMs [new religious movements] and may be functional in inspirational terms pertinent to member commitment, also tends to be a potent de-stabilizing force enhancing group volatility. Charismatic leadership has been said to be intrinsically precarious by the absence of both institutionalized restraints on the willfulness of the leader and institutionalized supports to sustain and stabilize the leader's authority. Venerated by devotees, relatively unconstrained by rules or customs, yet continually needing to "prove" his or her worthiness and uniqueness, the charismatic leader may be both empowered and pushed into deviant behavior. Beyond these considerations, it should be noted that charismatic authority, more or less by definition, involves *a break with received codes and customs*. Strong charismatic leadership often provides a positive sanction for behavior that contravenes the standards which would otherwise inhibit deviance.[10]

Not only do these charismatic leaders imbibe the heady narcotic of power, but religious groups themselves ofttimes legitimate themselves by understanding themselves as extra-special/extra-ordinary recipients of divine power and thus powerful by association. Again, Wellman and Tokuno:

> Religions throughout history and across cultures have formed themselves around a power or force that is experienced as within, outside, and above

the sources of "normal" forms of moral authority in human societies. Religions call on sources of moral and spiritual authority that cannot be empirically disconfirmed by means of ordinary verification, whether socially, culturally, politically, or scientifically. In this way, the power and force of religion is beyond question, analysis, or inspection. This gives to religion and leaders within religious communities enormous social and moral leverage to mobilize groups toward whatever metaphysical or political goals they experience or create.[11]

Thus, these latter two authors claim as well that religion—however defined and understood—does inherently contain within itself the seeds of discord and conflict, and, if taken to extreme conclusion as I argue in this text, becomes a *participating factor* in genocide, one among many. For Wellman and Tokuno, religions are best suited to thrive in a conflictual relationship, not only with the state but with other religious communities as well:

> The symbolic and social boundaries of religion (no matter how fluid or porous) mobilize individual and group identity in conflict, and sometimes violence, within and between groups...religion is ideally suited to survive and thrive under difficult circumstance...conflict tends to galvanize religious communities rather than subdue them. Our counterintuitive claim is that religion tends toward greater vitality when it is in tension with surrounding cultures...*it is part of the nature of religious communities to gain their identity through conflict and tension with out-group cultures*...This tension and conflict with out-groups does not always lead to violence. Forms of rhetorical and cultural conflict function to vitalize and mobilize religious identity as well.
>
> Religion in general, and monotheisms in particular, need social conflict and competition both to hone their symbolic boundaries and to keep them from imploding internally from internecine conflict...Religions as monopolies or as oppressed groups, use conflict to strengthen their identity and mobilize their groups to action...religion does produce conflict and less frequently violence.[12]

Thus, summarily, religions as social constructs possesses within themselves the potential for violence and, ultimately, genocide because of what is: a dividing subculture that validates the "us" and invalidates the "them", which honors the "us" and dishonors the "them", which privileges the "us" and de-privileges the "them".

What is all-too-often overlooked in discussions of religion and violence and the role of charismatic authoritarian leaders is that, according to Roy Rappaport, it is also an *expensive* proposition. To wit:

> Coercion is expensive and difficult, and compliance and docility are achieved more easily and inexpensively through first the encouragement

of religious experiences inspired by hopes of salvation in another life and, second, inculcation of the belief that the world's evils are the result of the worshipper's own sinfulness rather than a matter of external exploitation or oppression which the worshipper could possibly resist.[13]

Finally, Michael Jerryson reminds us that

> Charismatic religious leaders have translated mundane problems into larger, more cosmic issues. Within the religious rhetoric, concerns are no longer simply a matter of money or physicality. The religion, sacred land, or the balance between good and evil is under attack. The charisma of religious leaders are abstracted more than ever in the digital age. One can become influenced by videos or website online.[14]

For both Karen Armstrong and William Cavanaugh, however, such is simply not the case, but, rather, a *misreading* of what religion was and is, a hugely beneficial social construction which has, throughout history, brought God (and/or gods) and humanity together. Whatever excesses have resulted in the murderous deaths of millions "in the name of religion", its practitioners and devotees have misread and misunderstood the "true" nature of religion and substituted in its place the foibles of a flawed humanity, distorting religious texts, violating and perverting sacred rituals, corrupting both religious leaders, followers, and religious institutions, organizations, and agencies to serve the false gods of political, economic, and military nation-states, and/or powerful leaders (e.g., Adolf Hitler [1889–1945] in Germany, Josef Stalin [1878–1953] in Russia, Mao Zedong [1893–1976]) in China), committed to a secularizing and distancing of themselves and their peoples from the sacredness of life itself. At stake, it would seem, is the ages-old tension between purity and impurity: "pure" religion versus "impure" humanity. (Shades of the Christian concept of *original* sin—itself an interpretive attempt to assess and understand humanity's destructive actions and based on a reading of the sacred story of Adam and Eve found in the biblical book of Genesis.)

For British comparative religionist and popularizer Karen Armstrong (b. 1944), a former member of the Roman Catholic Sisters of the Holy Child Jesus (1962–1969), three of her most well-known texts that have established her reputation are *The Battle for God: Fundamentalism in Judaism, Christianity and Islam* (New York: Alfred A. Knopf, 2000), *A History of God: The 4,000 Year Quest of Judaism, Christianity, and Islam* (New York: Grammercy, 2004), and *Fields of Blood: Religion and the History of Violence* (New York: Alfred A. Knopf, 2014). As I have written elsewhere regarding this last text and relevant here:

> …in her "Afterword", Armstrong drives home her primary point that violence in the name of religion is not religious violence, but, rather,

religion abused in the name of politics. "The problem lies not in the multifaceted activity that we call 'religion' but in the violence embedded in our human nature and the nature of the state, which from the start required the forcible subjugation of at least 90 percent of the population".

(394)

The issue, therefore, is not whether religion as such is inherently violent or not; nor is it the question of its relationship to either politics or our biological nature. The question that Armstrong and others have not yet addressed fully frontally is whether there is something inherent in the construction of religion itself and religious communities upon which those who commit violence can too easily draw upon up to and including genocide. That book remains to be written.[15]

For William T. Cavanaugh (b. 1962), American Roman Catholic theologian, professor of Catholic studies and director of the Center for World Catholicism and Intercultural Theology at DePaul University, Chicago, IL, the "religion and violence debate" comes down to the classic contestation between religion (good) and secularism (bad). He has written numerous pieces in a variety of publications, both academic and non-academic, with such titles as "Girard and the Myth of Religious Violence" (2017); "Religion, Violence, Nonsense, and Power" (2017); "Religion and Violence" (2017); "Secularization of the Holy: A Reading of the 'Wars of Religion'" (2016); "Sins of Omission: What 'Religion and Violence' Arguments Ignore" (2004); "Religious Violence as Folklore" (2011); "The Violence of 'Religion': Examining a Prevalent Myth" (2004), and others. Most, if not all, of his persuasive and eloquently argued perspectives come together in his 2009 book *The Myth of Religious Violence: Secular Ideology and the Roots of Modern Conflict*,[16] though he has continued to address the topic subsequent to its publication as noted. One, therefore, cannot read them both, however, without finding oneself in an 'either-or' conundrum rather than an 'and' scenario. And while both have, at the very least, granted that, in both the past and present, we human beings have engaged in violent behaviors and perceived ourselves as doing so as religious person, we all-too-often have done so either by falsely understanding our reality or willingly (or unwillingly) allowing ourselves to too-easily be manipulated, corrupted, coerced by others far more powerful than ourselves who tempt us with rewards both here and beyond.[17]

While not wishing to belabor the points raised by both writers, and according them the credibility they deserve, again, they appear to go great lengths to "zero out" religion as a *legitimating* factor—what I refer to throughout this text as a *participating* factor—in the violence of humankind, especially in the extreme cases of genocide. Neither in their writing as well chooses to address, argue, or refute my ultimate claim that religion—as, again, always understood and interpreted—is a *flawed* social construction of our species, containing within it in part the seeds of our own destruction, and needs to be re-defined, re-thought, re-constructed, re-conceptualized, and re-practiced to overcome its inherent tribalism, its ownership by some of "truth", its appeals to authorities both human and divine, its preoccupations with the sacrosanctity of texts, its overarching by some of the validation of the past, and other related issues and causes. This is not to negate or denigrate the goods that religion has done and continues to do—post-traumatic healing being the most obvious—but, rather, attempting to make the case that, yes, religions have participated in genocide, are presently doing so, and will, in all likelihood, continue to do so unless this particular cycle of violence is broken.

Turning to Durkheim (1858–1917), the "father of modern academic sociology", however, his understanding of religion as a community binder sacralizing the relations among members also has the potential to lead to the othering of non-members and the potential to thus legitimate war, martyrdom, and sacrifice as sacred duties, including the concept of the scapegoat—a biblically-based idea—by which either an individual or a group either willingly or unwillingly takes upon itself or themselves the "sins" of the community in power and thus a violent resolution enabling the initiating group to go forward.

René Girard (1923–2015), French historian, literary critic, and philosopher of social science, built upon Durkheim's understanding in his 1986 text *The Scapegoat*, focusing on the relationship between myths—a central characteristic of all religious traditions—collective violence, innocent victimhood, and religious and persecutory texts, including the Hebrew Bible/Old Testament. In so doing, he draws religious communities into this long-standing circle of violence as inherently who, what, and why they are what they are.[18] Again, quoting John R. Hall:

> Girard theorizes sacrifice as a resolution of the cycle of violence that stems from mimesis—an imitative rivalry centered on the desire for the objects that the Other values. A 'surrogate victim' who stands in for wider ills, crimes, or malfeasance becomes the object of collective murder. Because the victims lack effective defenders, the ritual killing requires no further retribution, and the cycle is brought to an end, while simultaneously achieving a goal of sanctification—establishing the purity of the sacred in its positive aspects, and separating it from evil, and from the profane. The ritual cleansing so widespread in religious ceremony originally takes the form of sacrifice that destroys a representative bearer of evil. In essence, the core ritual practice of religion is a process of scapegoating.19

(One cannot read these words without immediately recalling the genocide against the Armenians, Assyrians, and Greeks by both secular Turks and Muslim-committed Turks; Tutsi Rwandese by their fellow Hutus, both infused by a history and Belgian White Father Hamitic theology; and the Holocaust against the Jews, the upshot of two-thousand years of Christian anti-Jewish hatred.)

Lastly, for Max Weber (1864–1920), German historian, jurist, political economist, and sociologist, he saw a distinct and direct relationship between the functional realities of both communal efforts by both political entities and religious entities by which, either separately or together, they attempt to *dominate* their constituencies. This authoritative domination could take the form of physicality to the point of repressive brutality or psychic overlordship, by either withholding or granting "favors", however defined. Thus, both contain and have demonstrated historically the use of violence as a means of social control by those in authority at the direction of their leaderships, and all-too-often focused on other outsider group, though, at times, inner directed toward "culling the herd" of dissidents within their own groups.[20]

Before turning to the next chapter— "What is Genocide?"—mention must also be made of terms that, over the course of the generations, have assumed places of importance in any explorations of religions and religious communities. These include (1) sacrifice, (2) martyrdom, (3) suicide, and (4) war and peace including so-called holy wars (the subject of Chapter 7).

The first two—sacrifice and martyrdom—are paramount in that both are, definitionally, violent acts done in the name of the faith, either willingly by which one surrenders one's life or unwillingly by which those in power force those without power—or religious validation—to surrender their lives. Individually, the death of the Christ is foundational to the faith, and there is a long history of Christian martyrdom *imitatio Dei*, in imitation of that original death. The refusal of religious Jews who refused to debase themselves in the presence of their Nazi and allied murderers and who went to their deaths *al kiddushat HaShem* (for the sanctification of the Holy Name of God) while affirming Deuteronomy 6:4 ("Hear O Israel, the Lord is our God, the Lord is One".) remains for many Jews and non-Jews an inspiring memory in the aftermath of the Holocaust/Shoah.

The third—suicide—is problematic in that, both Roman Catholicism and Judaism (and other religious traditions, but not all, e.g., Hindu widows practicing *sati* by throwing themselves on their husbands' funeral pyres), regard such life-taking as an affront to their God, and a desecration of the holy vessel of the human body "made in God's image" (Genesis 1:27). Islamic tradition, however, is of mixed perspective vis-à-vis the suicide bombers of the 20th and 21st centuries who willingly blow themselves up to inflict deaths on their enemies. Some see them as victims manipulated by those in power to achieve religious-political ends; others see them as emulatory models of faith commitment whose deaths are intended to inspire others. All are, no matter one's reading, violent acts.

Prussian general and military theorist Carl von Clauswitz (1780–1831) is said to be the author of the aphorism, "war is the continuation of politics by other means", to which one could quite easily insert the further understanding that, historically and contemporarily, it has been and is also the continuation of religious endeavors to achieve power or to maintain power subsumed beneath the legitimating and validating structures of exclusivist religious authority and unique ascription of the group's divine-human encounter. Taken to extreme conclusion, then, genocide becomes the means by which such groups can remove from their physical presence other religious communities whose own understandings of that same divine-human encounter are not in accord with their own, possess a perceived real threat to the structural integrity of the group's way of life including its religious leaders, its rituals and practices, its affirmations of the sacrality of its holy texts, and, ultimately, its very raison d'etre for being.

Thus, religion and violence—or religious violence—I would argue is inherently part of the very structure of the creation and construction of religions over the long course of human history, and, taken to their furthest and most negative implementations, contain within themselves the potentiality or opportunity to implement genocide against others when given the occasion and opportunity to do so.

What, then, is this thing called genocide is the subject of the next chapter.

Notes

1 The proverb itself has been traced back in English to 1742 and is first attested in the United States in the 1802 *Diary and Autobiography of John Adams* and an 1817 letter of Thomas Jefferson. However, the proverb was first expressed in ancient times, as far back as 485–410 BCE when Protagoras said that "there are two sides to every question". In about 428 BCE, Euripides also said, "In a case of dissension, never dare to judge till you've heard the other side". Gregory Y. Titelman, *Random House Dictionary of Popular Proverbs and Sayings* (New York: Random House, 1996).
2 Richard Dawkins, *The God Delusion* (New York: Mariner Books, 2008).
3 Sam Harris, *The End of Faith: Religion, Terror, and the Future of Reason* (New York: W. W. Norton & Company, 2004).
4 Christopher Hitchens, *God is Not Great: How Religion Poisons Everything* (New York: Twelve Books, 2007).
5 Vittorio Buffachi (2005), "Two Concepts of Violence", *Political Studies Review*, 3: 194.
6 Mary R. Jackman (2001), "License to Kill: Violence and Legitimacy in Expropriative Social Relations", in John T. Jost and Brenda Major, eds., *The Psychology of Legitimacy: Emerging Perspectives on Ideology, Justice and Intergroup Relations* (Cambridge: Cambridge University Press), 437–467.
7 John R. Hall, "Religion and Violence: Social Processes in Comparative Perspective", Chapter prepared for Michele Dillon, ed., *Handbook of the Sociology of Religion* (Cambridge: Cambridge University Press, 2005); emphases in original.
8 Terence E. Fretheim (2004), "God and Violence in the Old Testament", *Word & World*, 24(1): 19–20.

9 Quoted in John D. Carlson (2011), "Religion and Violence: Coming to Terms with Terms", in Andrew R. Murphy, ed., *The Blackwell Companion to Religion and Violence* (Malden and Oxford: Wiley-Blackwell), 16.
10 Thomas Robbins (1997), "Religious Movements and Violence: A Friendly Critique of the Interpretive Approach", *Nova Religio: The Journal of Alternative and Emergent Religions*, 1(1): 19; emphasis in original. NB: His insights are applicable not only to new religious movements, but *all* religious and political movements as well.
11 James K. Wellman, Jr., and Kyoko Tokuno (2004), "Is Religious Violence Inevitable?", *Journal for the Scientific Study of Religion*, 43(3): 294.
12 Ibid., 292–293; emphasis added.
13 Roy A. Rappaport (1971), "The Sacred in Human Evolution", *Annual Review of Ecology and Systematics*, 2: 41.
14 Michael Jerryson (2021), "Religious Violence as Emergency Mindset", *Journal of Religion and Violence*, 9(1): 8.
15 Steven Leonard Jacobs (2017), "Review of *Fields of Blood: Religion and the History of Violence* by Karen Armstrong, and *Did God Really Commit Genocide? Coming to Grips with the Justice of God* by Paul Copan and Matthew Flannagan", *Genocide Studies International*, 11(2): 264.
16 Oxford and New York: Oxford University Press, 2009.
17 While not addressed here, it is, certainly to a greater or lesser degree, worth contemplating why both Armstrong and Cavanaugh, at least initially in the case of Armstrong, come to their conclusions out of a Roman Catholic hierarchical context rather than a Protestant or non-Christian one.
18 René Girard, *The Scapegoat* (Baltimore: The Johns Hopkins University Press, 1986). Translated by Yvonne Freccero. Other texts worth examining in this context are Charlie Campbell, *Scapegoat: A History of Blaming Other People* (London and New York: Duckworth Overlook, 2011); Robert Daily, *Must There Be Scapegoats? Violence and Redemption in the Bible* (San Francisco: Harper & Row, 1978); Tom Douglas, *Scapegoats: Transferring Blame* (London and New York: Routledge, 1995); Andrea Dworkin, *Scapegoat: The Jews, Israel, and Women's Liberation* (New York and London: The Free Press, 2000); Kenneth M. Gould, *They Got the Blame: The Story of Scapegoats in History* (New York: Association Press, 1944); Marek Halter, *Why the Jews? The Need to Scapegoat* (New York: Arcade Publishing, 2020). Translated by Grace McQuillan; and Sylvia Brinton Perera, *The Scapegoat Complex: Toward a Mythology of Shadow and Guilt* (Toronto: Inner City Books, 1986).
19 John R. Hall (2003), "Religion and Violence: Social Processes in Comparative Perspective", available online. https://projects.iq.harvard.edu/files/wcfia/files/569_jhallreligionviolence11-01.pdf
20 Carlton J. H. Hayes, in his now-classic text, *Nationalism: A Religion* (New Brunswick and London: Transaction Publishers, 2016) sees in the exercise of nation-state power the very same tropes one regularly associates with religions and religious communities: commitment with validating identity, unique cultural primacy, and the centrality of specific language.

Chapter 5

What Is This Thing Called "Genocide"?

In his 1944 magnum opus *Axis Rule in Occupied Europe*, (Washington, DC: Carnegie Endowment for International Peace), Raphael Lemkin (1900–1959) introduced to the world "a new word for an old crime"—genocide—which would, ultimately, evolve, four years later, into the 1948 United Nations Convention on the Prevention and Punishment of the Crime of Genocide (the easily-remembered identification for which is the "Genocide Convention").[1] This chapter presents the very latest thinking and scholarship on genocide—as well as the under-explored concepts of "cultural genocide", "gender and genocide" (i.e., "gendercide"), and "trauma and memory"—and the nexus between religion and genocide, with the understanding that religion, too, like so much else, is a socio-cultural construct. Other topics noted in this chapter as well are the related concepts of "classicide"; "democide"; "ecocide" (the subject of Chapter 9); "eliticide"; "ethnic cleansing, and identity, political, and social cleansing"; "ethnocide"; "femicide"; "filicide"; "fratricide"; "homicide"; "libricide"; "linguicide";[2] "matricide"; "omnicide"; "patricide"; "policide"; "politicide", and "tyrannicide", among other terms, including three of its more unusual and controversial derivatives, "abortion genocide, feticide, infanticide, and neonaticide"; "Black genocide"; and "White genocide". (See Chart 1 "Geno-cides" for the full listing with definitions.)

Also, framing what we will call "anti-genocide", the work of the United Nations "Responsibility to Protect" (R2P), the Extraordinary Chamber in the Courts of Cambodia (ECCC), both the International Criminal Court (ICC) and the International Court of Justice (ICJ), the International Criminal Tribunal for Rwanda (ICTR), the International Criminal Tribunal for (the former) Yugoslavia (ICTY) are brought into this discussion, all undergirded by the International Military Tribunal (IMT)—the "Nuremberg Trials"—at the end of World War II (1945–1946), which "set the stage" for what was to follow.

We, therefore, begin by briefly reviewing Lemkin's own understanding as already introduced in Chapter 1 and based on his initial 1933 formulation, furthering addressing the subsequent critiques of what will, ultimately, become the "Genocide Convention" in both its less well-known Ruhashyankiko Report (1975; never distributed) and its more well-known Whitaker Report (1985).

Chart I "Geno-cides"

Term	Definition
Androcide	The systematic murdering of men and/or boys, or males in general.
Classicide	The deliberate and systematic destruction, in whole or in part, of a social class through persecution and violence.
Deicide	The murder of a god or gods by either humans and/or other gods.
Democide	The intentional murder of an unarmed to disarmed person by government agents acting in their authoritative capacity and pursuant to a policy of high command.
Ecocide	The destruction of the natural environment by deliberate or negligent human action.
Eliticide	The murdering of the leadership, the educated, and the clergy of a group.
Ethnocide	The extermination of national cultures as a component of genocide.
Femicide	The intentional murdering of women or girls because they are female.
Feticide	The act of murdering a fetus or causing an abortion.
Filicide	The deliberate act of a parent murdering their own child.
Fratricide	The act of murdering one's brother or stepbrother.
Gendercide	The systematic murdering of a specific gender.
Genocide	The intentional action to destroy a people—usually defined as an ethnic, national, racial, or religious group.
Genocide, abortion	The belief that all abortions are intentionally genocidal.
Genocide, auto-	The arbitrary or ideologically inspired mass murder of a country's citizens by its own ethnic group against its own ethnic group.
Genocide, Black	The belief that the ongoing mistreatment of African Americans by the US government and white Americans is genocide.
Genocide, cultural	The eradication and destruction of cultural artifacts, as well as the suppression of cultural activities that do not conform to the destroyer's notion of what is appropriate.
Genocide, White (conspiracy theory)	The theory that there is a deliberate plot to eliminate the white race.
Geronticide	The murdering of the elderly or their abandonment to death.
Homicide	The act of one human being murdering another.
Infanticide	The intentional murdering of infants.
Lesbicide	The intentional murder of women because of their lesbianism.
Libricide	The regime-sponsored destruction of libraries and their contents, especially books.

(Continued)

Chart 1 "Geno-cides" (Continued)

Term	Definition
Linguicide	The death of a language due to either the deaths of its first-generation speakers and/or the conscious state-sponsored prohibition of its use and cultural productivity.
Mariticide	The deliberate or intentional murder of one's husband or boyfriend.
Matricide	The act of murdering one's mother.
Neonaticide	The deliberate act of a parent murdering their own child during the first twenty-four hours of life.
Omnicide	The hypothetical complete end of the human species from either natural causes or human causes.
Parricide	The act of murdering a close relative.
Patricide	The act of murdering one's father or stepfather.
Policide	The intentional destruction of an independent political and social entity, such as a city or a nation.
Politicide	The deliberate physical destruction of a group whose members share the main characteristics of belonging to a political movement.
Regicide	The purposeful murdering of a monarch or sovereign of a polity to usurp power.
Religicide	The deliberate destruction of a religion, its community, its rituals and other practices, and its sacred texts and objects.
Sensicide	The murdering of the elderly or their abandonment to death.
Specicide	The hypothetical complete end of the human species from either natural causes or human causes.
Suicide	The act of intentionally causing one's own death.
Tyrannicide	The murdering or assassination of a tyrant or unjust ruler, purportedly for the common good.
Uxoricide	The intentional murder of one's wife or girlfriend.

Finally, we address the important question of "What constitutes genocide and what does not?" by initially examining the still-disputed case of Darfur in the Sudan, how the United Nations has attempted to answer that as well, and how such answering will take us into our concluding Chapter 11.

Already in 1933, at a conference on the codification of international law in Madrid, Spain, where he hoped to present his paper, Lemkin was prevented from attending, however, by his (antisemitic) superiors in the Warsaw prosecutors' office—attributing his concerns both to a Jewish self-serving preoccupation (in a country with a long history of antisemitism and antagonism between non-Jewish and largely Roman Catholic Poles and their fellow Jews) and an initial desire not to antagonize their German/Nazi neighbor to the west—Lemkin had already seen the twin crimes of "vandalism" (i.e., cultural genocide; Polish *wandalizm*) and "barbarism" (i.e., physical genocide; Polish *barbaryzm*) intertwined, though, tragically, he and others would later sacrifice the former concept as one of the original drafters of the Convention if it merited its passage. (NB: "Political groups" would also, ultimately become a casualty on that same altar, largely the result of Soviet unwillingness to legitimate and validate political opposition.) As his thinking would evolve, however, in his text *Axis Rule*, we still realize its echoes in his initial understanding of genocide as

> a coordinated plan of different actions aiming at the destruction of essential foundations of the life of national groups with the aim of annihilating the groups themselves. The objectives of such a plan would be disintegration of the political and social institutions of *culture*, language, national feelings, religion, and the economic existence of national groups, and the destruction of the personal security, liberty, health, dignity, and even the *lives* of the individuals belonging to such groups.[3]

Despite its flaws and serious critiques by both legal and nonlegal scholars of genocide, the Convention remains today the *only* legally mandated international definition of genocide and one which has been incorporated into any number of nation-states as well. Three of the more glaring difficulties with the Genocide Convention are (1) the notion/idea of *intentionality*, subject all-too-often to the absence of either available or hidden documentation, hearsay, subjective psychological assessment of perpetrators (though the international courts have ruled that repeated, well-planned, and organized genocidal behavior *does* in fact, show evidence of intentionality); (2) limiting acts of genocide to only the four groups listed—national, racial, religious and ethnical [sic]; and (3) further defining what constitutes *part* of a victim-group so as to be the recipients of genocide. More on this later.[4]

As for Chart 1, the very word Lemkin introduced almost four decades ago has spawned a "cottage definitional industry" as scholars, journalists, popularizers, and activists (and legislators) have all attempted to weigh in, modify, and/or refocus concerns more pointedly toward specific groups. Among those groups are males and females; parents and children, siblings, and other relatives; other groups not defined or excluded from the Genocide Convention; and, ultimately, the destruction of the human species itself (omnicide/specicide). Most relevant, however, to any discussion of an expansive understanding of genocide would be (1) *classicide* (destruction of a given social class); (2) *democide* (murder of unarmed persons by governmental entities); (3) *ecocide* (the destruction of our planetary home); (4) *eliticide* (murder of group leadership cadres, including clergy and other religious leaders); (5) *ethnocide* (cultural destruction); (6) *auto-genocide* (murder within one's own group); and (7)/(8) *libricide* and *linguicide* (cultural destruction). Even more relevant, perhaps would be (1) *deicide* (murder of the god or gods) and (2) *religicide* (murder of a religion or religion in general), and by extension, "religious cleansing", that is, the removal and/or relocation of a given population-group based on its religion.

Regarding these last two, Christianity itself begins 2,000 years ago with the (necessary) murder of its god (Jesus) by those Roman oppressors in Palestine who saw in him the potential possibility of a civil-political insurrectionist who would foment revolution, and, therefore, must be put to death. Tragically, however, the unknown gospel writers of the New Testament, perhaps out of their desire to establish their own religious bona fides, reframed their adversaries as the Jews of the time, specifically the Pharisaic leadership (seemingly) opposed to his teachings and his questionable blasphemous claim to divinity rather than Sadducean leadership who would have been supportive of the Roman power structure. The Romans then apparently become somewhat duplicitous in Jesus' death by crucifixion—a noted favored Roman form of capital punishment—and the Jews, their so-called masters, making of them either willing collaborators to Jewish power or unwilling and, thus, unsuspecting dupes of the Jews. Thus, the history of 2,000 years of Jewish-Christian relations is, by and large, a bad if somewhat uneven one, framed by an antisemitic orientation blaming the Jews for *deicide*—the death of the god—despite even modern theological claims that Jesus *had* to die to fulfill the divine promise of eternal life for sinful humanity. (More on the relationship between antisemitism and genocide in Chapter 8.)

Religicide, on the other hand, is best shown in the historical example of Soviet Russia in its unsuccessful attempts not only to remove Russian Christian Orthodoxy from its midst, but as well as its nearly-successful attempt to persecute and murder Jews and obliterate all traces of Jewish cultural productivity (music, the arts, literature, Yiddish language, books, newspapers, and scholarly works) as well as Jewish expressions of its own religiosity, both Hasidic and non-Hasidic Orthodoxy. The ongoing wars between Sunni and Shi'a Muslims, and the nearly successful genocide against the Yazidi religious community by the Islamic State are contemporary examples of religicide as is the historical example of the Roman Catholic Church's attempt to put down the Cathar reinterpretation of Christianity and persecute and murder its followers in the 13th century in France. In these examples—and there are others, to be sure—what is central to many is the alliance between dominant religious and nation-state political entities which exercise political, policing, economic and military power to, ultimately, further the aims of a given religious community—their own. Where, however, it is religion itself which is the enemy—the Soviet example—the full force of nation-state power is brought to bear against any expression of religion regularly perceived as an ongoing and distractive threat to those in power and weakening their hold on the populace. The auto-genocide practiced by the Khmer Rouge in Cambodia, specifically targeting Buddhism and Buddhist monks (as well as heretofore perceived intellectual elites—doctors, lawyers, teachers, and professors), themselves Cambodians, is an additional concrete manifestation of religicide.

Why so? Religions, by their very construction and definition, understand the commitment of their members to ideas and ideals not always in consonant and/or harmony with the ideas and ideals of the nation-state and its leaders, and ofttimes, even if not overtly expressed, challenging the very political agenda of the nation-state by their very existence. Economically, in order to maintain their institutional existences, they may be perceived as deflecting or defraying monies which would otherwise fill the nation-state coffers or treasuries, or, worst-case scenarios, line the pockets of corrupt officials. Politically, unless there is at least a perceived alignment between the dominant—at least population-wise—religious community and its leadership and those in power, religious voices and leaders may inspire opposition, revolution, rebellion, and overthrow. Thus, both classicide and eliticide come into play: political leaderships, desirous of maintaining their hold on power, would, logically, to their way of thinking, target religious leadership—clergy at all levels as well as theologians, writers, and teachers of a given religious tradition. Carried to extreme, then, genocidally directed and genocidally targeted violence against religious communities makes sense. Where dominant and dominating religious communities continue to exercise their own hold on power in a given nation-state (historical Roman Catholicism and contemporary Islam), in cooperation with those holding the reins of political power, not only minority religious communities are vulnerable and at risk, but dissident individual members and members of small dissident groups within a given religious community are equally vulnerable and at risk, perhaps even more so. Thus, more and more, my preferred term *participating factor* makes more and more sense on many levels, from theoretical constructions to lived realities.

Before proceeding, however, we return to the Genocide Convention and the two reports authorized to review its positives and negatives and offer a series of recommendations, all designed to strengthen its enforcement on the world stage—the Ruhashyankiko Report of 1978 and the Whitaker Report of 1985, supplemented and further enhanced in 2019 by United Nations Secretary-General António Guterres (b. 1949) in his "Report on the prevention of genocide" to the UN Human Rights Council.[5]

The Ruhashyankiko Report (1978)

Most scholars of genocide are more or less familiar with the Whitaker Report (1985), but far less so with the Ruhashyankiko Report (1978) for one amazingly simple and obvious reason: *it was never distributed*! The "back-story" to its omission, however, is important as well.

Nicodeme Ruhashyankiko, a Rwandan legal expert, was appointed Special Rapporteur in 1973 and tasked by the then-Secretary General of the United Nations and former Nazi Kurt Waldheim (1918–2007; SG 1972–1981) with, as it was titled, "Study of the Question of the Prevention and Punishment of the Crime of Genocide". His review of historical genocide ignited a political firestorm. But most of the criticism was for a change Ruhashyankiko made between the first draft and the final version of the report.

The first draft had cited the Armenian Genocide, but that reference was deleted from the final version due to pressure from Turkey, an omission that was supported by only one member of the UN Commission on Human Rights. Ruhashyankiko justified his omission of the Armenian Genocide at the time of the writing of the report but the inclusion of the Holocaust by explaining that the latter was universally recognized while the Armenian Genocide was not. Although the Commission accepted the recommendation and passed the resolution to enable its distribution, it never took place, leaving copies of the report gathering dust in various research and other libraries.

Professor of Public International Law at Kanazawa University, Japan, Mitsue Inazumi, in her book *Universal Jurisdiction in International Law* has argued that the debate surrounding the Ruhashyankiko Report was political in nature, and indicative of how divisive such disputes over historical genocides were and remain so today.[6] Ruhashyankiko's backing down in the face of such Turkish pressure was and is tragic nonetheless, and casts a shadow over what was, otherwise, an outstanding study and assessment.

Be that as it may, it is worth summarizing, at least in part, his finding, as well as those of the Whitaker Report as well.

In nearly two hundred densely packed and tightly written single-spaced typed pages, Ruhashyankiko *did* survey the Genocide Convention, the overall historical and political contexts which gave rise to it, arguments for and against various sections of the document, and his own assessments, before concluding with his own recommendations. For example, early on, he comments on the issue of the exclusion of political groups at the insistence of the USSR—an issue we know only too well to which Lemkin was committed to including but was persuaded, nonetheless, to surrender in exchange for its passage—by writing:

> Should the adoption of new international instruments on genocide be contemplated[7], the Special Rapporteur is of the opinion that it would not be desirable to include political and other groups among the protected groups, in that a consequence of such inclusion would be to prevent some States from becoming parties to the new instrument. He also believes that other international instruments, such as the Universal Declaration of Human Rights[8] and the International Covenant on Civil and Political Rights, effectively protect political groups without jeopardizing the objectives pursued with regard to the prevention of the crime of genocide.
> [#87; page 23]

Only three pages later, he comments on the still-thorny issue of "intent" and the difficulties ascertaining such, an issue still being discussed today, to wit:

> in the view of the Special Rapporteur, the elimination of the element of intent would efface any distinction between genocide and ordinary

murder and also, as will be explained below...between genocide and war crimes.

[#159; page 26]

Also contained within the Report are two concerns he addressed, neither of which are currently applicable: (1) the situation of Apartheid in South Africa; and (2) European colonialism.

Further into the body of the Report, Ruhashyankiko proffers the suggestion of an international criminal court, well in advance of its establishment in 2002 after its approval in 1999, by writing:

> The Special Rapporteur feel that, since no international criminal court has been established, the question of universal punishment should be reconsidered, if it is decided to prepare new international instruments for the prevention and punishment of genocide. While recognizing the political implications of the principle of the application of the principle of universal punishment for the crime of genocide, the Special Rapporteur remains convinced that the adoption of this principle would help to make the 1948 Genocide Convention more effective.
>
> [#211; page 56]

Perhaps more intriguing, though not fully spelled out, is his comment that "the Special Rapporteur believes that the 1948 Convention can only be considered a point of departure in the adoption of effective international measures to prevent and punish genocide" [#440; page 120]. Today, it must be noted that there is, indeed, a growing UN body of literature surrounding the concept of genocide, including a whole host of documents, reports, resolution, statements, speeches, events, and observances.[9] Yet genocides remain ever-present.

Significantly, in two different places, Ruhashyankiko addresses (1) cultural genocide, (2) "ethnocide",[10] and (3) "ecocide":

> On the basis of information at his disposal...the Special Rapporteur is unable to draw a definitive conclusion as to whether the acts regarded as cultural genocide or "ethnocide" are constituent elements of the crime of genocide and whether it is possible to include it in a revised convention on genocide.
>
> [#461; page 128][11]

Further:

> The fact [that the question of "ecocide" has been placed by States in a context other than that of genocide has led the Special Rapporteur to believe that is becoming increasingly obvious that an exaggerated extension of the idea of genocide to cases which can only have a very distant

connection with the idea is liable to prejudice the effectiveness of the 1948 Genocide Convention very seriously.[12]

Before concluding his Report with a series of Recommendations, Ruhashyankiko addressees three other substantive issues, however briefly:

[1] ...the Special Rapporteur proposes to make a general survey of opinions on the causes of genocide [which for him were four: war, racism, colonialism, *and religious intolerance*] and then on means of prevention other than those of a juridical nature.

[#568; page 172; emphasis added]

[2] The Special Rapporteur considers that the aetiology of genocide in all its aspects requires more detailed disciplinary studies.

[#590; page 178]

[3] The Special Rapporteur wishes, however, to lay stress on preventative measures of an educational and informative nature designed to combat prejudices, hatred and discrimination of any kind deriving from national, ethnic, racial or religious differences, and theories, ideologies and practices based on terror, racial incitement or any other form of collective hatred, and to promote a spirit of peace, understanding and mutual respect and comprehension between peoples and different human groups.

[#610; page 185]

Thus, summarily, in only two pages (184–185), Ruhashyankiko lays out his eight recommendations:

1 There is need for many more States to become parties to relevant Conventions.

[#612; page 184][13]

2 With a view to more effective prevention of the crime, the provisions in question should also make it a punishable offense to engage in propaganda in favor of genocide or to prepare for its commission.
[#613; page 184][14]

3 The Special Rapporteur feels that the Commission on Human Rights should consider the setting up of *ad hoc* committees to inquire into allegations of genocide brought to the knowledge of the Commission by a Member State or an international organization and supported by sufficient *prima facia* evidence.

[#614; page 184][15]

4   The Special Rapporteur considers that the causes and the prevention of genocide in all its aspects require more detailed interdisciplinary study.

[#615; page 184]

5   Groups and organizations which subscribe to Nazism or Nazi-like ideologies or engage in Nazi activities should be banned...It is recommended that the General Assembly call upon all competent United Nations organs, specialized agencies and other international or national organizations to increase public awareness of the danger of a re-emergence of Nazism.

[#616; page 185]

6   It is therefore proposed that the Sub-Committee on the Prevention of Discrimination and Protection of Minorities should request the Commission on Human Rights to accelerate the drafting of a declaration on the elimination of all forms of religious intolerance, with a view also to the later elaborating on a convention on the subject.

[#617; page 185][16]

7   The Special Rapporteur believes that the Convention can only be considered a point of departure in the adoption of effective international measures to prevent and punish genocide...and has proposed that the possibility be examined of adopting new international measures for the effective prevention and punishment of genocide.

[#618; page 185]

8   The Special Rapporteur would wish to add that, if it is decided to adopt new international instruments, it will be necessary to ensure that such instruments should be open to all States, whether members of the United Nations or not.

[619; page 185][17]

The Whitaker Report (1985)

Six years later, 1985, hardly time for the UN to have addressed the Ruhashyankiko Report much less implement his recommendations, UN Secretary General Javier Perez de Cuellar (b. 1920; SG 1982–1991) tasked British barrister and Labour Party politician Benjamin C. G. Whitaker (1934–1914) with producing what would become the "revised and updated report on the question of the prevention and punishment of the crime of genocide", and lending his name to the "Whitaker Report" as it has come to be called. Woven throughout are a series of recommendations, some building upon the work of Nicodeme Ruhashyankiko, others added to a growing list of recommendations and suggestions, summarily considered below. Significantly, Whitaker noted that "the 1948 Convention recognized that intervention may be justified to prevent or suppress such acts and to punish those responsible, 'whether they are constitutionally responsible rulers, public officials or private individuals'". (18)[18]

Thus, the following I would contend are the most important of his recommendations, each of which is worthy of further exploration:

1 The lack of clarity about which groups are, and are not, protected has made the Convention less effective and popularly understood than it should be...It is recommended that the definition should be extended to include a sexual group such as women, men, or homosexuals. [30]
2 Further consideration should be given to the question of cultural ethnicity and ecocide [an obvious difference of opinion from that of Ruhashyankiko], including, if there is no consensus, the possibility of formulating an optional protocol. [33]
3 It is suggested that a court should be able to infer necessary intent from sufficient evidence, and that in certain cases this would include actions or of such a degree of criminal negligence or recklessness that the defendant must reasonably be assumed to have been aware of the consequences of his conduct. [39]
4 The Special Rapporteur therefore proposes that there should be added to the end of Article II of the Convention words such as "in any of the above conduct, a conscious act or acts of advertent omission may be as culpable as an act of commission". [41]
5 ...the Special Rapporteur recommends that explicit wording should be added to the Convention, perhaps at the end of Article III, that "in judging culpability a plea of superior orders is not an excusing defense". [53][19]
6 It is therefore recommended...that when the Convention is revised, consideration shall be given to including a provision for a State's responsibility for genocide together with reparations. [54][20]
7 The Special Rapporteur...believes that countries or at least States parties should be required to amend their domestic laws to permit such extradition if they do not prosecute offenders themselves. [63]
8 Since genocide may be held at least no less serious that torture, the Special Rapporteur recommends that similar provisions to those addressing war crimes and crimes against humanity be made for offenses of genocide. [64]
9 Intelligent anticipation of potential cases could be based on a data bank or continuously updated information, which might enable remedial, deterrent or averting measures to be planned ahead...the development of a United Nations satellite communications network. [79][21]
10 Another highly important area of study is interdisciplinary study (to be coordinated perhaps by the United Nations University) into the

psychological character and motivations of individuals and groups who commit genocide or racism, or the psychopathic dehumanizing of vulnerable minorities or scapegoats. In all human rights work, it is essential to go beyond condemnation of violations to analyzing their causation. [80]
11 The results of such research could help form part of a wide educational programme throughout the world against such aberrations, starting at an early age in schools. [81]
12 …public awareness should be developed internationally to reinforce the individual's responsibility, based on the knowledge that it is illegal to a follow a superior order or law that violates human rights. [82; originally addressed in the Nuremberg War Crimes Trials of the Nazi leadership in 1945/46]]
13 …an effective early warning system could help save several thousands of lives. [83][22]
14 Cogent support has been expressed for the establishment of a new impartial and respected international body whose special concern would be to deal with genocide. [84][23]

Thus, combined, twenty-two well-thought-out and concrete recommendations to combat the scourge of ever-present genocide in our world in the aftermath of the 1948 Genocide Convention now more than seven decades have been in force. So few of these combined recommendations implemented, and, thus, support for South African attorney and, later, professor of sociology at University of California, Los Angeles (UCLA), the late Leo Kuper's (1908–1994) impassioned critique vis-a-vis the seeming impotence of the United Nations to address genocide in his 1985 book *The Prevention of Genocide*,[24] and building upon his earlier text *Genocide: Its Political Use in the Twentieth Century*.[25]

The Guterres Report (2019)

As Samuel Totten and those nearly forty contributors to his important text *Last Lectures on the Prevention and Intervention of Genocide* remind us, there is no dearth of creative and/or innovative suggestions how to prevent future genocides.[26] The very latest list is found in the June 2019 "advanced unedited version" of the "Report on the prevention of genocide" by the United Nations Secretary-General (António Guterres) to the Human Rights Council, and consists of the following, and framed by its own introduction that "investing in prevention is the only sustainable way to fulfill the pledge of 'never again' which speaks to the very core of the United Nations mandate and its principles".

1 Become parties to and implement key international agreements related to the prevention and punishment of the atrocity crimes and the protection of populations, especially the Convention on the Prevention and

Punishment of the Crime of Genocide and the Rome Statute of the International Criminal Court and, in particular, ensure that atrocity crimes and their incitement are criminalized by domestic law. [59]
2. Strengthen efforts to ensure accountability for atrocity crimes through establishing domestic mechanisms that grant victims the right to an effective remedy, as well as through the removal of statutory limitations, amnesties or immunities that obstruct the prosecution of State officials, including the security forces, and other individuals responsible for atrocity crimes. [60]
3. Review and strengthen constitutional arrangements as required to guarantee the protection of fundamental human rights, recognize the diversity of the population, and grant explicit protection to different groups, *including ethnic or religious minorities*. [61; emphasis added]
4. Conduct a national assessment of existing risks and resilience opportunities, using the "Framework of Analysis for Atrocity Crimes". [62]
5. Build the capacity of national institutions to prevent or halt atrocity crimes. [63]
6. Support civil society initiatives that contribute to the prevention of atrocity crimes. [64]
7. Join existing or create relevant regional or sub-regional initiatives on atrocity prevention. [65]
8. Continue cooperating with my Special Advisers on the Prevention of Genocide and on the Responsibility to Protect in the development of options to strengthen civilian action to prevent atrocity crimes. [66]
9. Invite the Special Adviser on the Prevention of Genocide to brief relevant bodies, including the Security Council and the Human Rights Council on situations of concern where elements of the risk of genocide or other atrocity crimes are present. [67]
10. Ensure that the Human Rights Council continues to pay attention to warning signs of potential genocidal or other atrocity related violence and engage at an early stage to pre-empt the escalation of tensions. [68]
11. Make use of the Human Rights Council's mechanisms, by extending open invitations to and cooperation with relevant Special Procedures as well as by incorporating in national reports to the Universal Periodic Review an assessment of measures being taken to address risks and build the resilience of societies to prevent the commission of atrocity crimes. [69]
12. Cooperate with the Human Rights Treaty bodies, particularly by submitting State's regular reports and acting upon relevant recommendations for implementation that contribute to the prevention of human rights violations and particularly, atrocity crimes. [70]
13. Ensure that educational systems reflect the ethnic, national and cultural diversity of their society and set up an example of inclusiveness in their policies. [71]

14 While promoting human rights education activities, disseminate knowledge of the principles of the Convention on the Prevention and Punishment of the Crime of Genocide, paying particular attention to the elements of prevention. [72]
15 Acknowledge atrocity crimes in which State officials were involved and include education on past violations in schools. [73]
16 Continue efforts aimed at memorialization and remembrance of past atrocity crimes as a way to prevent atrocity crimes through educating society and reminding us of our collective duty of "never again". [74]
17 Engage in efforts to prevent any misuse of the Internet and social media for spreading messages of hate that could drive individuals towards violence, including by making use of social media to educate and raise awareness about peace and global citizenship as well as by encouraging media, including social media platforms, to adopt professional ethical codes and standards that incorporate respect for the principles and norms of international human rights. [75]

Suggestions and recommendations abound; what remains lacking apparently is our collective acknowledgment of our common humanity—our collective right to life—and our willingness to translate meaningful words into concrete actions.[27]

Unpacking each and every one of these recommendations, their consequences and their implementation would mandate an even larger text than this one and refocus our efforts away from that of the nexus between religion as a participating factor and genocide itself. However, it should be noted that Rushashyankiko regards "religious intolerance" as one of the root causes of genocide, and Guterres is sensitive to the plight of "religious minorities".

Three of the more egregious permutations of genocide, however, are those used by those, conspiratorially, stridently advocating against (1) Abortion Genocide (sometimes also referenced as Abortion Holocaust); (2) Black Genocide; and (3) White Genocide. To a large degree, an announced public militancy is common to all three, as is, carried to extreme, not only the potential for violence but their actual implementation. For those opposed to both Black and White genocides, they regard themselves as victim-groups subject to the evil machinations of governmental entities, economic, military, and medical plots, designed not only to subjugate them but, ultimately, to cause their very extinction as well. Opponents of White genocide additionally not only see themselves in opposition to these aforementioned collectives but also attribute their potential demise to powerful groups, primarily "the Jews" as seen in the "Zionist Occupation Government" (ZOG) too-easily manipulating the processes of the US Government and manipulating as well as the Black population to do their bidding. Equally so, many see themselves as "Christian warriors" prepared to take up arms to preserve a historically privileged mode of power and authority dramatically shrinking away as both Black and Hispanic populations increase, especially in the United States. Opponents to what they regard as Black genocide go so far as to regard the use of the military appeal to Black youth in the United States as a not-so-covert means to decrease their population, and some further arguing that the AIDS/HIV epidemic was likewise a plot on the part of the power structure to sway potential gay Black youth and cause their demise. (Even the preventative and related vaccines were thus designed according to these opponents to cause early deaths.)

For those dramatically and forcefully opposed to abortion in any and all circumstances, until recently in the United States under the previous presidential administration (2016–2020) and passage of draconian anti-abortion laws in many states, they claim to speak for the unborn, affirming personhood at conception, categorizing abortion as murder (*including* in cases of rape and/or incest, and, for some, even where the life of the mother is at stake), what they regard as the easy availability and access to abortion and abortion providers is genocide, pure and simple. They, too, implicate the US federal government as calculatingly sanctioning this abortion genocide, and, for many, seeing such acts as, equally, a frontal assault on their Christian—and a small minority of Jews, their Jewish—faith.

Taken together, however, opponents to Abortion Genocide, Black Genocide, and White Genocide—the last being the most violent—remain minority voices within the entire spectrum of those addressing the various iterations of genocide within the global human community.

Of more import are both cultural and gender genocides. Hearkening back to Lemkin who understood culture in the broadest sense as reflecting the "genius" (his word) of a given collectivity, destroying a people's cultural productivity—of which religion was and is a part—was very much an expression of genocide. To rob a people of that which makes it distinctive and uniquely different from its neighbors is very much to rob the world as well of its overall contributions to the evolving civilizational march of humanity. Unfortunately, the very word "cultural genocide" is not part of the Genocide Convention, though, interpretatively, it is possible to regard II b ("Causing serious bodily or mental harm to members of the group"), II d ("Imposing measures intended to prevent births within the group"), and II e ("Forcibly transferring children of the group to another group"), if implemented, as hastening the cultural destruction of the group, causing such mental harm and anguish, and preventing the transmission of the group's cultural productivity and legacy from one generation the next.

The examination of the sordid history of male-female relations worldwide, including religious communities,[28] has come full circle, and has laid claim to past and present practices of gendercide, and a growing body of literature addressing it.[29] The term itself is attributed to Mary Ann Warren (1946–2010) in her book *Gendercide: The Implications of Sex Selection* (Lanham: Rowman & Allen, 1985), and while she herself saw the term as gender-neutral and applicable to both females and males (rather than "femicide" directed to women and girls only), in the popular imagination, it is primarily directed toward females, and, in many societies and cultures as well, it is centrally the abuse, subjugation, brutality, torture, and murder of females as well. (NB: If "femicide" is understood to specifically target females; then its opposite "androcide" is understood to specifically target males. In the current climate where transgendered persons are more at risk than perhaps ever before, one awaits the appropriate term.)[30]

Intricately linked to ethnocide is the concept of "ethnic cleansing" and its derivatives—identity, political and social cleansing. "Ethnic cleansing" has become an important term for denying genocide. It is not necessarily directed toward the murder of a given victim group even though mass murder may be either an intended consequence or byproduct of that behavior. "Ethnic cleansing" is the physical removal of a defined sub-group with the ultimate goal of creating or furthering the homogeneity of the larger population by removing all evidence of the sub-group's physical presence, its cultural contributions and ownership of its physical structures, e.g., churches, mosques, synagogues, and other easily-identifiable buildings and monuments. "Ethnic cleansing" usually means the forced displacement and migration of a victim group. It includes both physical removal and prevention of participation in both the political and judicial processes of the nation-state.

The infamous Nuremberg Laws of Nazi Germany in the 1930s identified Jews as the quintessential "others", excluding them from various professions and denying them access to civic participation. The laws effectively rendered them "non-citizens". They denied them access to the courts and most other rights. In many other countries, so-called "undesirable populations" are similarly "othered", justifying their removal or relocation—e.g., gays, the homeless, the mentally and physically challenged, Native Americans, etc. All such laws provide evidence of so-called "social cleansing".[31]

As regards the case of Native Americans in the United States (and the tragedies of residential schools for both First Nations in Canada and Aboriginal Peoples in Australia, equally designed to "root out" their cultural and physical distinctiveness prior to integrating their children into larger—spelled white Christian—societies), we find the intersection of such cleansings and religion in the use of the term "Manifest Destiny" whereby in the 19th century, again white Christian, largely Protestant US citizens, were seemingly favored by God to expand their territory and displace (and relocate) native resident populations, sometimes after first attempting to "civilize such savages" as to the advantages and benefits of full involvement in their expanding nation-state.[32]

Such "cleansing" activities while not necessarily and always genocidal do retain that potential and are ofttimes legitimated and validated by the dominant religious institutions sometimes co-opted and other times willingly cooperative with the power structures of the nation-state.

Before addressing those institutions which I have labeled anti-genocide and concluding this chapter with a final complex issue—what does and does not constitute genocide, how to address it, and the case of Darfur—mention must also be made of the responsibility of history and historians in presenting genocide, and the impacting roles of memory and trauma in the accurate understanding of such events. All bear directly on how we prevent future genocides, bring to swift conclusion the present genocides, and punish those responsible for perpetrating genocides.

The first responsibility of the historians of genocide is accurate assessment of the data at hand—whether that data is documentary including video and/or other media evidence, but most especially and importantly eye-witness testimony (oral and/or written) by both perpetrators and the victim. As human beings, *how* we recall/remember traumatizing events and ofttimes placing ourselves at the centers of those events when we may, in fact, be "peripheral players" influences our retelling and/or recording of those same events.[33] To be fair and honest, there is a certain subjectivity in the presentation of those same events, not only on the part of victims and perpetrators but also scholars, journalists, legalists and legislators, policy makers, and the like. We collectively bring to those events the microscopic lens of our own humanity; sometimes, for example, our moral judgment and indignation, even unrecognized in ourselves but apparent to others, may affect our choices of what to include and what to omit, especially when encountering evidence which may further problematize our assessments of both victim and perpetrator behaviors and the subject of the next chapter. Recognizing our own prejudices and biases serves as a somewhat cautionary break and reminds us that we are the products of a myriad of factors, which result in who we are and why we do what we do.[34] All of which is to say that history and memory are not the same entity, but rather collaborative partners in attempting to assess and understand a given genocidal moment, the contexts—historical, political, economic, *and religious*—in which genocidal events take place, the persons involved—leaderships and followerships on all levels—and the like.[35] The same set of responsibilities remains the same for political scientists, including governmental officials and policy advocates, psychologists, and sociologists, and all who accept a public dimension to their leadership roles including religious leaders. Thus, we come to several 20th- and 21st-century institutions created in the aftermath of the most documented genocide in human history, the Holocaust of World War II.

Chronologically, it is important to note the dates of their establishment as indicative of the continuing development of "world consciousness" regarding the awareness not only of the pervasiveness of genocides, but how best to address this scourge of humanity. Thus:

- International Military Tribunal (IMT)   1945–1946
- International Court of Justice ICJ)   1945
- International Criminal Tribunal for the former Yugoslavia (ICTY)   1993–2017
- International Criminal Tribunal for Rwanda (ICTR)   1994–2015

- Extraordinary Chambers in the Courts of
  Cambodia (ECCC)   1997–Present
- International Criminal Court (ICC)   1998–Present
- Responsibility to Protect (R2P)   2005–Present

In the aftermath of World War II and the recognition of the horrors associated with it, the Allied victors (France, Great Britain, Soviet Russia, and the United States) brought to the bar of justice the military and civilian leadership of Nazi Germany (Adolf Hitler [1889–1945] and his mistress-wife Eva Braun [1912–1945] having already committed suicide 30 April/1 May 1945). Four indictments were presented: (1) participation in a common plan or conspiracy for the accomplishment of a crime against peace; (2) planning, initiating, and waging wars of aggression and other crimes against peace; (3) participating in war crimes; and (4) crimes against humanity.[36] Twenty-four defendants were put into the dock; eleven were sentenced to death (two cheated the hangman's noose—Hermann Goering [1883–1946] and Heinrich Himmler [1900–1945] by committing suicide); seven were sentenced to prison terms; and six were acquitted. As noted in this chapter, neither physical genocide nor cultural genocide was publicly given voice.

Paralleling these trials, the newly formed United Nations, successor to the League of Nations, established the International Court of Justice and tasked it with settling disputes between nations in accord with international law and offering advisory opinions to aid in settling nation-to-nation disputes. Genocidally related issues are not part of its mandate.

The International Criminal Tribunal for the former Yugoslavia was established in May 1993 and dissolved in December 2017 to prosecute perpetrators of war crimes committed during that universally acknowledged genocide. One hundred sixty-one persons were indicted, including Roman Catholic priests and nuns and Seventh-Day pastors (though throughout the emphasis was on physical genocide/murder not on cultural destruction, even while acknowledging desecration and destruction of churches and artifacts and religious locales where those murders took place). Ninety defendants were convicted and sentenced; twenty-one were acquitted; thirteen had their cases transferred to other courts; and thirty-seven had their cases terminated due to either withdrawal of indictments or death.

The International Criminal Tribunal for Rwanda was established in November 1994 and dissolved in December 2015 to try those responsible for that genocide. Of the ninety-six persons indicted, eighty-five persons were ultimately convicted, including some pastors.

The Extraordinary Chambers in the Courts of Cambodia, established in 1997 and ongoing, was and is purposed to try the senior leaders and those most responsible members of the Khmer Rouge for their orchestration and participation in that "auto-genocide" and violations of international law.

As noted previously, as one of the agendas of the Khmer Rouge was to rid the recreated state of Cambodia of Buddhist religion and religious leadership (monks, nuns, and abbots), evidence of both physical and cultural genocide are very much in evidence in the prosecutorial presentations of those indictments.

The International Criminal Court which was initially affirmed by those nation-state signatories in the Rome Statutes of 1998 and came into force in 2002 with a mandate to prosecute individuals for the international crimes of genocide (five crimes), crimes against humanity (sixteen crimes), war crimes (eighteen crimes), and crimes of aggression (ten crimes); forty-nine possible indictable offenses in all. Again, the emphases are on physical assault not cultural destruction or genocide as such. It is, however, the logical successor to the International Military Tribunal at the end of World War II.

Affirmed by all United Nations signatories at the UN World Summit in 2005, the mandate of the Responsibility to Protect (R2P) is to address four key concerns: (1) to prevent genocide, (2) to prevent war crimes, (3) to prevent ethnic cleansing, and (4) to prevent crimes against humanity. By virtue of their signatures, nation-states commit themselves to a responsibility to protect their populations—citizens and non-citizens—from mass atrocities in accord with international law. That commitment rests upon three "pillars": (1) the protection responsibilities of the state; (2) international assistance and capacity-building; and (3) timely and decisive collective response (of which international armed intervention remains a possible and distinct solutions). To date, those responsible for R2P at the UN have produced a plethora of documents some of which will be addressed in Chapter 10.

Collectively, these various instruments, institutions, courts, and their collaborative agencies are the practical and realistic translators of whatever theories and ideas are initiated by others, academics, journalists, policy-planners, advocates, and the like, with a dual responsibility to not only address the *prevention* of the crimes of genocide and related violations of the human community but the *punishment* of those *genocidaires* who choose to implement those assaults against their fellow human beings.

Having now framed genocide both theoretically and pragmatically, these questions logically arise: How to assess a given volatile scenario? When is what is transpiring truly a genocide requiring/mandating an international response and when is it not? The distinctions drawn vis-a-vis the above organizations about crimes against humanity, war crimes, and crimes of aggression usher forth these same questions as well.

The United Nations Office on Genocide Prevention and the Responsibility to Protect, in attempting to answer these questions, has produced two documents of relevance "When to Refer to a Situation as 'Genocide'" (three pages) and "Framework of Analysis for Atrocity Crimes: A tool for prevention" (2014; thirty-two pages). After first examining them both, we will then apply them to the complex case of Darfur.

Regarding the first, its states that "this note aims to provide guidance on the correct usage of the term 'genocide' *based primarily on legal rather than historical or factual considerations*" (emphasis added).

Significantly, its further states that

> Lemkin developed the concept of genocide partly in response to the Holocaust, but also in response to previous instances in which he considered entire nations, and ethnic, *and religious groups*, had been destroyed, such as 'the destruction of Carthage; *that of religious groups in the wars of Islam and the Crusades*; the massacres of the Albigenses and the Waldenses and more recently, the massacre of the Armenians. (Emphases added)

Topics addressed include "Analysis—Origins of the concept"; "Criminalisation of genocide"; "Applicability of the Genocide Convention"; "The Genocide Convention and customary international law"; "Historical' cases of genocide"; "Use of the term 'genocide'";[37] "Other terminology; Other international crimes" before concluding that "it is up to a mandated judicial body to make a legal determination as to whether genocide did indeed occur, and who was responsible".

Drawing a further link to the second document, it states that "events that do not meet the definition of genocide may constitute war crimes or crimes against humanity, which are separate crimes under international law" and emphasizes that "there is no established 'hierarchy of gravity' of international crimes". Thus, the "Framework of Analysis for Atrocity Crimes" addresses all three—genocide, crimes against humanity, and war crimes—citing eight "Common Risk Factors" and two "Specific Risk Factors" for each. It further expands each of these fourteen Risk Factors by focusing on "Indicators" for each for a total of one hundred thirty-seven such potential "red flags" by which such crimes may or might take place. Taken together, collectively, such an analysis lays out a rather compelling grid by which to evaluate any given historical moment as to whether, in fact and in law, such an event may be labeled genocide, war crime, crime against humanity, or ethnic cleansing though this latter is not specifically addressed, having no standing in international law. The ongoing tragedy in Darfur meets this test of genocide.

However, as is well-known, the United States State Department under the then President Bill Clinton (b. 1946; served 1993–2001) dickered for three months as to whether the mass murder that was taking place in Rwanda was, indeed, a genocide, even while admitting that "genocidal-like events" were occurring there. On March 25, 1988, Clinton would later "apologize" at Kigali Airport, Rwanda by stating:

> All over the world there were people like me sitting in offices who did not fully appreciate the depth and the speed with which you were being

engulfed by thus unimaginable terror…Never again must we be shy in the face of the evidence.

He did not, however, utter the words "I am/we are truly sorry", acknowledge it as a genocide, nor leave the airport itself. A lesson obviously not learned.[38]

Yet in 2004, in an appearance before the US Senate Foreign Relations Committee, then Secretary of State General Colin Powell (1937–2021) declared the crisis in Darfur a genocide (after the US Congress had already passed a Resolution declaring it as genocide), as would the then President George W. Bush (b. 1946; served 2001–2009) in a speech three years later. Such a determination, the first time US leaders had used the word itself, did not result in a military response, either unilaterally or internationally. Then Secretary-General of the United Nations Kofi Annan (1938–2018; SG 1997–2006) described the genocide as a "massive violation of human rights". Analyzing the apparent impotence of all the un- or non-involved parties, Scott Straus would write:

> The genocide debate and the Darfur crisis are thus instructive for several reasons. First, they have made it clear that 'genocide' is not a magic word that triggers intervention…The lack of any subsequent action, however, showed that the Genocide Convention does not provide nearly the impetus that many thought it would…Second, the Darfur crisis points to other limitations of using a genocide framework to galvanize international intervention. Genocide is a contested concept: there is much disagreement about what qualifies for the term.[39]

It would, ultimately, fall to the International Criminal Court to issue charges against the President of the Sudan, Omar al-Bashir (b. 1944) and later other leaders of his entourage on charges of crimes against humanity, war crimes, and genocide. His trial on other charges began in Khartoum in 2020.

The cases of both Rwanda and Darfur thus reveal the complexities when attempting to evaluate and determine historical events through the lens of genocide, what factors play into those determinations—political, military, economic, and religious—and if and when such assessments call forth action on the part of individual nation-states and/or the international community.

We end this chapter by referencing Gregory Stanton's famous "Ten Stages of Genocide" (see Chart 2). Stanton is a former law professor, State Department official, past president of the International Association of Genocide Scholars (IAGS), and founder of Genocide Watch and the Alliance Against Genocide, the first international anti-genocide coalition, see www.genocidewatch.com.

Stanton first concretized his processual model of genocide in a lecture at Woodrow Wilson College, North Carolina, in 1987, later presenting it to the State Department in the aftermath of the Rwandan Genocide in 1996, and further adding to it in 2012. Thus, before examining the reality of those who *do* genocide—the *genocidaires*—we come to realize that genocide, like

Chart 2 A summary of Stanton's ten stages of genocide (for a fuller presentation of Stanton's model, see https://www.genocidewatch. com/tenstages)

#	Stage	Characteristics	Preventive measures
1	Classification	People are divided into "them and us".	"The main preventive measure at this early stage is to develop universalistic institutions that transcend… divisions".
2	Symbolization	"When combined with hatred, symbols may be forced upon unwilling members of pariah groups…"	"To combat symbolization, hate symbols can be legally forbidden as can hate speech".
3	Discrimination	"Law or cultural power excludes groups from full civil rights: segregation or apartheid laws, denial of voting rights".	"Pass and enforce laws prohibiting discrimination. Full citizenship and voting rights for all groups".
4	Dehumanization	"One group denies the humanity of the other group. Members of it are equated with animals, vermin, insects, or diseases".	"Local and international leaders should condemn the use of hate speech and make it culturally unacceptable. Leaders who incite genocide should be banned from international travel and have their foreign finances frozen".
5	Organization	"Genocide is always organized… Special army units or militias are often trained and armed".	"The U.N. should impose arms embargoes on governments and citizens of countries involved in genocidal massacres and create commissions to investigate violations".
6	Polarization	"Hate groups broadcast polarizing propaganda".	"Prevention may mean security protection for moderate leaders or assistance to human rights groups…Coups d'état by extremists should be opposed by international sanctions".
7	Preparation	"Mass killing is planned. Victims are identified and separated because of their ethnic or religious identity".	"At this stage, a Genocide Emergency must be declared. Full diplomatic pressure by regional organizations must be invoked, including preparation to intervene to prevent genocide".

(Continued)

#	Stage	Characteristics	Preventive measures
8	Persecution	"Expropriation, forced displacement, ghettos, concentration camps".	"Direct assistance to victim groups, targeted sanctions against persecutors, mobilization of humanitarian assistance or intervention, protection of refugees".
9	Extermination	"It is 'extermination' to the killers because they do not believe their victims to be fully human".	"At this stage, only rapid and overwhelming armed intervention can stop genocide. Real safe areas or refugee escape corridors should be established with heavily armed international protection".
10	Denial	"The perpetrators… deny that they committed any crimes".	"The response to denial is punishment by an international tribunal or national courts".

Source: Wikipedia: The Ten Stages of Genocide. https://en.wikipedia.org/wiki/Ten_stages_of_genocide

other humanly crafted and humanly constructed social processes, is an evolving process over time. Each of Stanton's stages could and should be further explored and analyzed however from an additional perspective: how religion plays a role in that construction. Each of these ten stages can, quite easily, be assessed and addressed though this additional lens. That which is applicable to the ten stages of genocide is equally applicable to the evolving nature of religious communities.

- Classification—stage one—is inherent in the construction of religious communities: "us *versus them*", "insiders *versus* outsiders", "true believers *versus* false believers".
- Both genocidal and religious groups draw upon the power of symbolization—stage two—to identify members of their group and maintain their hold on power.
- Both groups discriminate in favor of members of their group and against "others"—stage three.
- Leaders of both genocidal and religious groups may dehumanize the "others" as traitors, heretics, or even as dangerous creatures or diseases—stage four.
- Both genocidal and religious groups are organized—stage five.

- Leaders of such groups polarize—stage six—the distance between their group and the "others".
- They may organize planning to prepare—stage seven—their groups to engage in what follows.
- Persecution of the targeted groups—stage eight.
- If they have the power to do so, they may exhort their followers to exterminate members of a targeted group—stage nine. When they can gain state support, they may collaborate with the nation-state. Religious nationalism is the deadliest justification for genocide.
- Throughout the process and afterward, both genocidal and religious groups deny any evil in what they do and deny their own involvement in acts of genocide—stage ten.

Notes

1 Washington: Carnegie Endowment for International Peace. The emphasis in this Convention was, to be sure, on the *prevention* rather than the *punishment* of those nation-states and individuals and groups who perpetrated genocide, consistent with Lemkin's own faith that international law would itself serve as that prevention. It would then fall, ultimately, to those international legal institutions to further clarify the Convention by concretizing the specific punishments of those same entities found guilty of the crime of genocide. See, for example, Samuel Totten and Henry Theriault, *The United Nations Genocide Convention: An Introduction* (Toronto: University of Toronto Press, 2020).
2 See Steven Leonard Jacobs (2005), "Language Death and Revival after Cultural Destruction: Reflections on a Little Discussed Aspect of Genocide", *Journal of Genocide Research*, 7(3): 423–430.
3 Raphael Lemkin (1944), *Axis Rule in Occupied Europe*, 79; emphases added.
4 On the question of definitional complexity, see the following anthologized collections of important essays: Paul R. Bartrop, ed., *Modern Genocide: Analyzing the Controversies and Issues* (Santa Barbara: ABC-CLIO, 2018); Donald Bloxham and A. Dirk Moses, eds., *The Oxford Handbook of Genocide Studies* (Oxford and New York: Oxford University Press, 2010); Cathie Carmichael, and Richard C. Maguire, eds., *The Routledge History of Genocide* (New York and London: Routledge, 2013); and Dan Stone, ed., *The Historiography of Genocide* (New York: Palgrave Macmillan, 2008). As regards the contentiousness vis-à-vis issues surrounding the Genocide Convention itself, see Donald W. Bleacher, *The Genocide Debate: Politicians, Academics, and Victims* (New York: Palgrave Macmillan, 2011); and Edward S. Herman and David Peterson, *The Politics of Genocide* (New York: Monthly Review Press, 2010).
5 Much of this material was first presented by me in the opening lecture "Prevention of Genocide: Rethinking the (1948) Genocide Convention in Light of the Ruhashyankiko (1978) & Whitaker (1985) Reports—What Would Raphael Lemkin (1900–1959) Have Said?", International Conference on the Crime of Genocide: 100th Anniversary of the Genocide of the Greeks of Pontus, Athens, Greece, 6–8 December 2019.
6 Mitsue Inazumi, *Universal Jurisdiction in Modern International Law: Expansion of National Jurisdiction for Prosecuting Serious Crimes under International Law* (Cambridge: Intersentia Publishing LTD, 2005), 72–73.

7 This thread of additional anti-genocide instruments weaves itself throughout the report, though nowhere does Ruhashyankiko fully spell out what those instruments could or should be other than the creation of an "international criminal court".

8 It should also be remembered that Lemkin himself was quietly critical of the UNDHR, chaired as its committee was by Eleanor Roosevelt (1884–1962), widow of the late US President Franklin Delano Roosevelt (1882–1945). His legal argument was that such a Declaration had no standing in the judicial system while a Convention did; his literary metaphor was that of comparing an engagement to a marriage. For a fuller exploration of various facets, interpretations, and understandings, the work of Johannes Morsink vis-a-vis the UNDHR remains significant: *Inherent Human Rights: Philosophical Roots of the Universal Declaration* (Philadelphia: University of Pennsylvania Press, 2009); *The Universal Declaration of Human Rights and the Challenge of Religion* (Columbia: University of Missouri Press, 2017); *The Universal Declaration of Human Rights and the Holocaust* (Washington: Georgetown University Press, 2019); and, fundamentally, *The Universal Declaration of Human Rights: Origins, Drafting & Intent* (Philadelphia: University of Pennsylvania Press, 1999). It should, however, be noted that Article 18 states that

> everyone has the right to freedom of thought, conscience, and religion; this right includes freedom to change his [sic] religion or belief, and freedom, either alone or in community with others and in public or private, to manifest his [sic] religion or belief in teaching, practice, worship and observance;

and Article 27 states

> (1) everyone has the right freely to participate in the cultural life of the community, to enjoy the arts and to share in scientific advancement and its benefits; (2) everyone has the right to the protection of the moral and material interests resulting from any scientific, literary, or artistic production of which he [sic] is the author.

9 In the Index to the UN Office on Genocide Prevention and the Responsibility to Protect, "Key Documents" include (1) Founding Documents (4); (2) Secretary-General's Reports (10); (3) Resolutions by UN organs: (a) General Assembly (2); (b) Security Council (1); (c) Human Rights Council (6): (d) Resolutions and reports by other organizations (5); (e) Articles by the Special Advisors (3) Other documents (1). The UN Regional Information Center (UNRIC) in its "Backgrounder" on "Genocide" includes the following: (1) Entities (1); (2) Treaties and Declarations 6); (3) Selected UN Documents (11); (4) Selected Statements and Speeches by UN Officials (21); (5) Events and Observances (4). The late Leo Kuper, however, was overly critical of the ongoing production of such documentary material:

> Indeed, the ceaseless manufacture of normative documents without implementation may be a disservice. It deflects action away from implementation, encouraging abstract formulation as a substitute for practice; and formal adherence to ideal norms may engender a self-righteousness that serves as license for gross violation of human rights...representatives of governments in the United Nations seem to experience no qualms (indeed, to the contrary, they seem to experience a moral exaltation) in castigating the very sins in other countries that their governments freely practice in their own.

Leo Kuper (1985), *The Prevention of Genocide* (New Haven and London: Yale University Press, 2010).

10 Lemkin's first footnote in Chapter 9 of *Axis Rule* uses this very term as an alternative to genocide:

> Another term could be used for the same idea, namely ethnocide, consisting of the Greek word "ethnos" –nation—and the Latin word "cide".
>
> (79)

11 There is today a growing body of literature addressing this very question, consistent with Lemkin's own orientation including both physical and non-physical genocide. See, for example: Jeffrey S. Bachman, ed., *Cultural Genocide: Law, Politics, and Global Manifestations* (Abingdon and New York: Routledge, 2019); Lawrence Davidson, *Cultural Genocide* (New Brunswick and London: Rutgers University Press, 2012); Elisa Novic, *The Concept of Cultural Genocide: An International Law Perspective* (Oxford and New York: Oxford University Press, 2016). Lemkin himself would write in *The American Scholar* (publication of the Phi Beta Kappa honorary society) in 1946, for example:

> Cultural considerations speak for international protection of national, religious, and racial groups. Our whole cultural heritage is a product of the contributions of all nations. We can best understand this when we realize how impoverished our culture would be if the peoples doomed by Germany, such as the Jews, had not been permitted to create the Bible, or give birth to an Einstein, a Spinoza; if the Poles had not had the opportunity to give the world a Copernicus, a Chopin, a Curie; the Czechs, a Huss, a Dvorak; the Greeks, a Plato, and a Socrates; the Russians, a Tolstoy, and a Shostakovich.

Raphael Lemkin (1946), "Genocide", *The American Scholar*, 15(2): 228.

12 Contemporarily, at least in the United States, the most dramatic and explosive example of such linkage is the attempt by anti-abortion advocates to link the destruction (read "murder") of fetuses *in utero* to that of genocide. Carried to extreme and absurd interpretive understandings,

> In a weekend feature in August 2019, the *Washington Post* tied the popular fall pumpkin spice latte from coffee giant Starbucks to massacres, *genocide*, and savagery against the people of the Banda Islands, now part of Indonesia, hundreds of years ago,

as reported by the politically conservative and ofttimes inflammatory *Washington Examiner* of 19 August 2019 (emphasis added). Additionally, the UN Office on Genocide Prevention and the Responsibility to Protect, under "Guidance Note 1", indirectly addresses this issue with its "When to Refer to a Situation as Genocide", and states that

> the situation as to whether a situation constitutes genocide is thus factually and legally complex and should only be made following a careful and detailed examination of the facts against relevant legislation…This must be done by a competent international or national court of law with the jurisdiction to try such cases, after an investigation meeting appropriate due process standards.

Its failure, however, to rule genocide in the case of Darfur, South Sudan, negates the positivity of its own expressed intention.

13 As of May 2019, 151 States out of 195 have ratified the Genocide Convention.
14 On this under-explored topic, see Frank Chalk (1999), "Hate Radio in Rwanda", in Howard Adelman and Astri Suhrke, eds., *The Path of a Genocide: The Rwanda Crisis from Uganda to Zaire* (New Brunswick and London: Transaction Publishers),

93–110; and Christine L. Kellow and H. Leslie Stevens (1998), "The Role of Radio in the Rwandan Genocide", *Journal of Communications*, 48(3): 107–128.
15 Though not specifically addressed, the concept of genocide early warning systems should have also been brought to bear in this recommendation. See Steven Leonard Jacobs (2011), "Franklin H. Littell's and Israel W. Charny's Early Warning Systems", *Journal of Ecumenical Studies*, 46(4): 599–608; and Hayward R. Alker, Ted Robert Gurr, and Kumar Rupersinghe, eds., *Journey Through Conflict: Narratives and Lessons* (Lanham: Rowman & Littlefield, 2001).
16 On 23 September 2019, at its 74th Session, the General Assembly of the UN was presented with the Interim Report of its Special Rapporteur on Freedom of Religion and Belief, Ahmed Shaheed (b. 1964), entitled "Elimination of all forms of religious intolerance", with a central focus on antisemitism. Earlier, May 2019, UN Secretary-General António Guterres (b. 1949) announced "A Strategy and Plan of Action on Hate Speech" with a two-fold objective: (1) Enhance UN efforts to address root causes and drivers of hate speech; and (2) Enable effective UN responses to the impact of hate speech on societies. That strategy would address the following "Key commitments": (1) monitoring and analyzing hate speech; (2) addressing root causes, drives, and actors of hate speech; (3) engaging and supporting the victims of hate speech; (4) convening relevant actors; (5) engaging with new and traditional media; (6) Using technology; (7) using education as a tool for addressing and countering hate speech; (8) fostering peaceful, inclusive and just societies to address the root cause of hate speech; (9) engaging in advocacy; (10) developing guidance for external communications; (11) leveraging partnerships; (12) building the skills of UN staff; and (13) supporting Member States.
17 Neither Vatican City nor Palestine are members of the United Nations as such. Six other countries are not members of the UN: Taiwan, Western Sahara, Kosovo, South Ossetia, Abkhazia, and Northern Cyprus.
18 So, notes Leo Kuper as well,

> given the many failures of the United Nations to act against regimes engaging in continuous massacres of their subjects, it seems to me that there is a great need for individual nations, or preferably groups of nations, to reassert under carefully defined conditions the right of humanitarian intervention against genocide and other gross, consistent, and murderous violations of human rights.

Leo Kuper, *The Prevention of Genocide* (New Haven and London: Yale University Press, 1999), 226.
19 An obvious nod to the International Military Tribunal War Crimes Trials held in Nuremberg, Germany, against the Nazi leadership in 1945–1946.
20 A less well-known case was that brought before the United Nations by a US African American organization charging the United States with genocide and seeking reparations. See Steven Leonard Jacobs (2017), "'We Charge Genocide': An Historical Petition All but Forgotten and Unknown", in Scott W. Murray, ed., *Understanding Atrocities: Remembering, Representing, and Teaching Genocide* (Calgary: University of Calgary Press), 125–143.
21 See Steven Leonard Jacobs (2011), "Franklin H. Littell's and Israel W. Charny's Early Warning Systems", *Journal of Ecumenical Studies*, 46(4): 599–608, which examines two such examples of genocide early warning systems. No such system, to date, has thus far been fully implemented, installed, or put into place to the best of knowledge of this researcher.

22 In Paragraph 84, Whitaker lists five (5) benefits from the implementation of such an early warning system:

- The investigation of allegations.
- Activating different organs of the United Nations and related organizations, both directly and through national delegations, and making representations to national Governments, and to interregional organizations for active involvement.
- Seeking support of the international press in providing information.
- Enlisting the aid of other media to call public attention to the threat or actuality of genocidal massacre, asking relevant racial, communal, *and religious leaders*, in appropriate cases to intercede, and arranging the immediate involvement of suitable mediators and conciliators at the outset. (Emphasis added)
- Sanctions could be applied with public support, by means of economic boycotts, the refusal to handle goods to or from offending States, and selective exclusion from participation in international activities or events. Representations would also be made to enlist their support in the application of sanctions.

23 Whitaker concludes his Report with "the principal recommendations of the present Special Rapporteur are contained in paragraphs 41, 50, 54, 55, 57, 64, 70, 79, 80, 82, 83–84, 86–88, 90, and 91" [92]. Both the International Criminal Trial for Rwanda (ICTR) and the International Criminal Tribunal for the (Former) Yugoslavia (ICTY) are the concrete manifestations of this recommendation.

24 Leo Kuper, *The Prevention of Genocide* (New Haven and London: Yale University Press, 1985). Recently, Professor Edward C. Luck of Columbia University, New York, and the First UN Advisor on the Responsibility to Protect (R2P, 2008–2012) has suggested eight possible reasons for that impotence:

- One obvious reason was the matter of timing.
- A second was the distinction between the focus of human rights on the individual victim and of genocide on crimes against a group.
- A third plausible explanation was that the inclusion of genocide or other mass crimes against groups might have raised uncomfortable questions about the limits of national sovereignty, as seen as fundamental pillars both of the new world body and of the larger inter-state system based on Westphalian principles.
- Fourth, by the time of the San Francisco meeting, the four convening powers—the United States, the UK, the USSR, and China—were determined to push for broad international acceptance of the draft Charter as quickly and painlessly as possible.
- Fifth, it was quite plausible, given the existential wartime struggle with the Axis powers and the core peace and security purposes of the organization, to conclude that the surest way to stop ongoing genocide was to defeat militarily those states that were committing such horrific acts.
- A sixth rationale—though the author has not seen any historical evidence to directly document this conjecture—would have been that the numerous references to human rights and fundamental freedoms, without distinction to race, sex, language, or religion, in the Charter could have been seen as sufficient.
- Seventh, it should be recalled that Raphael Lemkin himself favored keeping genocide prevention on a separate track.

- Eighth, and finally, it is quite possible that the convening powers and others were reluctant to have their lack of response to the Holocaust questioned or highlighted on the highly visible stage of the San Francisco conference.

Edward C. Luck (2019), "Roots of Ambivalence: The United Nations, Genocide, and Mass Atrocity Prevention", in Barbara Harff and Ted Robert Gurr, eds., *Preventing Mass Atrocities: Policies and Practices* (London and New York: Routledge), 158–159.

25 Leo Kuper, *Genocide: Its Political Use in the Twentieth Century* (New Haven and London: Yale University Press, 1983).
26 Samuel Totten, ed., *Last Lectures on the Prevention and Intervention of Genocide* (London and New York: Routledge, 2018). An interesting addition to the literature on prevention is that of the Jacob Blaustein Institute for the Advancement of Human Right of the American Jewish Committee, New York, entitled "Manual on Human Rights and the Prevention of Genocide" (2015).
27 The life-affirming writings of psychotherapist and Founder and Executive Director of the Institute on the Holocaust and Genocide, Jerusalem, Israel W. Charny (b. 1931) are particularly relevant and insightful here. See, for example, *How Can We Commit the Unthinkable: Genocide, the Human Cancer* (Boulder: Westview Press, 1982); *Fascism and Democracy in the Human Mind: A Bridge Between Mind and Society* (Lincoln: University of Nebraska Press, 2006); *The Genocide Contagion: How We Commit and Confront Holocaust and Genocide* (Lanham: Rowman & Littlefield, 2016); *A Democratic Mind: Psychiatry with Fewer Meds and More Soul* (Lanham: Rowman & Littlefield, 2016); and *Psychotherapy for a Democratic Mind: Treating Intimacy, Tragedy, Violence, and Evil* (Lanham: Rowman & Littlefield, 2018).
28 See Daniel C. Maguire and Sa'diyya Shaikh, eds., *Violence against Women in Contemporary World Religion: Roots and Cures* (Cleveland: Pilgrim Press, 2007).
29 Two important recent texts are Paula A. Michaels, and Christina Twomey, eds., *Gender and Trauma since 1900* (London and New York: Bloomsbury Academic, 2021); and Amy E. Randall, ed., *Genocide and Gender in the Twentieth Century: A Comparative Survey* (London and New York: Bloomsbury Academic, 2015).
30 Some writers, for example, Mariarosa Della Costa in her edited collection use the more dramatic term "gynocide" to address this ongoing assault against women and girls: *Gynocide: Hysterectomy, Capitalist Pariarchy and Medical Abuse of Women* (Brooklyn: Autonomedia, 2007).
31 See Andrew Bell-Fialkoff (1993), "A Brief History of Ethnic Cleansing", *Foreign Affairs*, 110–121; Andrew Bell-Fialkoff, *Ethnic Cleansing* (New York: St. Martin's Griffin, 1999); Norman M. Naimark, *Fires of Hated: Ethnic Cleansing in Twentieth-Century Europe* (Cambridge and London: Harvard University Press, 2001); Stefan Wolfe, *Ethnic Conflict: A Global Perspective* (Oxford and New York: Oxord University Press, 2006).
32 Broadening the scope of manifest destiny beyond but including the United States, see Gary Clayton Anderson, *Ethnic Cleansing and the Indian: The Crime That Should Haunt America* (Norman: University of Oklahoma Press, 2014); Roxanne Dunbar-Ortiz, *An Indigenous Peoples' History of the United States* (Boston: Beacon Press, 2015); Todd Gitlin and Liel Leibovitz, *The Chosen People: America, Israel, and the Ordeals of Divine Election* (New York and London: Simon and Schuster, 2010); Amy S. Greenberg, *Manifest Destiny and American Territorial Expansion: A Brief History with Documents* (Boston: Bedford/St. Martin's 2012); William D. Hutchinson & Hartmut Lehmann, eds., *Many Are Chosen: Divine Election and Western Nationalism* (Harrisburg: Trinity Press International, 1994); Deborah L. Madsen, *American Exceptionalism* (Jackson: University Press of Mississippi, 1998); Anthony D. Smith, *Chosen Peoples: Sacred Sources of National Identity* (Oxford and New York: Oxford University Press, 2003); Anders Stephanson, *Manifest Destiny:*

American Expansion and the Empire of Right (New York: Hill and Wang, 1995), Albert K. Weinberg, *Manifest Destiny: A Study of Nationalist Expansionism in American History* (Chicago: Quadrangle Books, 1935).
33 Deryn Strange and Melanie K. T. Takarangi note that "people tend to remember more trauma than they experienced, and those who do, tend to exhibit more of the 're-experiencing' symptoms associated with post-traumatic stress disorder (PTSD)". "Memory Distortion for Traumatic Events: The Role of Mental Imagery", *Frontiers in Psychiatry*, (2015), 6(27): 1.
34 As Donald W. Beachler writes on this very point:

> Scholars journalists, and politicians are often motivated by political interests in choosing what issues to emphasize and what matters to ignore. It is perhaps human nature, or at least a common weakness, to be cognizant only of the facts or events that fit our preconceived worldview or promote our interests. All too often, few of us want to be bothered by information that may be inconsistent with our political or material interests. It is difficult to process information that contradicts our worldview.

The Genocide Debate: Politicians, Academics, and Victims (New York: Palgrave Macmillan, 2011), 9. See, also, Kjell Anderson, *Perpetrating Genocide: A Criminological Account* (London and New York: Routledge, 2018), specifically pages 8–9 on the complexities of interviewing perpetrators; Cathy Carruth, *Unclaimed Experience: Trauma, Narrative, and History* (Baltimore and London: The Johns Hopkins University Press, 1996); Didier Fassin & Richard Rechtman, *The Empire of Trauma: An Inquiry into the Condition of Victimhood* (Princeton and Oxford: Princeton University Press, 2009); Sue Grand and Jill Salberg, eds., *Trans-generational Trauma and the Other: Dialogues Across History and Difference* (London and New York: Routledge, 2017). Further, a scientific exploration as to whether or not trauma can be physically transmitted—the exploration of *epigenetics*—is the work of pioneering researcher Rachel Yehuda; see David Samuels (2014), "Do Jews Carry Trauma in Our Genes: A Conversation with Rachel Yehuda), www.tablemag.com. Accessed January 21, 2021. In that interview, she defines epigenetics as

> the study of alterations on genes that change the way the genes function. An epigenetic mark is literally a change to the gene or to the DNA environment that will affect the way the DNA is read into RNA, and subsequently how RNA is expressed into a protein.

35 See Richard Crownshaw, Jane Kilby, and Antony Rowland, eds. *The Future of Memory* (New York and Oxford: Berghahn Books, 2010); Geoffrey Cubitt, *History and Memory* (Manchester: Manchester University Press, 2007); Janet Jacobs, *Memorializing the Holocaust: Gender, Genocide, and Collective Memory* (London and New York: I. B. Tauris, 2010); Daniel Levy, and Natan Sznaider. *The Holocaust and Memory in the Global Age* (Philadelphia: Temple University Press, 2016); Oren Baruch Stier. *Committed to Memory: Cultural Meditations on the Holocaust* (Amherst: University of Massachusetts Press, 2003); and Joan Tumblety, ed., *Memory, and History: Understanding Memory as Source and Subject* (New York and London: Routledge, 2013).
36 It should be noted that Lemkin himself was an advisor to US Justice Robert H. Jackson (1892–1954) and was able have the word "genocide" inserted into the official record of the proceedings seventeen times. It was *not* included in the formal indictments, however. Nor was the focus specifically directed against the near-extermination/annihilation of the Jewish people and the nearly-successful attempt to eradicate all evidences of Judaic culture—religious and non-religious—from those places under Nazi hegemony.

37 "According to Article IX of the Genocide Convention, disputes related to its interpretation, application and fulfillment, including State responsibility, should be addressed to the ICJ [International Court of Justice]. With regards to individual criminal responsibility, Article VI determines that persons charged with genocide shall be tried by a competent court of the State in the territory of which the act was committed or by a competent international penal tribunal whose jurisdiction is accepted by State Parties."
38 See Samantha Power, *"A Problem from Hell": America in an Age of Genocide* (New York: Basic Books, 2013) for her rather trenchant critique of American complicity in genocide.
39 Scott Straus (2005), "Darfur and the Genocide Debate", *Foreign Affairs*, 84(1): 131–132. See, also, John Hagan, and Wenona Rymond-Richmond, *Darfur and the Crime of Genocide* (Cambridge: Cambridge University Press, 2008), which further explores and expands why, when all the evidence was presented, nation-states still refused to act, including the United Nations.

Chapter 6

Who Are These Human Beings Who *Do* Genocide—the Perpetrators?

Like the comment on the growing body of literature regarding religion and violence—the subject of Chapter 4—there is an increasing body of literature regarding perpetrators—who they were and are and why they did and do what they did and do—including the *Journal of Perpetrator Research* published by Winchester University Press, Great Britain, and affiliated with the Perpetrators Studies Network of Utrecht University in The Netherlands (five issues thus far, 2017–2021).[1] This chapter examines some of that extensive literature, replete with biographical examples, to determine what role, if any, religion has played or does play in the determination of those whom we now label *genocidaires*. Definitionally, therefore, one must agree with Kjell Anderson that "a perpetrator is that individual who commits such acts that *directly* contribute to genocide".[2] Though not specifically addressed by him or many others, a secondary "player" is that of the *collaborationist*—or the equally negative "non-participant" that of the *bystander*—who we may thus define as that individual or group who *indirectly* contribute to genocide by either their silence, public support, and approval of those who do the actual physical work of genocide or feign ignorance (i.e., "I/we did not truly know what was happening").[3] Religionists—especially clergy—with whom we are especially concerned in this chapter fall into both categories.

We begin, of course, with the Holocaust (Hebrew, *Shoah*), keeping in mind the rather trenchant and perhaps some acerbic comment of James Waller:

> According to Jewish-Christian tradition, the first time that death appeared in the world, it was murder. Cain slew Abel. "Two men", says Elie Wiesel, perhaps the most widely read writer on the Holocaust, "and one of them became a killer". The book of Genesis goes on to record that Cain was banished from Eden. He subsequently founded our first city—in the land of Nod, east of Eden—and named it Enoch, after his firstborn son. Through Enoch, Cain's line continued and prospered. Thousands of years later, *we all can be considered the children of Cain*. At the very least, we bear the taint of the violent legacy he ushered into the world when he killed his brother.[4]

Even more on track and relevant perhaps specifically to this chapter is the observation by Kjell Anderson:

> Religious figures may verbalize genocide using the language of sin or divine malevolence. All this mystification of evil has the effect of making genocide seem an inexplicable and, consequently, inexorable force. It also eternalizes the causes of genocide, rather than locating them in the realm of human social interaction. Genocide is not an act of God, any more than it is a natural disaster or a manifestation of mass hysteria.
>
> With the mystification of genocide also comes the mystification of the perpetrators. They are demonized as monsters arising from authentic and metaphysical evil rather than human society. This demonization of the perpetrators contains an aspect of righteous condemnation. Such condemnation is morally justifiable, yet when manifested as this sort of demonization, it is also misleading.[5]

Keeping both the insights of Waller and Anderson in mind, we turn to the work of Michael Mann, sociologist at the University of California, Los Angeles, whose pioneering work *The Dark Side of Democracy: Explaining Ethnic Cleansing* remains controversial.[6] In a paper prepared for the International Sociological Association Conference, Brisbane, Australia, in 2002, entitled "Explaining Murderous Ethnic Cleansing Eight Theses", in his eighth thesis, Mann suggests that "'ordinary people' are brought by 'normal' social structures into committing murderous ethnic cleansing" (and, thus, can be clustered into the following groups, applicable as well to *genocidaires*):

a **Ideological killers** believed in the righteousness of cleansing.
b **Bigoted killers** are motivated by more causal, less ideologically driven stereotypes of the victim group.
c **Violent killers** are drawn to killing.
d **Fearful killers** felt themselves threatened, with harm to life or limb, if they did not kill.
e **Careerist killers** were employed in organizations involved in murderous cleansing.
f **Materialist killers** were lured by the prospect of direct economic gain by looting or taking the victims' jobs, businesses, or property.
g **Disciplined killers** are caged within legitimate organizational authority, where non-compliance with orders is considered deviant.
h **Comradely killers** are caged inside conformity by peer-group pressure, especially by fear of the peer-group withdrawing its emotional support.[7]
i **Bureaucratic killers** are caged inside the "bureaucracies of modernity".[8]

Guenter Lewy, in his (2017) book *Perpetrators: The World of the Holocaust Killers*, drawing upon letters, diaries, recollections, and trial transcripts, writes of those who "worked" in the Nazi camps:

> The large majority of the guards abused the inmates because cruelty was the routine of the camps and therefore expected. The guards flogged, tormented, and killed because they were allowed and expected to do so. Violence and brutality were considered proof of commitment. Being rough with prisoners could further one's career in the camp system, whereas being soft would hurt and expose the SS man to derision and mockery from his fellow guards. Some guards harassed prisoners because they were bored or because it gave them a feeling of power. Many of the guards had little education, and the ability to have a member of the intellectual or professional class at their mercy provided a ready way to overcome a feeling of inferiority.[9]

Insightful and dramatic as Lewy's assessment is, however, it does not address the psychosociological reality of why such persons do so.

Robert Ericksen also goes on to suggest that

> "there is a powerful religious view which stresses the presence in all humans of "original sin", the human capacity for evil. Indeed, placed in the "right" circumstances and core constituencies, we are almost all capable of such evil—perhaps even of "enjoying" it".[10]

He cautions, however, that "'original sin' would be an insufficient explanation for this, since our capacity of evil only becomes realized in certain social circumstances".[11] Even recognizing that the earlier 20th century debate regarding "nature versus nurture" has long since died a rather ignoble death with the recognition that our physical, biological, and genetic natures play significant parts in our behaviors as do *all* of the cultural, familial, and societal influences that contribute to our individual and collective identities, there are still grounds for addressing what key factors—if any—in our psychological and sociological makeup contribute to shaping and forming us into the kinds of human beings who we are and the actions and activities in which we engage. Our focus, however, is not on the many, many different kinds of Holocaust/Shoah genocidal perpetrators there were, but rather on those we may label as "religionists", that is, those for whom their religion played a major role in their development, as the following troubling examples would seem both to indicate and support our thesis that religion—however defined and understood—remains a *participating* (and, in these specific cases, influencing) *factor* in genocide.[12] Those chosen are, most assuredly, not all in this category but, rather, representatives of a certain class/kind of *genocidaire*. Their notoriety speaks for itself but does not include members of the SS (*Schutzstaffel*, "Protection Squadron"), SA (*Sturmabteilung*, "Storm Troopers"), Gestapo (*Geheime Staatspolizei*, "Secret State Police"), or *Wehrmacht* ("Defense Force", i.e., Military)[13] who also participated in this genocide and for whom their Christianity—Roman Catholicism, Lutheranism, Protestantism—and, in the case of al-Husseini, Islam were central to their self-identity.

1 **Paul Althaus** (1888–1966), Lutheran theologian, World War I chaplain, and professor of theology at the University of Göttingen, Althaus welcomed Adolf Hitler's ascension to the Chancellorship of Germany as a "gift and miracle of God". His advocacy of German quasi-mystical peoplehood (*das Volk*) was consistent with his advocacy of National Socialism (Nazism), his pre-Nazi antisemitism, and his denigration of Judaism. After World War II, he was removed from his position during the de-Nazification process, but, in 1948, he returned to teaching at the University Erlangen where he remained until his retirement in 1966. In 1953, he was elected to the Bavarian Academy of Sciences and Humanities; six years later, 1959, he would be awarded the Bavarian Order of Merit.

2 **Mohammed Amin al-Husseini** (1897–1974) was the son of Jerusalem's Mayor and anti-Zionisit Tahir al-Husseini (1842–1908), himself strongly anti-Zionist, and a Muslim cleric. (During World War I, he would serve in the Ottoman Army.) He would go on to become Grand Mufti of Jerusalem and President of the Supreme Muslim Council (1921–1937/1948). Palestinian Arab nationalist, leader of the community in British Mandatory Palestine. He was both fiercely nationalistic and virulently antisemitic and opposed to both the Jewish presence in Palestine and immigration of Jews. Though sentenced in 1920 to ten years imprisonment for his participation in anti-British riots, he was pardoned shortly thereafter, and, in 1921, he was appointed Grand Mufti by the British High Commissioner Sir Herbert Samuel (1870–1963). Though initially perceived as an ally of the British, by 1936, he had turned against them, and allied himself with both Fascist Italy and Nazi Germany. Before the start of World War II in 1939, al-Husseini was intimately involved in fomenting anti-British and anti-Jewish/Zionist activities, including riots and murders throughout the Middle East, most especially in Palestine. By 1941, he was already resident in Berlin, broadcasting on Radio Berlin that killing the Jews of Palestine was a Muslim duty and trying (futilely) to convince Adolf Hitler (1889–1945) that exporting the Nazi annihilatory/exterminatory agenda should accompany their successful takeover of the Middle East. ("Arabs, fight as one man and fight for your sacred rights. Kill the Jews wherever you find them. This pleases God, history, and religion. This saves your honor. God is with you".)[14] He was also responsible for supporting the organization of the Handschar Regiment, the Kama Regiment, and the Skanderberg Regiment of like-minded

Muslims to fight alongside Hitler's troops as well as supporting the Azerbaijani Legion. Though not a great scholar, he buttressed his hatred of the Jews by regularly quoting verses from the Qur'an. After World War II, and especially after the Israeli-Arab/Palestinian War of 1948, his power and influence were significantly diminished and he died in Beirut, Lebanon, on 4 July 1974. (Though originally arrested by the French at the war's end, he successfully escaped, and was, ultimately, granted asylum in Egypt.)

3 **Adolf Bertram** (1859–1945), Roman Catholic Archbishop of Breslau, Poland (1914–1945) and later elevated to Cardinal, Bertram, very much pro-German, was a strong supporter of Hitler, Nazi Germany, and National Socialism. Early, he received doctorates in both theology and Canon Law. In the aftermath of World War I, he replaced Polish priests with German ones in this realm and sided with Germany vis—vis Polish-German political tensions. In 1932, he was denied papal permission to join the Nazi Party. As the Nazis' military successes increased in World War II, he ordered celebration in the churches under his control (e.g., Poland and France). At times, however, he did criticize Germany and National Socialism for both thoughts and actions, which he regarded as anti-Christian, while, at the same time, defending the Nazi state and Hitler's leadership. Among his papers found after his death was a handwritten note calling for a Requiem Mass for Germans who died during the war, including Hitler; the Mass was never held.

4 **Walter Grundmann** (1906–1976), Protestant theologian, antisemite, avowed Nazi, active member of *Deutsche Christen*, and later the *Stasi* (East German State Security Service) collaborator/informer for the German Democratic Republic (GDR) of East Germany and spying and reporting on other theologians, resident in both the East and the West. Grundmann was already a member of the Nazi Party by 1930. In 1939, he was appointed as a head of the Institute for the Study and Elimination of Jewish Influence on German Church Life in Jena whose acknowledged intent was to "deJudaize" the Bible (both Old and New Testaments) and legitimatize antisemitic theological training and Nazi propaganda efforts.[15]

5 **Emanuel Hirsch** (1888–1972), Protestant theologian and member of the Nazi Party, who, already in 1933, swore his allegiance to Adolf Hitler and the National Socialist State, officially joining the Party in 1937, and also became a "Patron Member" of the SS. Hirsch was a professor at the University of Göttingen from 1921 to 1945, but, rather than go through the de-Nazification process of the Allies, he resigned his position, supposed for health reasons, and forfeited his pension. A leader of the *Deutsche Christen* movement, he was also an advisor to *Reichbischof* Ludwig Müller.

6 **Alois Karl Hudal** (1885–1963), Austrian and Bishop of the Roman Catholic Church and holder of both a doctor of sacred theology degree

and a doctor of sacred scripture degree, was serving as a military chaplain during World War I. He was the head of both the Austrian-German congregation Santa Maria dell'Anima (until 1952) and rector of the Collegio Teutonico in Rome for the training of German and Austrian seminarians for the priesthood (1923–1952, the result of a forced resignation). An early supporter of Hitler and National Socialism, he helped establish the so-called ratline, which allowed prominent Nazis, both military and political, to escape capture and trial by the Allies, including Franz Stangl (1908–1971), Commandant of both the Sobibor and Treblinka death camps; Josef Mengele, MD/PhD (1908–1979), the notorious "Angel of Death" at Auschwitz death camp; Alois Brunner (1912–2001[?]/2010[?]), Commandant at the Drancy internment camp, France, and, later assistant to Eichmann; and Adolf Eichmann (1908–1962), himself, one of the major organizers of the Holocaust; among many others. Toward the end of the war, he sheltered escaping Nazis at the Santa Maria dell'Anima. In 1937, he published *The Foundations of National Socialism*, praising Hitler and his leadership while indirectly attacking Vatican policies, but which would, ultimately, draw the ire of both the Vatican and the Nazis. Hudal was also an advocate for what he termed "Christian National Socialism". The book, however, was banned in Germany for its disagreements/attacks on the leading Nazi theoretician Alfred Rosenberg (1893–1946). He would later go on to give vocal and public support to the German takeover of Austria (*Anschluss*, 12 March 1938). He was also notoriously outspoken in his antisemitism, anti-liberalism, and anti-Communism, and fully supportive of the German invasion of Soviet Russia ("Operation Barbarossa", 22 June–5 December 1941). Hudal remained convinced until his death that what he did was right: supporting and protecting Nazism and Nazis and fighting "godless Communism".

7 **Gerhard Kittel** (1888–1948), Lutheran theologian, lexicographer world-famous for his *Theological Dictionary of New Testament*, he was a professor of Evangelical Theology and New Testament at the University of Tübingen. He was the son of the great Hebrew Bible/Old Testament scholar Rudolf Kittel (1853–1929). Openly antisemitic, he defended himself by maintaining that his historical work was "scientific" in nature and arguing that his research showed the problematic evolution of early Judaism and its corruption of the beginning of Christianity and on into the modern period. He was also a member of the Institute for the History of the New Germany. In 1933, he published *Die Judenfrage* (*The Jewish Question*) wherein he advocated stripping Jews of their citizenship, removing them from professional life, and excluding contact between non-Jewish Germans and Jews. He never repudiated his text.

8 **Johan Heinrich Ludwig Müller** (1883–1945), Lutheran theologian and leader of the *Deutsche Christen* ("German Christian) movement, in 1933—the year Hitler came to power as Chancellor of Germany—was

appointed *Reichbischof* ("Reich Bishop") of the (Protestant) *Deutsche Evangelische Kirche* ("German Evangelical Church"). He remained both a committed Nazi and antisemite up to and including his suicide in 1945. After World War I, he became a military chaplain to the paramilitary *Der Stahlhelm* ("Steel Helmets") and was an already-committed National Socialist (Nazi) in the 1920s, and officially joined the new Nazi Party in 1931. Theologically and religiously, he was already committed to "purging" Christianity of the Jewish "corruption" of the faith and fully supported the revisionist understanding that the Christ was an Aryan rather than a Jew.

9 **Jozef Gaŝpar Tiso** (1887–1947), Roman Catholic priest and President of the Slovak Republic (1939–1945), was aggressively involved in the deportation of Slovakian Jews to extermination/death camps in both Germany and Poland, and later executed by hanging in Czechoslovakia for treason.[16] After World War II, Tiso was thus executed for both war crimes and crimes against humanity in the town of Bratislava. After the Nazi takeover of the Sudetenland the Nazis in 1938 and the breakup of Czechoslovakia, by 1939, Tisa was President of Slovakia and would become heavily involved with the deportation of its Jews. Initially a master of languages including Hungarian, German, and Latin, he also mastered Hebrew, Aramaic, and Arabic while at the University of Vienna and received his doctor of theology degree in 1911. Always politically active, he was a member of the Catholic People's Party in Slovakia after having been a member of the Slovak People's Party in 1918 and blamed the Jews for the rise of alcoholism in Slovakia. During World War I, he served a priest in the Austro-Hungarian Army, seeing firsthand the horrors of war and the increasing interests necessity for good government and good military organization. After the collapse of the Austro-Hungarian empire and monarchy, he saw himself part of the movement for Slovakian autonomy within the Czecho-Slovakian framework and became a popular and articulate political-religious figure and steadily evolving toward both authoritarianism and totalitarianism in his political outlook while, increasingly, becoming even more publicly antisemitic. Initially, he would become the prime minister of the new Slovakian Republic in 1939 before becoming its president that same year after the German invasion of Poland on 1 September 1939. Rather than an equal nation-state with Nazi Germany, the new republic under his leadership was more a client- or puppet-state. By 1942, close to 60,000 Slovakian Jews were deported and murdered.

These obvious examples saw no conflicts whatsoever between their faith—Islam or Catholic or Protestant Christianity—and their active collaborationist involvement with Nazism and the murder of millions of Jewish children, women, and men.[17] One must also recognize the 2,000-year bad histories of

Christian-Jewish relations stemming from the New Testament assessment of Jews as primarily responsible for the death of the Christ and the antagonism, early on, between the founder of Islam (Muhammed, 570–632) and the Arabian Jewish tribes rejecting his religio-theological vision reflected in any number of Qu'ranic verses and continuing to the present day on the part of some, not all, practitioners of both faiths. The slaughter of Jews and Jewish victim-groups by both was legitimated by their religious faiths and thus remains both a *participating and influencing factor* in such genocidal activities, an observation with which both Ericksen and Lewy would concur.[18] In the case of the Nazis and Nazi Germany, such "work" was further legitimated by those who manned the death camps—both men and women[19]—as well as those squads of men who was part of the *Einsatzgruppen* ("mobile killing units"), throughout Eastern Europe, primarily Soviet Russia. Thousands were involved in the day-to-day task of murder and many of their biographies cannot be divorced from the birth faiths in which they were baptized and to which they remained committed throughout their lives. Not all but many.[20]

Turning to genocide, the case of the 1994 Rwandan Genocide further faults those religionists/clerics who were *active* participants and, today, find themselves in prison, cleared, or released for their crimes after having been indicted, convicted, or cleared by the International Criminal Tribunal for Rwanda (ICTR, 8 November 1994–31 December 2015) and/or other jurisdictions. One notes the following:

1 **Maria Kisito** (b. 1964, Julienne Mukabutera), Rwandan Benedictine nun sentenced to twelve years in prison for her active participation in the murder of 500–700 people who sought refuge in her convent. Along with Mother Superior Mukangango, she not only directed the murderers to the convent, but supplied the petrol/gasoline to burn down the building itself.
2 **Augustin Misago** (1943–2012), Roman Catholic Bishop of the Diocese of Gikongoro, was accused of active participation in the genocide, but later cleared of all charges and died in office.
3 **Gertrude Mukangango,** Benedictine Mother Superior at the same convent as Maria Kisito was sentenced to fifteen years for the same crime.
4 **Wenceslas Munyeshyaka** (b. 1958), Roman Catholic priest, was convicted of genocide, rape, and aiding the murderers in their slaughter by a Rwandan military court, which sentenced him to life in prison. Relocating shortly after the genocide, he has continued to function as a priest in France since 2001. Though the French initially pursued him in court in 2006–2007, the evidence was found problematic. He was again brought to court in 2015, but the presiding judge dismissed the case in 2016 at the request of the prosecutor.
5 **Elizaphan Ntakirutimana** (1924–2007), Senior Pastor of the Seventh-Day Adventist Church and the first cleric to be sentenced along

with his son, a physician, Dr. Gérard Ntakirutimana. He was found guilty of transporting the murderers to his religious complex. He completed his ten-year sentence and died one month after his release at age eighty-two.

6 **Emmanuel Rukundo** (b. 1959), Roman Catholic priest. Originally, he was found guilty and sentenced to twenty-five years for active participation in genocide, rape, murder, and crimes against humanity. His sentence was later reduced to twenty-three years in 2010. He was released in 2016 having served sixteen years. Prior to the genocide, he has served as a military chaplain. Having initially fled to Switzerland, he was denied refugee status and deported to Arusha, Tanzania, to stand trial before the ICTR.

7 **Athanase Seromba** (b. 1963) Roman Catholic priest convicted of enabling the *genocidaires* to bulldoze his church where 1,500–2,000 Tutsis were taking refuge. Found guilty of genocide and crimes against humanity, he was sentenced to fifteen years in prison.[21] He first fled to Italy and changed his name but surrendered himself to the ICTR. His trial took place between 2004 and 2006. As of 2009, he was serving his life sentenced in prison in Porto-Novo, Benin.

Again, these seven—six convicted and one cleared—represent only some, not all, of those clerics brought before the ICTY and accused, convicted, or not. That those convicted saw no conflict between their faith and its teachings and their *active* involvement and complicity in the crime of genocide is at issue.[22] In another context, equally arguing that religion is a flawed sociocultural construction which too-easily lends itself to genocide by virtue of sharing with it many of the same characteristics (e.g., "us versus them", systematic organized structures, leadership cadre orientations, sense-making worldviews, moral/ethical behavioral expectations, symbolization, and the like), ultimately, religion thus remains a too-easily adaptable tool in the genocide toolbox.[23]

Furthermore, the seventeen persons briefly described above were *leaders* of their respective communities, and one must not underestimate or undervalue the role, responsibility, and influence of leadership in enabling followers to implement and carry out their own genocidal visions. Daniel Chirot in his (1994) text *Modern Tyrants* makes the following points:

> Once a tyrant is in power, whatever his original motivation, the tendency toward increasing isolation from reality, growing impatience and frustration at the reverses he inevitably suffers, and mounting intolerance of criticism, tend to make him suspicious of all those around him. We see this in the career of every tyrant, and in fact, of every individual who is in power for too long.
>
> (144–145)

The position of those in authority to appoint yes-men is widespread and is one of the most common of failures of leadership in all social systems. But turning the one in power into a god whom everyone fears and who can justify his actions by claiming and eventually believing himself to represent the force of fated history, magnifies the problem.

(164)[24]

He then goes on to enumerate eight "Propositions" applicable as he understands it to tyrants in the political arena:

1. The more chaotic the economy and political system, the more they seem to be failing, the more likely it is that a tyrant will emerge as a self-proclaimed savior.
2. The weaker the administrative apparatus of the state, the more likely it is that there will be the kind of chaos that leads to the emergence of a powerful potential national savior; and the easier it will be for him to turn into a tyrant once he has seized power.
3. For any nation, new or old, we can judge the extent to which its political and intellectual elite's identity is based on jealous and vengeful resentment, on memories of past wrongs, real or imagined, and estimate that the more this is so, the higher the probability of future tyrannies.
4. The more strongly communal values are held to be superior to individual rights, and the more it is believed that every individual is determined by traits he or she automatically inherits from his or her community, the more likely it is that tyranny will be found morally acceptable for the greater good of the community.
5. The stronger the ideologies of inevitable conflict between communities—by they races, nations, economic classes, *or religions*—the more likely it is that tyranny will occur.
6. Reactive nationalism that is based on fear and resentment of the outside world, that demands communal solidarity of the entire nation, regardless of the cultural and individual differences which exist, and that faced serious internal ethnic *and religious* diversity is likely to impose itself by force. This will produce resistance, and in turn, acceptance of increasingly tyrannical methods of rule by those in power in order to sustain the nationalist ideal.
7. Nationalist elites who believe that discipline and social purity, defined as the exclusion of "foreign" values and habits, can solve the complex problems of adapting to the modern world are likely to become both increasingly frustrated and tyrannical once they achieve power.[25]
8. A tyrant who is not an intellectual, or ceased to identify himself as one, and who rejects the influence of the ideological intelligentsia, will be corrupt because that will become the only basis of his power. He will feel

threatened by intellectuals and persecute them because they have more coherent ideological programs that threaten his rule.

(409 ff.; emphases added)[26]

Clerics are not tyrants, though some, throughout history, have acted tyrannically. Regarding the above, however, the following observations are relevant.

1. Religious leaders, ofttimes by dint of their own personality structures and orientations to the world around them, *do* see themselves as "saviors" of a disenchanted and disenfranchised humanity.
2. The chaotic world in which they find themselves—the breakdown of the societies of which they are a part—may very well energize them to present their vision of the "divine-human encounter" for humanity as the last, best hope for survival.
3. The perceived moral-ethical solution is to "right the wrongs" of the past in keeping with their strong believe that the god (or gods) to whom they are committed has/have "tapped them" (communicated with them?) for this special purpose.
4. For those already a part of the favored religious community, they are "saved". Others who are not are invited into the community of the saved, or worst-case scenario, excluded from the community of the saved, and then left to their own survival devices, or physically removed, up to and including sanctioning genocide.
5. The somewhat trite cliché "our way or the highway" is applicable here as well. Only *this* religious vision of *this* religious leader and only *this* religious community hold out the promise of salvation, however defined and understood.
6. Fear itself remains a component of the religious leader's argument with "hell" either in this world or the next being the reality awaiting one and one's group failing to get on board or excluded from getting on board.
7. Purification, too, remains a strong component of the cleansing process along this road to salvation. The individual must engage in specific activities to thus cleanse and purify himself or herself and continually prove worthy of membership as the cleric/leader understands it.
8. If British Lord Acton (John Dalberg-Acton, 1834–1902) was even minimally correct that "power corrupts and absolute power corrupts absolutely", then religious leadership, like all other forms of leadership, has in itself the potential to corrupt over time those who occupy those positions of power and those who follow them.

★ ★ ★ ★ ★

With what then are we left? Attempting to asses those who perpetrate genocide, we turn first to psychology and then to sociology, and we begin with the comment of German-American philosopher, sociologist, psychologist, musicologist, and composer known for his critical theory of society, Theodor Adorno (1903–1969). In a radio interview in 1966, which would later be printed as "Education After Auschwitz", he addressed his concern regarding "the psychology of those who do such things":

> The roots must be sought in the persecutors, not in the victims who are murdered under the paltriest of pretenses. What is necessary is what I once in this respect called the turn to the subject. One must come to know the mechanisms that render people capable of such deeds, must reveal these mechanisms to them, and strive, by awakening a general awareness of these mechanisms, to prevent people from becoming so again.

As Robert P. Ericksen notes as well:

> There is *something* about ordinary people that leaves them willing to commit murder when asked to do so. There is *something* about people with spiritual commitments and abundant education that yet lets them be willing to support extraordinarily harsh policies if it seems consistent with their national duty.[27]

It is to that "something" that we now turn.

An important distinction, at the outset, is that posed by Kara Critchell and her colleagues in their Editors' Introduction to the inaugural issue of the *Journal of Perpetrator Research*, namely that between "motive" and "motivation":

> *Motive* is used to mean the specific reasons for performing a specific action, an incentive, a particular goal or objective…*Motivation* is generally what drives a person, at a deeper level, to pursue certain broader goals of self-actualization in life.[28]

Thus, psychologically, while Robert Lifton uses the term "doubling" to refer to those Nazi medical doctors (and other personnel) who could perform their hideous labors inside the various concentration, labor, and death camps (Note 19), I use the term "bifurcation" to describe these and other individuals who were able to go about their genocidal tasks not seeing their fellow human beings—members of the human community—but as enemies for whom the only solution to the threat to their own existence and that of their own community was destruction, annihilation, extermination; death.[29] Placing themselves and their group at the very center of human existence—for which we now have the new term "selfing"—they remain evidently easily able to engage in "othering", ofttimes without penalty or remorse.[30] That mindset, despite perhaps even having been schooled in the ability to distinguish between right and wrong, going so far as to, at least initially, experience distaste, discomfort, or even revulsion at taking the lives of others, enables such murderers to draw upon both an innate xenophobia (i.e., fear of that which is different and therefore threatening) and our very human ability to rationalize (justify, legitimate) such activities in their own eyes and the eyes of other group members for whom such membership is of importance. *We are not genocidally predisposed by our very nature, but all factors considered, we may very well be violent by nature, and our ability to curb that instinctual behavior when confronted by the appearance of seemingly threatening behaviors "triggers" the very behaviors, which are at the heart of this text.* Possessed of these very same innate attributes, religionists both those in leadership positions and those who follow them draw upon them when perceived as warranted to both distance themselves from their enemies—ofttimes labeled as inferior or wrong expressions or understandings of the divine-human encounter—and thus participate in the very genocidal activities, which render them complicit or, at the very least, collaborationists or bystanders.

Then, too, sociologically, group-think comes into play. As members of a living species, we are not isolates, except in the rarest of circumstances, and participation and membership in groups, large or small, marks us as humans even as it does not distinguish us from other animal species who, like us, follow the dictates and demands of leaders. Sociologists talk in terms of both *achieved* leadership and *ascribed* leadership: those whose positions are the result of their own doing—ofttimes with the assistance of a coterie of others—Mann's so-called elites—and those who inherit their positions by others who preceded them—family members—who themselves may have arrived through either portal. Threats to either leaders or followers are met when religious power is coupled with state power by violent responses and legitimatized by sacred texts (Old or New Testament, Qur'an, and others), rituals (scapegoating), and the like, and the "knowledge" that their God or gods has/have smiled favorably upon them and validated them as well.

Who then are those who *do* genocide? Those whose very human-ness draws upon innate qualities in the service of corrupt or corrupted leaders whose own hunger to achieve and maintain power demands of those who follow them acts which in other circumstances may not necessarily result in such life-threatening and or life-taking behaviors and activities. Girded by seemingly uncontested divine legitimation, religionists, like others in other groups (political, social, economic, and military[31]), are potentially genocidal actors, but, unlike others, draw upon distinctively unique tools—their own socio-cultural construct—which all-too-easily marks them as participants or, depending upon the historical circumstances (e.g., Cathar threat to Roman Catholicism), initiators.

Summarily, social psychologist James Waller provides something of a progressive template or model attempting to answer this question of how seemingly "ordinary" people come to engage in genocide.

Chart 3 A model of how ordinary people commit genocide and mass killing

How do ordinary people commit genocide and mass killing?		
Which leads to: Ultimate influences: The Evolution of Human Nature *Which leads to:*		
Proximate Influence: Cultural Construction of Worldview	Proximate Influence: Psychological Construction\of the "Other"	Proximate Influence: Social Construction of Cruelty
Which leads to:		
1 Collectivistic Values	1 Us-Them Thinking	1 Professional Socialization
2 Authority Orientation	2 Moral Disengagement	2 Group Identification
3 Social Dominance	3 Blaming the Victims	3 Binding Factors of the Group[32]

Yet, despite everything written, every conjecture, every attempt at understanding why some individuals and groups—leaders and followers as well—perpetrate genocide and others do not, we may be no closer to that understanding. But that lack of clarity does not absolve us of attempting to try.

Notes

1 In their Editors' Introduction to 1:1, Kara Critchell, Susanne C. Knittel, Emiliano Perra, and Uğur Umit Üngör raise the following questions:

> How do we define, understand and encounter perpetrators of political violence? What can be learned from studying the perpetrators? How are perpetrators made and unmade? Which sociological, psychological, historical, and political processes are relevant in understanding perpetrators and perpetration? What can we discern about their motivations, and how can that help society and policy-makers in countering and preventing such occurrences? How are perpetrators represented in a variety of memory spaces including art, film, literature, theatre, commemorative culture, and education?

Kara Critchell, et al. (2017), "Editors' Introduction", *Journal of Perpetrator Research*, 1(1): 2–3.

2 Kjell Anderson, *Perpetrating Genocide: A Criminological Account* (London and New York: Routledge, 2018), 6; emphasis added.

3 In 2019, Oxford Academic put together an online collection entitled "History of Collaborators: Loyalists to Oppressive Regimes" taken from various journals addressing sixteen such instances of collaboration in the modern era. https://academic.oup/ahr/pages/history_of_collaborators. Accessed 6 February 2019. See, also, for example, Sheila Fitzpatrick, ed., *Accusatory Practices: Denunciation in Modern European History* (Chicago: The University of Chicago Press, 1997); and Jan Grabowski, *The Polish Police: Collaboration in the Holocaust* (Washington, DC: United States Holocaust Memorial Museum, 2016).

4 James Waller, *Becoming Evil: How Ordinary People Commit Genocide and Mass Killing* (Oxford and New York: Oxford University Press, 2007. Second Edition), xiv; emphasis added.
5 Kjell Anderson, *Perpetrating Genocide: A Criminological Account* (London and New York: Routledge, 2018), 2.
6 Cambridge: Cambridge University Press, 2005. John Breuilly, David Cesarani, Siniŝa Maleŝević, Benjamin Neuberger, and Michael Mann (2006), "Debate on Michael Mann's *The Dark Side of Democracy: Explaining Ethnic Cleansing*", *Nations and Nationalism*, 12(3): 389–411.
7 Christopher Browning's *Ordinary Men: Reserve Police Battalion 101 and the Final Solution in Poland* (New York and London: Harper Perennial, 2017. Second Edition) comes readily to mind, wherein he argues that those "ordinary middle-aged, working-class men who committed these atrocities" did so "out of a mixture of motives, including the group dynamics of conformity, deference to authority, role adaptation, and the altering of moral norms to justify their actions".
8 Social psychologists Roy F. Baumeister and Kathleen D. Vohs suggest that there are "four main reasons people do what they do (commit genocide):

> First, there is 'instrumentality' or violence and evil-doing as 'means to an end'—to get something (power, money, land, or resources, etc.) or to influence someone else in a competitive situation where violence is one of the options for resolving the conflict.
>   Second, the reason for the attack could be 'threatened egotism' when the 'image of self' is threatened or there is 'wounded pride' or honour.
>   Third is 'idealism' and 'doing good by doing bad'.
>   Finally, 'sadism: the joy of hurting' is listed here as 'the most common account in victims' testimonies and fictional depictions but the least common in everyday life.

Olaf Jensen (2008), "Introductory Thoughts and Overview", in Olaf Jensen and Claus-Christian W. Szewjnmann, eds. *Ordinary People as Mass Murderers: Perpetrators in Comparative Perspective* (New York: Palgrave Macmillan), 8.
9 Guenter Lewy, *Perpetrators: The World of the Holocaust Killers* (Oxford and New York: Oxford University Press, 2017), 17.
10 This same thesis is also presented by Hans Ashkenasy in his book *Are We All Nazis?* (New York: Lyle Stuart, 1978).
11 His first seven theses (and equally applicable to genocide) are:

  1 Murderous ethnic cleansing is modern because it is the dark-side of democracy.
  2 Ethnic hostility rises where ethnicity trumps class as the main form for social stratification, in the process "capturing" and "channeling" class-like sentiments toward ethno-nationalism.
  3 The "danger zone" of murderous cleansing is reached when (a) large movements claiming to represent two fairly "old" ethnic groups have both persistently laid claims to "their own" state of all or part of the same territory; and (b) this claim seems to them to have substantial legitimacy and some plausible chance of being implemented. [NB: One of the complicating factors in the ongoing Israeli-Palestinian divide.]
  4 The "brink" of murderous cleansing is reached in one of two alternative scenarios.

>   a The less powerful side is bolstered to fight rather than to submit by believing that aid will be forthcoming from outside.
>   b The stronger side believes that it has such overwhelming military power and ideological legitimacy that it can achieve its own cleansed state violently at little physical or moral risk to itself.
>
> 5 "Going over the brink" into perpetrating murderous cleansing occurs when the state exercising sovereignty over the contested territory has become factionalized and then radicalized amid an unstable geopolitical environment leading into a war in which the outgroup is seen as one of the enemies.
> 6 Murderous cleansing is rarely the initial intent of the perpetrators. [NB: The case of the Nazis versus the Jews and the former's exterminatory/ annihilatory agenda would appear to dispute this thesis even while many reputable historians would date its true beginnings with the German invasion of Russia— "Operation Barbarossa"—in 1941.]
> 7 But there are three distinct levels of perpetrators:
>   a Radical elites commanding "party-states"
>   b Bands of militants forming violent "paramilitaries"
>   c "Core constituencies" of ethno-nationalism providing mass though not usually majority popular support.

12 Pieter Nanninga inserts into this discussion an important caveat, to wit:

> Attributing a particular role to 'religion' in explaining the event is inconsistent, as there are no objective criteria to decide about what constitute religious motivations and what not. Rather than focusing on religion as an abstract category, we should ask how and why particular traditions, beliefs, and practices deemed religious by the perpetrators have been appropriated to shape, justify, and give meaning to their actions.

Pieter Nanninga (2019), "Religion and International Crimes: The Case of the Islamic State" in Alette Smeulers, Maartje Weerdesteijn, and Barbora Hola, eds., *Perpetrators of International Crimes: Theories, Methods, and Evidence* (Oxford and New York: Oxford University Press), 2019.

13 See, for example, Alex J. Kay, and David Stahel (2020), "Crimes of the Wehrmacht: A Re-evaluation", *Journal of Perpetrator Research*, 3(1): 95–127.
14 Quoted by Howard Morley Sachar, *Aliyah: The Peoples of Israel* (Cleveland: World Publishing Company, 1961), 231.
15 For a close examination of Grundmann and his Institute, see Susannah Heschel, *The Aryan Jesus: Christian Theologians and the Bible in Nazi Germany* (Princeton and Oxford: Princeton University Press, 2008).
16 The most comprehensive study of these and other Christian theologians and biblical scholars in Germany is that of Anders Gerdmar, *Roots of Theological Anti-Semitism: German Biblical Interpretation and the Jews, from Herder and Semler to Kittel and Bultmann* (Leiden and Boston: Brill, 2009).
17 Three times in their article "German Catholic Bishops and the Holocaust, 1940–1952" (1988), Frank M. Buscher and Michael Phayer fault many of the bishops of the Roman Catholic Church for failing "to exercise their authority effectively and constructively" (463), "shouldered no responsibility and accepted no share of guilt for failing to exercise their moral authority during the Holocaust" (472); "against advice from within their own ranks, they kept silent about it…they decided against indicting themselves for not speaking out" (479). *German Studies Review*, 11(3). Further muddying these waters, Doris Bergen (2001) examines

the roles, from marginal to active supporters, of the Wehrmacht chaplains in World War II: "German Military Chaplains in World War II and the Dilemma of Legitimacy", *Church History*, 70(2): 232–247. And while the important Catholic document *Nostra Aetate* ("in Our Time"), absolving Jews of responsibility in Christ's death and declaring antisemitism as anti-Christian, in 1965 and "We Remember: A Reflection on the Shoah" in 1998 mark important advances in Jewish-Catholic (and Protestant) relations, the Church as an institution has yet to address its own 2,000-year history of involvement in the progression of an antisemitism that, ultimately, directly or indirectly, may have provided a foundational underpinning for the Holocaust itself.

18 Robert Ericksen:

> It should be stated clearly than Germans became Nazis because they wanted to become Nazis and because the Nazis spoke so well to their interests and inclinations. Numerous studies now show that the level of Christian support for Hitler and the Nazi state during most of the Third Reich. Even when some Christians questioned some aspects of the regime, most retained overall support and appreciation for Hitler's successes.

Robert P. Ericksen (2019), "'Ordinary Christians' in Nazi Germany", in Thomas Pegelow Kaplan, Jürgen Matthäus, and Mark W. Hornburg, eds., *Beyond 'Ordinary Men': Christopher R. Browning and Holocaust Historiography* (Leiden: Ferdinand Schöningh/Brill), 54.

Guenter Lewy:

> It appears that not a few of those who objected to the murder of the Jews and actively tried to help were believing Christians, but we know that being a Christian did not prevent numerous others from participating in the killing. Virtually all Nazis were the baptized children of Christians, and the continued adherence of the great majority of the German people to the Christian faith did not constitute an effective bulwark to the relentless process of destruction. Almost eighteen thousand Catholic priests, theology students, and lay brothers served in the Wehrmacht as military chaplains, but not one of them voiced dissent from the policy of annihilation. The record of Protestant military chaplains has not yet been examined in detail, but it appears not to be any different. For all these men, dedication to the fatherland and promoting the salvation of Christian souls was more important than challenging the genocidal practices of the Nazi regime. These policies were antithetical to everything their faith stood for, but this theoretical conflict failed to prevent their deportment of accommodation and compromise.

Guenter Lewy, *Perpetrators: The World of the Holocaust Killers* (Oxford and New York: Oxford University Press, 2017), 86.

19 See, for example, the well-known text by Robert Jay Lifton, *The Nazi Doctors: Medical Killing and the Psychology of Genocide* (New York: Basic Books, 1986) whereby he suggests that those medical professionals who carried on their work in the Nazi death camps fell prey psychologically to the concept of "doubling", essentially splitting their personalities into two—an individual variation and rationalization, perhaps, of the "good cop/bad cop" theme—which enabled them to do their work without moral qualms. Wendy Lower's *Hitler's Furies: German Women in the Nazi Killing Fields* (New York: Houghton Mifflin Harcourt, 2011); Izabela Steftja, and Jessica Trisko Darden, *Women as War Criminals: Gender, Agency and Justice* (Stanford: Stanford University Press, 2020); and Flint Whitlock, *The Beasts of Buchenwald: Karl & Ilse Koch, Human-Skin Lampshades, and*

the War Crimes Trial of the Century (Brule, WI: Cable Publishing, 2011) serve to remind readers that men alone are never solely responsible, no matter how much they predominate, in genocide, war crimes, and crimes against humanity.

20 Michael Mann has addressed this in his (2000) article "Were the Perpetrators of Genocide 'Ordinary Men' or 'Real Nazis'? Results from Fifteen Hundred Biographies", *Holocaust and Genocide Studies*, 14(3) 331–366, especially, 347–350, "Religion" and Table 3 "Religion of Family of Origin and Birthplace Census District". See, also, Robert Gellately, *Hitler's True Believers: How Ordinary People Became Nazis* (Oxford and New York: Oxford University Press, 2020) vis-à-vis supporters/ collaborationists/bystanders; Peter Fritsche, *Germans into Nazis* (Cambridge: Havard University Press, 1999); Guenter Lewy, *Perpetrators: The World of Holocaust Killers* (Oxford and New York: Oxford University Press, 2017), forcefully arguing for the very "ordinariness" of those who did the actual work of Nazi genocide. Further expanding this overall discussion are Victoria Barnett, *Bystanders: Conscience and Complicity during the Holocaust* (Westport: Praeger, 2000), Amos N. Guiora, *The Crime of Complicity: The Bystander in the Holocaust* (Lanham: Ankerwyke Publishing, 2017); and Raul Hilberg, *Perpetrators, Victims, Bystanders* (New York: Harper Perennial, 1993).

21 Though Wikipedia always remains a questionable academic resource due to both the anonymity of its authors and the too-easily editing of its articles, interestingly enough, under the category of "Genocide perpetrators", it includes 19 Armenian genocide perpetrators; 11 Bosnian genocide perpetrators; 59 Holocaust perpetrators, but 114 "major perpetrators of the Holocaust"; 11 Nanjing Massacre perpetrators; 37 Romani genocide perpetrators; and 6 Seyfo (Assyrian Genocide) perpetrators, all told, more than 250 such persons, and a veritable gold mine database worthy of further explorations as to their religious upbringing, their status, and their active involvement or lack thereof during the time of their participation in genocidal criminality.

22 Felix Bigabo and Angela Jansen (2020) interviewing imprisoned Rwandan Genocide perpetrators write of them continuously working on ways to acknowledge, rationalize or justify those acts as part of their biography. "From Child to Genocide Perpetrator: Narrative Identity Analysis among Genocide Prisoners Incarcerated in Muhanga Prison, Rwanda", *Psychology Research and Behavior Management*, 13: 759–774.

23 Steven Leonard Jacobs, "The Religion-Genocide Nexus", in Ben Kiernan, Tracy Lemos, eds., *The Cambridge World History of Genocide* (Cambridge: Cambridge University Press), forthcoming.

24 Princeton: Princeton University Press, 1994. Richard Weikart makes this very point regarding Adolf Hitler (1889–1945) in *Hitler's Religion: The Twisted Beliefs that Drove the Third Reich* (Washington: Regnery History, 2016). See, also, Anna Della Subin, *Accidental Gods: On Men Unwittingly Turned Divine* (New York: Metropolitan Books, 2021.)

25 Jacques Semelin addresses this very idea in his *Purify and Destroy: The Political Uses of Massacre and Genocide* (New York: Columbia University Press, 2007).

26 Benjamin Valentino equally argues regarding the importance of the leader in organizing, fomenting, and implementing genocide and noting that "the impetus for mass killing usually originates from a relatively small group of powerful leaders and is often carried out without the active support of broader society". *Final Solutions: Mass Killing and Genocide in the 20th Century* (Ithaca and London: Cornell University Press, 2004).

27 Robert P. Ericksen (2019), "'Ordinary Christians' in Nazi Germany", in Thomas Pegelow Kaplan, Jürgen Matthäus, and Mark W. Hornburg, eds., *Beyond*

"Ordinary Men": Christopher R. Browning and Holocaust Historiography (Leiden: Ferdinand Schöningh/Brill), 54; emphases added.
28 Kara Critchell, Susanne C. Knittel, Emiliano Perra, and Uğur Umit Üngor (2017), "Editors' Introduction", *Journal of Perpetrator Research*, 1(1): 16.
29 Steven Leonard Jacobs (2008/2009), "Revisiting hateful Science: The Nazi 'Contribution' to the Journey of Antisemitism", *Journal of Hate Studies*, 7(1): 47–75.
30 In order effectively perpetrate a genocide, dehumanization must come into play. As Lewy notes:

> The dehumanized victim is deprived of his human status and is no longer perceived as a feeling suffering person. Dehumanization creates psychological distance between the perpetrator and evildoing. The victim becomes expendable. Dehumanization also implies that the victims deserve such extremes measures as death. When they are depicted as demons or other threatening types, whatever is done to them is justified. Seen against an imaginary deadly menace, deportation and mass murder could become pre-emptive self-defense. The best way of protecting us from the effect of witnessing the pain and suffering of others is to convince ourselves that the victims must have done something to bring it on themselves.

Guenter Lewy, *Perpetrators: The World of the Holocaust Killers* (Oxford and New York: Oxford University Press, 2017), 123.
31 Here, one cannot, at least in the American context, but think of the My Lai massacre during the Viet Nam debacle (March 16, 1998), or the Abu Ghraib prison humiliation including torture of Iraqi detainees during the Iraqi "War on Terror" (2003–2004)—now realized as an unsubstantiated and failed search for weapons of mass destruction (WMDs). Far less well-known is that of the Korean massacre by American troops at No Gun Ri during the Korean War (26–29 July 1950). Such assaults upon humanity, as distinct from genocide, however, fall into the category of so-called war crimes. They are, ofttimes, no less genocidal having the goal of fully destroying the victim-group. See, for example, Michael Bryant, *A World History of War Crimes: From Antiquity to the Present* (London and New York: Bloomsbury Academic, 2021); Roy Guttman, David Rieff, and Anthony Dworkin, eds. *Crimes of War 2.0: What the Public Should Know* (New York and London: W. W. Norton and Company, 2007. Revised and Updated Edition); and Aryeh Neier, *War Crimes: Brutality, Genocide, Terror, and the Struggle for Justice* (New York: Random House, 1998).
32 James Waller, *Becoming Evil: How Ordinary People Commit Genocide and Mass Killing* (Oxford and New York: Oxford University Press, 2007. Second Edition), 138; and (2008), "The Ordinariness of Extraordinary Evil: the Making of Perpetrators of Genocide and Mass Killing", in Olaf Jensen and Claus-Christian W. Szejnmann, eds., *Ordinary People as Mass Murderers: Perpetrators in Comparative Perspective* (New York: Palgrave Macmillan), 149.

Chapter 7

"Holy" Wars and "Religious" Wars
Is There a Connection?

Seemingly, we have developed a plethora of terms to describe "mega-death", both historically and contemporarily, including such terms as "ethnic cleansing" (previously addressed) and "mass murder", but, most especially, "holy wars" and, perhaps more inclusively, "religious" wars, this latter term being ramped up since the tragedy of 9/11 in the United States—and worldwide. The questions posed in this chapter are (1) whether these terms and what they present/represent—and conceivably others, including, quite possibly, Holocaust/*Shoah*—are subsumed under the larger category of genocide, and (2) whether religion plays a distinctive role in each of them individually or all of them collectively. This chapter also examines the various groups we label "terrorists" (e.g., al-Qaeda, ISIS/ISIL, and Taliban) and takes into consideration both the Western and Eastern religious traditions as we understand them. Thus, this chapter will address the following terminological topics: (1) Crusades; (2) Geneva Conventions; (3) Inquisition (Spanish and Portuguese); (4) Jihad; (5) Just War Theory and its Egyptian, Greek, Roman, and Judaic predecessors; (6) massacres; (7) religious wars/holy wars; and (8) terrorism and terrorists. Though enumerated here alphabetically, our point of reference/framework is that of the *longue durée* (French, "long view"), historically considered.

Even before Just War Theory (Latin, *ius belli justi*), most closely associated with the Roman Catholic Church and the writings of saints Augustine (354–430 CE) and Thomas Aquinas (1225–1274)—though in actuality having a pre-Catholic history—the rabbis of the post-biblical Judaic *religious* tradition had already addressed notions of war by drawing a significant distinction between what they labeled *milkhemet mitzvah* or *milkhemet hovah* or "obligatory war" and *milkhemet reshut* or "permitted" or "optional" war, the former understood as necessary for defensive reasons but the latter for non-defensive reasons, for example, the desire to expand a nation-state's boundaries or the acquisition of additional resources. For them as well, there was no distinction between the sacred and secular; all was subsumed in a theocratic understanding where the singular deity—God—was first, last, and always, an interactive and guiding player for humanity, holding it accountable for its actions either in concert with divine guidance and demand/command or in opposition to it. Their own religio-ethical sensitivities, however, found support in what is often overlooked, the opening verses of Deuteronomy 20:

> When you go forth to war against your enemies and see horses and chariots and an army larger than your own, you shall not be afraid of them; for the LORD your God is with you, who brought you up out of the land of Egypt.[2] And when you draw near to the battle, the priest shall come forward and speak to the people,[3] and shall say to them, 'Hear, O Israel, you draw near this day to battle against your enemies: let not your heart faint; do not fear, or tremble, or be in dread of them;[4] for the LORD your God is he that goes with you, to fight for you against your enemies, to give you the victory.'[5] Then the officers shall speak to the people, saying, 'What man is there that has built a new house and has not dedicated it? Let him go back to his house, lest he die in the battle and another man dedicate it.[6] And what man is there that has planted a vineyard and has not enjoyed its fruit? Let him go back to his house, lest he die in the battle and another man enjoy its fruit.[7] And what man is there that has betrothed a wife and has not taken her? Let him go back to his house, lest he die in the battle and another man take her.'[8] And the officers shall speak further to the people, and say, 'What man is there that is fearful and fainthearted? Let him go back to his house, lest the heart of his fellows melt as his heart.'

Equally so in the treatment of women captives as specified in Deuteronomy 21:

> [10] When you go forth to war against your enemies, and the LORD your God gives them into your hands, and you take them captive,[11] and see among the captives a beautiful woman, and you have desire for her and would take her for yourself as wife,[12] then you shall bring her home to your house, and she shall shave her head and pare her nails.[13] And she shall put off her captive's garb and shall remain in your house and bewail her father and her mother a full month; after that you may go in to her, and be her husband, and she shall be your wife.[14] Then, if you have no delight in her, you shall let her go where she will; but you shall not sell her for money, you shall not treat her as a slave, since you have humiliated her.

Taken together, biblical passages such as these and their rabbinic commentaries over the generations on the conduct of war reflect not only a tragic acceptance of the reality of war but a stance that it must be both conducted and framed by moral and ethical behavior.[1]

Paralleling somewhat, perhaps, these biblical passages, we already find in Egyptian, Chinese, and Japanese, Indian/Hindu, Greek, and Roman literatures discussions of war and proper and improper/inappropriate behaviors.

For example, in studying the Egyptian Old Kingdom (2686–2181 BCE), the Egyptian Middle Kingdom, 2055–1650 BC), and the Egyptian New Kingdom (1552–1069 BCE), Rory Cox concluded that

> The ethics of war in ancient Egypt was founded upon three tenets of Egyptian culture that displayed remarkable longevity and consistency: (1) the cosmological role of Egypt, (2) the divine office of the pharaoh, and (3) the superiority of the land of Egypt and its inhabitants over all other lands and peoples. These ideological foundations led the Egyptian political elite to develop an ethics of war that possessed elements analogous to later Western concepts of proper authority and just cause so-called *ius ad bellum* criteria.[2]

Cox's use of the words "culture" and "ideology" as regards ancient Egypt equate well with our word "religion" and cannot be divorced from it.

For the Chinese, during the Zhou Dynasty (1046–256 BCE), its philosophical scholars produced much literature regarding war as only a last resort and only at the unquestioned decision of the emperor. Military success validated the decision. In turn, the Japanese would themselves draw upon this same philosophical body of knowledge.[3]

In the classical Indian Hindu text, the *Mahabharata*, a lengthy discussion of "just" or "righteous" war is entertained with an eye toward establishing *just conduct, just proportionality, just means*, and *just cause*, framed by the question of whether suffering in war can ever be justified. Equally, Sikhism, too, discussed legitimating defensive wars fought for just, righteous, or religious reasons to preserve the faith and the faithful.[4]

For these four as well—Chinese, Japanese, Hindu, and Sikh, and other ancient religious traditions— "religion" is inextricably bound up with the realities of war and proper/improper behavior when engaged in its practice.

For Cian O'Driscoll, "Ideas homologous to a range of core *jus ad bellum, jus in bello*, and *jus post bellum* principles were evident in classical Greek political thought and practice".[5] His rather expansive focus addresses such questions as (1) proper authority, (2) just cause, (3) right intention, (4) discrimination, and (5) proportionality. Throughout and foundational to the Greeks' conduct of war was the role, purpose, function, and interplay of the gods, as it was for the Romans as well.

Turning then to the Christian and most well-known understanding of Just War Theory, we begin with Augustine. His own starting point was found in Paul's Letter to the Romans, 13:1–7 vis-a-vis the authority of the ruler not only to engage in violent acts, but to collect taxes as well, and the responsibility of the citizen to "subject [himself] to the governing authorities", to wit:

Let every person be subject to the governing authorities. For there is no authority except from God, and those that exist have been instituted by God.[2] Therefore he who resists the authorities resists what God has appointed, and those who resist will incur judgment.[3] For rulers are not a terror to good conduct, but to bad. Would you have no fear of him who is in authority? Then do what is good, and you will receive his approval,[4] for he is God's servant for your good. But if you do wrong, be afraid, for *he does not bear the sword in vain; he is the servant of God to execute his wrath on the wrongdoer.*[5] Therefore one must be subject, not only to avoid God's wrath but also for the sake of conscience.[6] For the same reason you also pay taxes, for the authorities are ministers of God, attending to this very thing.[7] Pay all of them their dues, taxes to whom taxes are due, revenue to whom revenue is due, respect to whom respect is due, honor to whom honor is due.

(RSV translation; emphasis added)

In Augustine's writings, he argued for protecting the peace and punishing those who did/do evil as legitimate functions of legitimate and authoritative government *in obedience to the will of God* as just activities. In his crucial text *On the City of God Against the Pagans* (Latin: *De civitate Dei contra paganos*), written in 426 CE, we find the actual phrase "Just Wars".

Drawing upon not only the writings of Augustine, but Aristotle, Plato, other Greek and Roman philosophers, as well as the Bible—both Hebrew Bible/Old and New Testaments—the Dominican Thomas Aquinas drew as well upon the 12th-century legal textbook *Decretium Gratiani* written by the jurist Gratian (1100? –1150?) who also based himself upon biblical materials. In his own text *Summa Theologica* ("Theological Summary"), written in 1485, he laid out three criteria for just wars: (1) legitimated by rightful sovereigns, (2) legitimated by just causes, and (3) legitimated by the proper intent of the fighters themselves (i.e., promoting good and vanquishing evil). As was also the case with many of his predecessors, war itself was only to be engaged in as a last resort. The violence itself was thus not to be practiced with cruel intention, but, rather, to further the cause of justice, even if tragically, the innocent (non-combatants) suffered (i.e., non-combatants).

As it has evolved, not only in Roman Catholic doctrine but also in the result of principled engagement by secular scholars—especially political philosophers—by the 19th century and onward, "Just War Theory", and its extension "International Law Theory", has established itself in Western thought and concretized in a specific set of rules in the arenas: *Jus ad bellum* ("the right to go to war"), *Jus in bello* ("the right conduct within war"), and *Jus post bellum* ("ending war"). Chart 4 indicates the various categories addressed:

Thus, "Just War Theory", both in its origination and its evolution, cannot be divorced from the religious framework, which gave rise to its discussions. One consequence/upshot in very real terms is the development of the Geneva

Chart 4 Just War Theory

Jus ad bellum
- Just cause
- Comparative justice
- Competent authority
- Right intention
- Probability of success
- Last resort
- Proportionality

Jus in bello
- Distinction
- Proportionality
- Military necessity
- Fair treatment of prisoners of war
- No evil methods of war

Jus post bellum
- Just cause for termination
- Right intention
- Public declaration and authority
- Discrimination
- Proportionality[6]

Conventions explored below, and which specifically address the concerns of both civilians (non-combatants) and prisoners in the context of war. Practical European necessities and realities, however, sidelined discussions of Just War Theory somewhat when it came to two historical moments, neither of which can be separated from their own religious understandings: (1) the Crusades and (2) the Inquisitions (Spanish and Portuguese), both of which were undergirded by religious thought and validation.

The following crusades can quite easily be characterized as "religious wars" or "holy wars" (see below for a further expansion of these terms) between 1095 and 1291 according to this outline, and initiated by the Western Roman Catholic Church against the Arab/Muslim/Islamic populations of the Middle East, most specifically in the geographic area, we today refer to as Palestine/Israel, and primarily centered on "reclaiming" the holy city of Jerusalem—the site of Jesus' crucifixion—from those regarded as "infidels", "pagans", and even "heretics" living there.[7] However, political and economic reasons cannot be separated from those who actually engaged in these battles—for example, the poor who foresaw an opportunity to erase long-standing debts, rulers and knights who saw the same, as well as occasions to fill or refill their own coffers. Such militaristic efforts were at times initiated but always sanctioned by papal authority and thus initiating and inserting a certain "religious fervor" into the mix.

"Holy" Wars and "Religious" Wars 101

Chart 5 "The Crusades"

Crusades and the Holy Land, 1095–1291

- First Crusade, 1095–1099
- Kingdom of Jerusalem, 1099–1144
  - The Crusade of 1101
  - Consolidation of the Latin States, 1101–1118
  - The reign of Baldwin II, 1118–1131
  - Fulk and Melisende, 1131–1143
  - The rise and fall of Zengi, 1127–1146
  - The Siege of Edessa, 1144
  - Second Crusade and aftermath, 1144–1187
- The Second Crusade, 1147–1149
  - Campaigns in Iberia and Northern Europe, 1147
  - The career of Nūr-ad-Din, 1146–1174
  - The Kingdom of Jerusalem from Baldwin III through Sibylla, 1143–1190
  - The rise of Saladin, 1137–1193
  - The Battle of Hattin and the loss of Jerusalem, 1187
- Third Crusade, 1187–1197
  - The call for a Crusade, 1187
  - The Sieges of Tyre and Acre, 1187–1190
  - Crusade of Frederick Barbarossa, 1190
  - Crusade of Richard the Lionheart, 1187–1192
  - Crusade of 1197
  - The Kingdom of Acre com Isabella through Almaric II, 1190–1212
- Fourth Crusade and the Latin Empire, 1197–1204
  - Fourth Crusade, 1202–1204
- Struggle for Recovery: Fifth and Sixth Crusades, 1205–1247
  - Fifth Crusade, 1217–1221
  - Sixth Crusade, 1228–1229
  - Barons' Crusade, 1239–1241
- Crusades of Saint Louis and Edward I, 1249–1290
  - Seventh Crusade, 1248–12154
  - Eighth Crusade, 1270
  - Lord Edward's Crusade, 1271–1272
- Decline and fall or the Crusader States, 1201

Parenthetically, one less-explored consequence of these religious-military attacks was the evisceration of the various European Jewish communities along the route to the East, the most well-known three Germanic cities of Speyer-Worms-Mainz, known as the "Rhineland Massacres" during the First Crusade of 1096. The mindset of those who perpetrated these barbarous atrocities was why wait until their arrival far from home when those "guilty" of the murder of their Christ were near at hand. Thus, both religion and theology come into play here in what was clearly an extended case of genocidal intent in keeping with that part of the UN Genocide Convention, which declares the goal of the *genocidaires* is the destruction of a well-defined group "in whole *or in part*" (emphasis added).[8]

On a somewhat discordant note, however, Jonathan Riley-Smith suggests that

> Holy war has the tendency, whatever the religion involved, to turn inwards sooner or later and to be directed against the members of the society that generated it. The fear grows that any chance of victory may be vitiated by corruption or divisions at home, so that only when society is undefiled and is practicing uniformly true religion can a struggle on its behalf be successful.[9]

The Inquisitions held in Spain and Portugal, though originally begun in France, were designed to ferret out heretics or "insincere Christians", many of them Jews who had converted (*marranos;* pejoratively, "swines" or "pigs") rather than face expulsion at the end of the 15th century, and, in so doing, expanded the circle of victims as Riley-Smith suggests. In the eyes of the Roman Catholic Church, the Waldensian Heresy of the 15th century, and, earlier, the Cathar or Albigensian Heresy of the 14th century, both in France, were themselves subject to the brutalities, including tortures, and deaths at the hands of those in power and with the sanction of the Church. It is, therefore, not inappropriate to argue that the victims were themselves dead or maimed at the intersection of religion and physicality, and that the ultimate obliteration of both the Waldensians and the Albigensians equally smacks of genocidal intent.[10]

Add to this heady historical brew the Thirty Years' War—1618–1648— and its deaths of somewhere between 4,500,000 and 8,000,000 persons, both military *and civilian,* within the *Holy* Roman Empire, and which, ultimately led to the idea/ideal of the sovereignty of the modern nation-state, leads us logically to the Geneva Conventions plural (1864, 1907, 1929, 1949), which were all designed to protect both non-military civilian non-combatants and military prisoners of war (both wounded and sick). Careful readings of each of these Conventions will find echoes of earlier biblical concerns (both Hebrew Bible/Old and New Testaments), For example, concern for the widow, the fatherless, the orphan, and the poor—a common biblical thread—in this case in wartime, is reflected in those innocent civilians being addressed. The military exemptions referenced at the outset of this chapter also find their echoes in further defining who is and who is not a combatant.

Moving to the East, however, and perhaps backward somewhat, we encounter the Arabic term *jihad* ("striving", "effort" or "struggling", from the word *jihada*), rooted as it is in the Qur'an, the Hadith (commentary), and the traditions of Islam. Possessed of two meanings—the internal one of self-struggle and maximum self-actualization, and the external one of war against the enemies of God (unbelievers) and defensively so—tragically, the West makes far more of the latter than the former.[11] Some Islamic authorities have even characterized the latter as "jihad by the sword". During the so-called Classical Period of Islam (610, starting with Muhammad's call from God, until 1258 with the conquest of Baghdad by the Mongols), some scholars referred to the former as the "greater jihad" and the latter as the "lesser jihad". Others, however, reversed this understanding and, alongside it, themselves developed rules of military engagement, including prohibitions against harming those not directly involved in these conflicts (i.e., women, the aged, and children). However, and importantly, in the 2002 Gallup Poll of the Islamic World that surveyed more than 10,000 adults primarily in four Muslim countries (Lebanon, Kuwait, Jordan, and Morocco), pollsters concluded that "across the *Ummah*—Islamic global community of believers—the concept of *jihad* is considerably more nuanced than the single sense in which Western commentators invariably invoke the term".[12] Individually, a person engaged in *jihad* is referred to as a *mujahid*; collectively *mujahideen*. While one may prefer to acknowledge the religiosity of the former and the secularity of the latter, such is simply not the case: Like Judaism but perhaps less so in the various iterations of Christianity, Islam, too, is a total all-encompassing way of life built into which is what we in the West commonly understand as "religion" (a word which does not appear in either Islam or Judaism). Thus, war itself up to and including its most perverse expression—genocide—simply cannot be divorced from its religious frameworks, as duly noted in the works of two important contemporary radical Islamist thinkers, Egyptians Hassan al-Banna (1906–1949), founder of the Muslim Brotherhood (Society of the Muslim Brothers, *al-Ikwān al-Muslimūn*), and its chief ideologue Sayyid Qutb (1906–1966), both of whom wrote on the necessity of violent jihad. Osama bin Laden (1957–2011), founder of al-Qaeda ("The Base"), in his now-infamous "Declaration of the World Islamic Front against the Jews and the Crusaders" equally called for violent jihad, primarily against the West. Significantly, jihad is *not* included in the Five Pillars of Islam: (1) *Haj* (pilgrimage), (2) *Shahada* (testimony), (3) *Zakat* (alms), (4) *Salat* (prayer), and (5) *Sawm* (fasting). Classical Islam, like that of both Judaism and Christianity, is far more complicated than normative, and all-too-often simplistic, Western understandings would have one believe.

Thus, one must hesitatingly be careful to invoke such terms haphazardly or sloppily as "religious wars" or "holy wars" and, therefore, implying that "religion" is the cornerstone of such conflicts. Terminologically and historically speaking then, the central thesis of this text remains: that religion—however defined and understood—is a *participating factor* not only in warfare but in genocide as well, an *odium theologicum* if one prefers the Latin phrase for "theological/religious hated". Jeffrey Burton Russell refers to such involvement in his 2012 book *Exposing Myths about Christianity* as a "contributing factor" alongside such others as ethnic, political, social, and economic differences.[13] In some cases, the influence of religion on conflict and genocide may be greater or obvious; in others less so or more subtle reflecting an historical or contemporary tendentious orientation to the collective *Weltanschauung* (world perspective) of civilization.[14] Therefore, the incumbent responsibility of the researcher(s) in this area is to determine what impact—if any, and, if so, to what degree—religion plays, has played, is playing, or potentially will play in these violent physical conflicts and confrontations. Religion, an aspect of human cultural creativity and productivity, cannot be "isolated out" of such examinations. In 2011, the Human Rights Council of the General Assembly of the United Nations adopted a Resolution entitled "Combatting intolerance, negative stereotyping and stigmatization of, and discrimination, incitement to violence and violence against, persons based on religion or belief", further bringing to the attention of that world body the need to address the very nexus between religion and violence. Enlarging the circle somewhat, the same might very well be said when using the words "massacre" or "mass murder" (derived from the French word *macecre*, "butchery" or "carnage" and already in use by the 11th century) and which the *Oxford English Dictionary* defines as "the indiscriminate and brutal slaughter of people or (less commonly) animals; carnage, butchery, slaughter in numbers".[15] Commonly understood, however, though not universally agreed upon, we may define massacre as "the killing of multiple individuals and is usually considered to be morally unacceptable, especially when perpetrated by a group of political [*sic*] actors against defenseless victims".[16]

Equally problematic is the use of the words "terrorism" and "terrorist" not only in the light of the oft-used cliché "one person's terrorist is another person's freedom fighter", or, perhaps, even, "one person's terrorist is another person's revolutionary", but the ramping up of such uses in the aftermath of the 9/11 tragedy in the United States and elsewhere (e.g., Madrid train bombing in 2004, the London subway bombing in 2005, and, even earlier, abortion clinic bombings in the United States in the 1990s). And, as we have already encountered, there is no universally agreed upon definition of either "terrorism" or "terrorist". In the main, however, terrorism is understood to be the use of violence to accomplish specific ends, be they political, religious, economic or social, and thus the actor or actors who engage in such violence are understood to be terrorists, and the recipients of such acts by such actors are all-too-often understood to be innocent civilians (the offensive military term "collateral damage" may be applicable here) when direct objects of such attacks are those holding the reins of power in the nation-state, religious officials presenting their affirmations of the "correct" understandings of the divine-human encounter, or economic elites enlarging their own coffers at the expense of others. Interestingly enough, many scholars trace the beginnings of terrorism to 2,000 years ago when, during the oppressive Roman subjugation and control of Palestine, groups of Jews known as *Sicarii* (usually translated as "Zealots", but better understood as "dagger men" because of the curved daggers hidden within the folds of their robes which they brought out to murder Roman soldiers and their fellow Jews whom they regarded as collaborators, before melting back into the ofttimes appreciative crowds who supported them). In 2004, then UN Secretary General Kofi Annan (1938–2018) in a report to the General Assembly defined terrorism as "any action intended to cause death or serious bodily harm to civilians or non-combatants with the purpose of intimidating a population or compelling a government or an international organization [not defined] to do or abstain from doing any act". In the United States, even earlier, 1975, the Task Force on Disorders and Terrorism of the Law Enforcement Assistant Administration National Committee on Criminal Justice Standards and Goals defined those so-called disorders (here understood as more a political term—dis-order—rather than a psychological one) as:

- Civil disorders
- Political terrorism
- Non-political terrorism
- Anonymous terrorism
- Quasi-terrorism
- Limited political terrorism
- Official or state terrorism

The 1999 Government Report on Profiling Terrorists developed its own typology as follows:

- Political terrorism
  - Sub-state terrorism
- Social revolutionary terrorism
- Nationalist-separatist terrorism
- **Religious extremist terrorism**
  - **Religious fundamentalist terrorism**
  - **New religious terrorism**
- Right-wing terrorism
- Left-wing terrorism
  - Communist terrorism
- State-sponsored terrorism
- Regime to state terrorism
- Criminal terrorism
- Pathological terrorism[17]

The 2015 report from the Southern Poverty Law Center (Montgomery, Alabama) entitled "Age of the Lone Wolf: A Study of Lone Wolf and Leaderless

Resistance Terrorism" significantly concluded that "more people have been killed in America by non-Islamic domestic terrorists than jihadists", and connected any number of specific acts to the virulent racist and antisemitic Christian Identity Movement, which argues that European whites are the literal and biblical descendants of the ancient Ten Lost Tribes of Israel.[18] Terrorist groups, especially those with connections to religious communities, including somewhat ironically Jews and the modern State of Israel (e.g., the so-called settler movement), are found throughout the world, not only in the Middle East.[19] Largely unsuccessful in their ultimate objectives, the present (August 2021) takeover after a twenty-year absence and routing of the Taliban in Afghanistan may prove the exception and thus communicate to other terrorist groups in waiting the possibilities and potential for their own success. al-Qaeda and ISIS/ISIL from whom a more militant and violent interpretive understanding of Islam cannot be divorced from their overall political ideology and commitment are only the two most prominent examples, but not the only ones to include Islam, Christianity, Hinduism, Judaism, and Buddhism in their very raison d'etre for their existence.

Lastly and complicatedly, terminologically speaking, is the case of the Holocaust (*Shoah*-having never existed before its own moment and never repeated in its own exactitude by other seemingly comparative looking events) regarded by some as *sui generis* (totally unique unto itself) and which may or should be subsumed within the broader category of genocide. Two at times quite vociferous and quite argumentative scholarly, popular, and communal camps have arisen: Those in support of that uniqueness and unquestionably setting it apart from all other instances of genocide, and those comparativists who argue for its inclusion as one way to analyze instances of genocide by "lining up" it with other examples of genocide to determine both similarities and differences.[20]

Thus, words matter, and this chapter is intended to emphasis that importance, not only the various words we chose and the implications and consequences of those choices and how we proceed to investigate and interrogate instances of genocide. It is also intended to "complexify" rather than "simplify" these discussions by further emphasizing the participating factor of religion in these choices by not excluding it from but including it in these discussions.

The next chapters address important topics not usually talked about in many texts covering the question of genocide: antisemitism, biology and geography, including climate change and disease.

Notes

1 See my contribution to Sara E. Brown and Stephen D. Smith, eds., *The Routledge Handbook of Religion, and Genocide* (New York and London: Routledge, 2021), entitled "Holy Wars, Judaism, Violence, and Genocide: An Unholy Quadrinity?", 37–43, especially the bibliography.

2 Rory Cox (2017), "Expanding the History of the Just War: The Ethics of War in Ancient Egypt", *International Studies Quarterly*, 61: 372; emphasis added.
3 See, for example, Karl F. Friday, *Samurai Warfare, and the State in Early Medieval Japan* (London and New York: Routledge, 2004), 21–22.
4 Louis E. Fenech and W. H. McLeod, *Historical Dictionary of Sikhism* (Lanham: Rowman & Littlefield, 2014), 99–100.
5 Cian O'Donnel (2015), "Rewriting the Just War Tradition: Just War in Classical Greek Political Thought and Practice", *International Studies Quarterly*, 59: 1.
6 https://en/wikipedia.org/wiki.Just-war_theory.
7 See, for example, Karen Amstrong, *Holy Wars: The Crusades and Their Impact on Today's World* (New York: Anchor Books, 2001); and Amin Maalouf, *The Crusades through Arab Eyes* (New York: Schocken Books, 1984. Translated by Jon Rothschild.).
8 Among the literatures which have arisen addressing this particular aspect of the Crusades are the following: Robert Chazan, *European Jewry and the First Crusade* (Berkeley: University of California Press, 1987); Robert Chazan, *God, Humanity, and History: The Hebrew First Crusade Narrative* (Berkeley: University of California Press, 2000); Jeremy Cohen, *Sanctifying the Name of God: Jewish Martyrs and Jewish Memories of the First Crusade* (Philadelphia: University of Pennsylvania Press, 2004); Shlomo Eidelberg, ed. & trans., *The Jews and the Crusades: The Hebrew Chronicles of the First and Second Crusades* (Hoboken: KTAV Publishing House, 1996); Eva Haverkamp (2009), "Martyrs in Rivalry: The 1096 Jewish Martyrs and the Theban Legion", *Jewish History*, 23: 319–342; Steven Leonard Jacobs (2020), "Crusades", in *Antisemitism: Exploring the Issues* (Santa Barbara: ABC-CLIO), 29–32; Benjamin Z. Kedar (1998), "Crusade Historians and the Massacres of 1096", *Jewish History*, 12(2): 11–31; David Malkiel (2001), "Destruction or Conversion: Intention and Reaction, Crusaders and Jews, in 1096", *Jewish History*, 15: 257–280; and Norman Roth (1994), "Bishops and Jews in the Middle Ages", *The Catholic Historical Review*, LXXX(1): 1–17.
9 Jonathan Riley-Smith (2000), "Rethinking the Crusades", *First Things*, www.firstthings.com. Accessed 4 August 2021. Furthermore, "the use of crusader symbolism as a source of inspiration, activism and even justification of violence as a religious duty in Europe and in the Middle East" is addressed by Ariel Koch (2017) in his article "The New Crusaders: Contemporary Extreme Right Symbolism and Rhetoric", *Perspectives on Terrorism*, 11(5): 13–24.
10 Jonathan Kirsch's important text *The Grand Inquisitor's Manual: A History of Terror in the Name of God* (New York: Harper One, 2008) comprehensively clearly lays out this argument. Henry Kamen in his book *The Spanish Inquisition: A Historical Revision* (New Haven and London: Yale University Press, 2014), however and not without controversy, attempts to rebut many of the more popular and well-known myths associated with these two Inquisitions (e.g., their primary focus on the Jews and Muslims; the secular justification of the Inquisitions to increase economic treasuries).
11 Important, too, are the distinctions classically drawn between *dar-al-Islam*, *da-al-'Adl* or *dar-al-Salaam* (House of Islam/Justice/Peace) and *dar-al-Harb* or *dal-al-Jawr* (House of War/Injustice/Oppression), *and dar-al-Suhl*, *darl-al-'Ahd* or *dal-al-Muwada'ah* (House of Peace/Covenant/Reconciliation).
12 https://news.gallup.com/poll/7333/jihad-holy-war-internal-spiritual-struggle.aspx? Accessed 21 July 2021.
13 Jeffrey Burton Russell, *Exposing Myths about Christianity* (Downer's Grove: InterVarsity Press, 2012), 56.

14 Such, in fact, is the very claim of David Nirenberg in his 2013 book *Anti-Judaism: The Western Tradition* (New York and London: W. W. Norton & Company) wherein he argues that the very mindset of 2,000 years of Western Christianity has affected/infected/colored/influenced how the various societies and nation-states have understood reality, not only toward the Jews but themselves as well.
15 An historical note: Already in 1947, Raphael Lemkin (1900–1959) rejected "sterilization", "mass murder", and "extermination" in favor of "genocide", writing

> Mass murder or extermination wouldn't apply in the case of sterilization because the victims of sterilizations were not murdered, rather a people was killed through delayed action by stopping propagation. Moreover, mass murder does not convey the specific losses to civilization in the form of the cultural contributions which can be made only by groups of people united through national, racial or cultural characteristics.

Raphael Lemkin (1947), "Genocide as a Crime under International Law", *The American Journal of International Law*, 41(1): 147.
16 https://en.wikipedia.org/wikid/dMassacre. See as well, Alex J. Bellamy, *Massacres & Morality: Mass Atrocities in an Age of Civilian Immunity* (Oxford and New York: Oxford University, 2012); Donald G. Dutton, *The Psychology of Genocide, Massacres, and Extreme Violence: Why "Normal" People Come to Commit Violence* (Westport and London: Praeger Security International, 2007); Phillip G. Dwyer and Lyndall Ryan, eds., *Theatres of Violence: Massacres, Mass Killing, and Atrocity Throughout History* (New York and Oxford: Berghahn, 2012); Christian Gerlach, *Extremely Violent Societies: Mass Violence in the Twentieth-Century World* (Cambridge: Cambridge University Press, 2010); Mark Levene and Penny Roberts, eds., *The Massacre in History* (New York and Oxford: Berghahn Books, 1999); and Jacques Semelin, *Purify and Destroy: The Political Uses of Massacres and Genocide* (New York: Columbia University Press, 2007. Translated from the French by Cynthia Schoch).
17 Rex Hudson. *Who Becomes a Terrorist: The 1999 Government Report on Profiling Terrorists*. Lanham: The Lyons Press, 2002.
18 SPLC, "Age of the Lone Wolf", 4 ff.
19 With regard to Jews and Judaism and their own violent religious history, see Steven Leonard Jacobs (2020), "Judaism", in Michael Jerryson, ed., *Religious Violence Today: Faith and Conflict in the Modern World* (Santa Barbara: ABC-CLIO), 463–546.
20 See Steven Leonard Jacobs (2010), "Holocaust or Genocide/Holocaust and Genocide: The Controversy Continues", in Nancy Rupprecht and Wendy Koenig, eds. *Holocaust Persecution: Responses and Consequences* (Cambridge: Cambridge Scholars Press), 213–221.

Chapter 8

Antisemitism as Genocide

Julie Nathan, research director of the Executive Council of Australian Jews (ECAJ), in a 2019 opinion piece online entitled "The genocidal propensity of antisemitism" wrote the following:

> The genocidal nature of antisemitism is rooted in the maniacal and perverse belief that "the Jews" are inherently evil and absolutely powerful. This derives from superstitions and mythologies about Jews that have blighted and shamed both European and Islamic civilizations since medieval times, and which have produced unspeakable barbarities. Modern-era conspiracy theories about "the Jews", portrayed as nefarious and powerful, plotting to control the world, have added another layer to, and reinforced, these older theological and cultural myths. Jews have been among the most vulnerable and persecuted people in history, yet their tormentors continue to betray their own inner darkness by portraying Jews collectively as innately evil and absolutely powerful.[1]

The two most egregious examples of genocidal antisemitism to be sure (and there are others) are the Nazi genocide *against* the Jews—the Holocaust or in Hebrew *Shoah* ("Devastation" or "Destruction")—and the Islamist Hamas' ongoing genocidal delusionist fantasy orchestrated from their base in Gaza. With regard to the first, as both Randall L. Bytwerk[2] and Jeffrey Herf[3] have clearly shown, the genocidal agenda of the Nazis was grounded in both their antisemitism and their thorough conviction that "the Jews'" own agenda was that of the destruction of the German people and their culture, and, ultimately, a planned takeover of the world—whether Hitler and his inner circle subscribed to the facticity of the 19th-century forgery *The Protocols of the Learned Elders of Zion*.[4] They have also shown that while it is difficult if not impossible to conclusively determine the success of their ongoing efforts to convince the German people, including the military (*Wehrmacht*), SS (*Schutzstaffel* or "Protection Squadron", SA (*Sturmabteilung* or "Storm Detachment"), Gestapo (*Geheime Staatspolizei* or "Secret State Police") in real

DOI: 10.4324/9781003168799-8

numbers, the impact of the constant media barrage (newspapers, radio, public speeches) resulted in both active support of their goals and/or indifference or silence vis-à-vis the fate of the Jews.

What is absent in their otherwise excellent analyses is the anti-Jewish/anti-Judaism and thus European Christian religious factor of 2,000 years of antisemitism, which conditioned Europeans generation after generation to regard the Jews in their midst as the quintessential Others and worthy of whatever fate was to befall them as the people primarily responsible for *deicide* (i.e., the murderous death of the Christ). While this is not the place to rehearse the whole sordid history of antisemitism as foundationally significant, succinctly, that factor itself evolved from its earliest beginnings in the Middle East in Egyptian, Greek, and Roman times as follows but with no clear borders or separations, all four apparently interwoven as negativizing the Jews spread westward:

> *Social-Cultural*: "We don't like Jews because they are different from us, and they do things differently that we do".
>
> *Political-Economic*: "We don't like Jews because they are a threat to the stability of both our political and economic ways of life".
>
> **Religious-Theological: "We don't like Jews because they worship differently than we do, believe differently than we believe, and practice a religion different than ours".**
>
> *Racial-Biological*: "We don't like Jews because they are different than we are physically and genetically". [The Nazi "contribution" to antisemitism.][5]

After World War II and the rebirth of the Third Jewish Commonwealth, the State of Israel on May 14, 1948, a fifth factor presented itself:

> *Anti-Zionist-Anti-Israel*: "We don't like Jews because their allegiance, no matter where they live, is to a nation-state that is not us".[6]

Further important issues involving the intersections between Nazism and Christianity during World War II include (1) the "silence" of Pope Pius XII (Eugenio Pacelli, 1876–1958; reigned 1939–1958) in never publicly condemning the Nazis' murder of the Jews even with knowledge; (2) the appointment by the German government of Johan Heinrich Ludwig Müller (1883–1945) as *Reichbischof* (Reich Bishop) of the *Deutsche Evangelische Kirche* (German Evangelical Church); (3) the support of prominent German theologians and religious scholars in support of the Nazi regime: e.g., Gerhard Kittel (1888–1948), Paul Althaus (1888–946), and Emanuel Hirsch (1888–1972), and the Institute for the Study and Eradication of Jewish Influence on German Religious Life.[7]

However, the paradigmatic example of genocidal antisemitism is, supposedly, Adolf Hitler's Reichstag (Parliament) speech on January 30, 1939, in which he stated:

> If international finance Jewry within Europe and abroad succeed once more in plunging the peoples into a world war, then the consequence will be not the Bolshevization of the world and therewith a victory, but on the contrary, *the destruction of the Jewish race in Europe*.[8]

However, importantly, Bytwerk correctly notes:

> There are three significant things about this passage. First, Hitler claimed that the war, should it come, would be caused by the Jews.... Second, he asserted that although the Jewish goal would be to destroy Germany, war would instead lead to the "destruction of the Jewish race in Europe"... Third, the date is important—this was seven months *before* the war began. Within the context of the speech, it is not necessary (or even reasonable) to conclude that Hitler is speaking of the physical destruction of Jews. Rather, he suggested that the rest of Europe would solve the "Jewish Question" in the way Germany had done—through propaganda.
>
> However, when Hitler quoted the passage in his speeches during the war, he always said he had made the remark on September 1, 1939 (the outbreak of World War II) rather than January 30, 1939. The repeated slip of memory is significant. The "prophecy" has a different meaning if in peace, and Hitler wanted to make it clear that he was absolutely serious about his threat to destroy the Jews. In dating the statement at the outbreak of war, he gave it a new context, and a harsher import.[9]

Other pronouncements by Hitler would echo the theme of his original 1939 speech—e.g., January 30, 1941 ("all of Jewry will be finished in Europe"), January 1, 1942 ("the Jew will become the victim of his own plot"), January 30, 1942 ("the result of this war will be the annihilation of Jewry"), November 8, 1942 ("the extermination of Jewry in Europe"); February 24, 1942 ("the extermination of the Jew in Europe").

Thus, the bottom-line conclusion is that, ultimately, the Hitlerian agenda undergirded by its own forms of virulent antisemitism and supported by its elites, the state bureaucracy, its multifaceted organizational structures, and both the support and indifference or acquiescence of its people would result in the genocide of more than 6,000,000 European Jewish children, women, and men.

Before turning to the Middle East, however, with both its anti-Judaic and radicalized Islamist traditions and the importation of Western antisemitism and even going so far as to build somewhat upon the legacy of Nazism, and the genocidal potential of that agenda as well, it is important to keep in mind the following comment proffered by the Anti-Defamation League (ADL) in their (2002) piece "Islamic Anti-Semitism in Historical Perspective":

> To explain the demonization of contemporary Jews we must look not to the roots of Islam but to the West: the ancient blood libel, and charges of ritual murder and well-poisoning as well as the belief that Jews are engaged in a fantastic world conspiracy.[10]

To which one should add "host desecration" to these villainous charges. All four have their roots in the world of Western European Roman Catholic Christianity and do resonate somewhat in the Middle East today up to and including the importation and translation of *The Protocols of the Elders of Zion* into Arabic beginning in the 1920s.[11] The above noted ADL Report further states:

> Anti-Semitism that bases itself on religion, however, is different. The constant trumpeting of the anti-Semitism Islamist paradigm since the late 1960s and the apparent absence of an opposing, moderate voice of Islam emanating with any real force from the Middle East, suggest that this new theologically based demonization of Jews is being accepted by masses of Muslims throughout the region. Weaving together a theological metahistorical opposition to Jews with the worst of Western anti-Jewish conspiracy theories, today's anti-Semitism in the Middle East cannot be easily resolved. Religions are self-propagating, and theologies possess remarkable staying power across generations. A theologically based anti-Semitism gripped Christian Europe for hundreds of years: it took further centuries of reformation and revolution and an all-encompassing reordering of society for is domination to be broken. Even today its after-effects linger. It would be prudent not to underestimate its potency.[12]

Blood libel is the accusation already prevalent in the Middle Ages that Jews murdered (and murder) Christian children to drain their blood as the "secret ingredient" used in the making of the *matzot* (unleavened bread) associated with the Festival of Passover.[13] Ritual murder, ofttimes associated directly with blood libel, equally accused Jews of murdering Christians in a highly styled ceremonial act of death. Well-poisoning was associated with the tragedy of the Black Death/bubonic plague where ghettoized Jews were accused of poisoning the wells of the gentile serfs outside their walls.[14] Host desecration was the accusation that Jews stole the wafer used in the Eucharist of the Catholic Mass and attempted to destroy it by piercing it through. Transported to the Middle East: Israelis have been accused of murdering Palestinian children and using their blood in secret rituals and poisoning the water supplies of Palestinian villages as well.

Joseph S. Spoerl, recently writing in the *Jewish Political Studies Review* (2020), finds six "Parallels between Nazi and Islamist Anti-Semitism", and focusing primarily on Hamas:

> First, anti-Semitism is central to Hamas propaganda, and Hamas has not renounced or ceased producing such propaganda.
>
> Second, Hamas has made it clear that is has not revoked its 1988 Covenant which remains its statement of foundational principles.
>
> Third, strictly speaking, the Hamas Covenant of 1988 focused its anti-Semitic language on Zionism.
>
> Fourth, the release of the May 2017 "Document" coincides with a tightening of the grip of hardliners on the Hamas Politburo.
>
> Fifth, Hamas has a well-documented history of dissembling, especially when addressing non-Muslims.
>
> Finally, there is the unmistakable fact that the May 2017 "Document of General Principles and Policies" proclaims Hamas' intent to commit *politicide* against the world's only Jewish state.[15]

Given the antisemitism of the Nazis and taken to their genocidal conclusion, it is not difficult to substitute Hitler, the Nazis, and their own relevant documents as applicable, and thus reframe Spoerl's conclusions of Hamas' own genocidal intent.

Hamas is not alone in its antisemitic genocidal intent, however, and one must also trace its roots back to Hassan al-Banna (1906–1949, assassinated by the Egyptian Secret Police), the founder of the Muslim Brotherhood in 1928 (Society of Muslim Brothers/*Jamāʿat al-Ikhwān al-Muslimīn*);[16] its ideological mainstay Sayyid Qutb (1906–1966; hanged by the Egyptian Government);[17] even earlier to the Grand Mufti of Jerusalem Haj Amin al-Husseini (1897–1974); its contemporary expositors Egyptian Islamic scholar Yusuf Al-Qaradawi (b. 1926) and the late Shia cleric Seyyid Nawaf-Savafi (1924–1956); and its other genocidally intent organizations: Hezballah (Lebanese Shia military group founded in 1982),[18] Islamic Jihad (founded in 1983), Al-Qaeda (founded in 1988 by the late Osama bin Laden [1957–2011]; assassinated by the US), ISIS (Islamic State of Iraq and the Levant, founded in 1999)—all intent on the genocidal destruction of the Jewish State of Israel and its Jewish inhabitants, and, if given the opportunity, transporting their murderous agenda of death to Jews the world over. Not to be outdone, however, in agenda or intent was the late Ruhollah Musavi Khomeini (1900–1989), Ayatollah Khomeini, founder of the Islamic Republic of Iran and the leader of the 1979 Iranian Revolution, and its later President Mahmoud Ahmadinejad (b. 1956) who publicly stated his desire "to wipe Israel off the map".[19]

Moving to the United States with its own history of so-called White Nationalism and the proliferation of extremist groups (e.g., KKK, Army of God, Phineas Brotherhood, and others which merge their hated of Jews with their supposed Christian identity), even more so within the last decade, coupled with their ongoing spewing of antisemitism, one is powerfully reminded of the chants accompanying the August 2019 "Unite the Right" rally in Charlottesville, VA: "Jews will not replace us", and "Blood and Soil", the latter a direct translation of the Nazi slogan "*Blut und boden*" (the Nazis' own goal of a racially pure nation-state). Violence is part and parcel of these groups and Jews continue to be viewed as enemies attempting to wrest control of the US, and, for some, having already done so (i.e., references to the ZOG—"Zionist Occupation Government"—in the literature of many of these organizations). Taken collectively, were these organizations, small as most of them are, successful, they would recast the United States as *Judenrein*/Jew-free.

One should thus argue that one should not dismiss out of hand the genocidal agenda accompanying this antisemitic hatred, which has historically and contemporarily traveled with the Jews from their earliest beginnings until the present day, and which mandates much more research regarding the interrelationship between the two.

Lastly, positively, one of the more creative solutions addressing genocidal antisemitism is that of Ambassador Alan Baker, Israel's former ambassador to Canada, and director of the Institute for Contemporary Affairs at the Jerusalem Center for Public Affairs. Unfortunately, his 2015 "Draft International Convention on the Prevention and Punishment of the Crime of Anti-Semitism"—modeled as it is on the 1948 United Nations Genocide Convention—has gone nowhere. A close reading of its introductory materials, its 21 Articles, and its extensive supporting notes, however, further underscores the relationship between genocide and antisemitism and should give all of us pause as other relationships between hatred and genocide have already begun to assert themselves (Islamophobia throughout the world; anti-Asian prejudices resulting in violence in the US and elsewhere as people attribute the COVID-19 pandemic to the Chinese but transfer that animus to other Asians, including Koreans, as well).

The words of 2nd-century Rabbi Tarphon provide a fitting and appropriate conclusion to this chapter:

> The day is short, and the labor is plenty; the laborers are slothful, while the reward is great, and the master of the house is pressing. You are not obliged to complete the work, but neither are you free to desist from it.[20]

Notes

1 Julie Nathan (2019), "The Genocidal Propensity of Antisemitism", www.abc.net.au. Accessed 1 November 2021.
2 Randall L. Bytwerk (2006), "The Argument for Genocide in Nazi Propaganda", *Quarterly Journal of Speech*, 91(1): 37–62.
3 Jeffrey Herf (2005), "The 'Jewish War': Goebbels and the Antisemitic Campaign of the Nazi Propaganda Ministry", *Holocaust and Genocide Studies*, 19(1): 51–80.

4 For a detailed overview and analysis of the Protocols—of which there is a vast and growing literature—see Steven Leonard Jacobs and Mark Weitzman, *Dismantling the Big Lie: The Protocols of the Elders of Zion* (Los Angeles and Jersey City: Simon Wiesenthal Center and KTAV Publishing House, 2003).
5 See also, Steven Leonard Jacobs (2009), "Revisiting Hateful Science: The Nazi 'Contribution' to the Journey of Antisemitism", *Journal of Hate Studies*, 7(1): 47–75.
6 Steven Leonard Jacobs, *Antisemitism: Exploring the Issues* (Santa Barbara: ABC-CLIO, 2020), xxi. See, also, Gunther Jikeli, ed., "The Return of Religious Antisemitism", available online at www.mdpi.com/journal/religions; and Cary Nelson and Michael C. Gizzi, eds., *Peace and Faith: Christian Churches and the Israeli-Palestinian Conflict* (Philadelphia and Boston: Academic Studies Press, 2021), especially Chapter 8 by David Fox Sandmel, "The Kairos Palestine Document, Anti-Semitism, and BDS" (277–295); David Fox Sandmel, "Preface to a Timeline: A Brief History of Anti-Semitism" (482–490); and Cary Nelson, "Annotated Timeline of Jewish-Christian Relations and the History of Anti-Judaism" (491–529).
7 See Robert Ericksen, *Theologians under Hitler* (New Haven and London: Yale University Press, 1985); Susannah Heschel, *The Aryan Jesus: Christian Theologians and the Bible in Nazi Germany* (Princeton and Oxford: Princeton University Press, 2008); Richard Steigmann-Gall, *The Holy Reich: Nazi Conceptions of Christianity, 1919–1945* (Cambridge: Cambridge University Press, 2003); and Richard Weikart, *Hitler's Religion: The Twisted Belief that Drove the Third Reich* (Washington: Regnery History, 2013).
8 Max Domarus, *Hitler: Speeches and Proclamations 1932–1945* (Wauconda: Boldhazy-Carducci, 1960–2004), Volume III, 1439; emphasis added.
9 Bytwerk, "The Argument for Genocide in Nazi Propaganda", 39; emphasis added.
10 Anti-Defamation League (2002), "Islamic Anti-Semitism in Historical Perspective", 6.
11

> The Protocols had been translated into Arabic from the French, probably for the first time, by al-Khuri Antun Yamin in the 1920s under the title *Mu'amarat al-Yahudiyya'ala al-shu'ub* (The Plot of Jewry against the Nations). Another translation, by Frederick Zurfaiq, recently appeared under the title *Ahdaf al-Sahyuniyya* (The Aims of Zionism), published by *Jam'iyyat al-tamaddujn al-Islami* in Damascus. A third translation was serialized in the newspaper *Minbar al-Sharq*, and later published in book form. One other translation, at least, has been made by Muhammad Khalifa al-Tunisi, a Moslem, under the title *Al-Khatar al-Yahudi au protocolat hukama sahyun* (The Jewish Peril or the Protocols of the Elders of Zion). But it is not clear from the favorable comments on the translation in *Majal-lat al-Azhar* whether it has actually been published. It seems that Moslems as well as Christians have devoted their talents to the translation of the Protocols, but Eastern Christians were unquestionably the first to give currency to this fabrication.

Sylvia G. Haim (1955), "Arabic Antisemitic Literature: Some Preliminary Notes", *Jewish Social Studies*, 17(4): 308–309. On the relationship between Protocols and the Hamas Covenant, see Steven Leonard Jacobs (2007), "The Protocols of Hamas", *Reform Judaism*, 26–31. See, also, Menahem Milson (2011), "A European Plot on the Arab Stage: The Protocols of the Elders of Zion in the Arab Media", Inquiry & Analysis Series No. 690, MEMRI (Middle East Media

Research Institute); also, *Posen Papers in Contemporary Antisemitism* No. 12, The Vidal Sassoon International Center for the Study of Antisemitism, The Hebrew University of Jerusalem.
12 Anti-Defamation League (2002), "Islamic Anti-Semitism in Historical Perspective", 16.
13 To date, the most comprehensive account of the blood libel is that of Madga Teter, *Blood Libel: On the Trail of an Antisemitic Myth* (Cambridge: Harvard University Press, 2020).
14 See Joshua Trachtenberg, *The Devil and the Jews: The Medieval Conception of the Jew and Its Relation to Modern Anti-Semitism* (Philadelphia: The Jewish Publication Society of America, 2002. Reprint.)
15 Joseph S. Spoerl (2020), "Parallels between Nazi and Islamist Anti-Semitism", *Jewish Political Science Review*, 31(1): 216 ff; emphasis added.
16 Markos Zografos (2021), "Genocidal Antisemitism: A Core Ideology of the Muslim Brotherhood", ISGAP (The Institute for the Study of Global Antisemitism and Policy, NY) Occasional Paper Series No. 4. See also Bassam Tibi (2010), "From Sayyid Qutb to Hamas: The Middle East Conflict and the Islamization of Antisemitism", ISGAP Working Paper, ISBN: 978-0-9819058-8-4.
17 See, importantly, Ronald L. Nettler, *Past Trials and Present Tribulations: A Muslim Fundamentalist's View of the Jews* (London: Pergamon, 1987) which includes an extensive commentary on Qutb's essay "Our Struggle with the Jews"; and John Calvert, *Sayyid Qutb and the Origins of Radical Islamism* (Oxford and New York: Oxford University Press, 2018).
18 Its 1985 "The Hizballah Program: An Open Letter" has as its final section "The Necessity for the Destruction of Israel" and includes such statements as "It is the hated enemy that must be fought until the hated ones get what they deserve"; and "Our struggle will end only when this entity is obliterated".
19 Elihu Richter and Alex Barnea (2009), "Tehran's Genocidal Incitement against Israel", www.meforum.org/2167/iran-genodical-incitement-israel. Accessed 1 November 2021.
20 *Pirke Avot* ("Sayings of the Fathers"), 2:15.

Chapter 9

Why Should Biology Matter?

Correlation Is *Not* Causation!

The overarching question that needs to be addressed in any discussion of genocide is what, in truth, is a human being or a people group that is capable of such atrocity. Paralleling somewhat the question of a predisposition toward religion is the question of a predisposition toward such violence—pre-wired, hard-wired, or genetically cohered. Can we learn from the latest scientific thinking about our very "humanbeingness", which may shed further light on why genocide has been and remains very much a part of the human story, and why this author and this text maintain a "nexus" (i.e., *participating factor*) between religion and genocide.

Yet the debate remains, cantankerous at its worst, between those whose favor environmental over genetic/biological factors as primary influencers and those who favor genetic/biological factors over environmental factors as primary influencers. More than fifty years ago, in his presidential address to the Western Political Science Association (2 April 1970), University of Oregon professor, sociologist and political scientist, James Chowning Davies (1918–2012) summarized well the divide:

> One of the usually unspoken premises in the thought and writing of everyone, including social scientists and social philosophers, is a general view of man [sic]. Some people base their views and their actions on a belief that man is hostile, aggressive, violent, and selfish. Other people base their views and actions on a belief that man is friendly, peaceful, nonviolent, and cooperative.
>
> As participants, people who view man as violent are probably inclined to confirm their view of man by acting violently in the pursuit of political and social and private goals. As observers, people who view man as violent are probably inclined to confirm their views by supporting laws and police and military action which will maximize the violence of the response to violence. Correlatively, people as participants and observers who view man as nonviolent are probably more likely to confirm

DOI: 10.4324/9781003168799-9

that view by acting nonviolently themselves and approving nonviolent responses to violence on the part of government.

Those who view man as hostile toward their fellow men are likely to be hostile and those who view man as friendly are likely themselves to be friendly. Both kinds will seek and will find intellectual support for their pre-existing views...For those who are hostile, a reading of Thomas Hobbes [English philosopher, 1588–1679] and J[ean]-J[acques] Rousseau [Swiss philosopher, 1712–1778] will make little difference. They will agree with Hobbes and disagree with Rousseau. For those who are friendly, the response will be to disagree with Hobbes and agree with Rousseau.[1]

His conclusion:

The absurd position that the tendency to aggress is any more natural than the tendency to cooperate. Man, as I said, does both.

Men often turn violent when their needs are intensely frustrated, but the sources of the frustration invariably include events that occur in the environment and block the fulfillment of the innate tendency. Man does have an innate tendency to fulfill his needs, not an innate tendency to fulfill them by violent means.[2]

On the other hand, National Institutes of Health (NIH) neurobiologist and professor at the University of Maryland, College Park, MD, R. Douglas Fields in his book *Why We Snap: Understanding the Rage Circuit in Your Brain* has written:

Step back and view our species objectively from the outside, the way a zoologist would carefully observe any other animal or see us the way every other creature perceives human beings.[3] The brutal reality could not be more evident or more wrong. Our violence operates far outside the bounds of any other species. Human beings kill anything. Slaughter is a defining behavior of our species. We kill all other creatures, and we kill our own. Read today's newspaper. Read yesterday's or read tomorrow's. The enormous industry of print and broadcast journalism serves predominantly to document our killing. Violence exists in the animal world, of course, but on a far different scale. Carnivores kill for food; we kill our family members, our children, our parents, our spouses, our brothers and sisters, our cousins, and in-laws. We kill strangers. We kill people who are different from us, in appearance, beliefs, race and social status. We kill ourselves in suicide. We kill for advantage and for revenge, we kill for entertainment: the Roman Coliseum, drive-by shootings, bullfights, hunting, and fishing, animal roadkill in an instantaneous reflex for sport. We kill friends, rivals, coworkers, and classmates. Children kill children, in school and on the playground. Grandparents, parents, fathers, mothers—all kill and all of them are the targets of killing.[4]

Weighing in as well are the academic disciplines of epigenetics, evolutionary psychology, sociobiology, and social psychology as well as biology and genetics (and, of course, anthropology, economics,[5] geography,[6] history, and political science), and all attempting to ascertain who, what, when, where, and why and who we are what we are, violent or not.

Before doing so, however, worth further pondering is the question whether there are human "commonalities" across the globe, independent of cultural and geographic variations, and which, therefore, are related directly to the questions with which this chapter is concerned. In 1991, emeritus professor of anthropology at the University of California, Santa Barbara, Donald E. Brown (b. 1934), published his text *Human Universals* wherein he contended that they "comprise those features of culture, society, language, behavior, and psyche for which there are no known exceptions, and, thus definitionally, common to all human societies".[7] Norenzayan and Heine define them as "core mental attributes shared by humans everywhere" and seek to provide "a conceptual analysis and methodological framework to guide the investigation of genuine universals through empirical analysis of psychological patterns across cultures".[8] In the Appendix to his 2002 *The Blank Slate*, Harvard Professor of Psychology Steven Pinker (b. 1954) author as well of *The Better Angels of Our Nature: Why Violence Has Declined* included the full list of Brown's Universals.[9] Abstracted from that full list and relevant to this text are following universals:

- Belief in supernatural/religion
- Beliefs, false
- Beliefs about death
- Beliefs about fortune and misfortune
- Collective identities
- Conflict
- Conflict, consultation to deal with
- Conflict, means of dealing with
- Conflict, meditation of
- Death rituals
- Distinguishing right and wrong
- Ethnocentrism
- Fear of death
- Identity, collective
- In-group distinguished from out-groups
- Language employed to manipulate others
- Language employed to misinform or mislead
- Language as translatable
- Laws (rules of membership)
- Magic
- Magic to increase life
- Magic to sustain life

- Magic to win love
- Males engage in more coalitional violence
- Males more aggressive
- Males more prone to lethal violence
- Murder proscribed
- Music related in part to religious activity
- Myths
- Prestige inequalities
- Redress of wrongs
- Resistance to abuse of power, to dominance
- Rites of passage
- Rituals
- Sanctions
- Sanctions for crimes against the collectivity
- Sanctions include removal from the social unit
- Symbolism
- Territoriality
- Violence, some forms of proscribed
- Weapons
- World view[10]

Thus, any discussion of our "humanbeingness" ought to take into consideration these commonalities as well. As is therefore correct and as James C. Davies argued above, we human beings, inherently complicated as we are, are—at least at the psychological level—a mix of both positive and well-meaning attributes and negative and destructive attributes, up to the ultimate expression of negativity, genocide.[11]

Further, the interaction between our physical selves and our "cultural selves" leads us logically to the new field of *epigenetics*, and, for our particular purposes, the experience of trauma, which initially affects directly its victims, and evidently becomes transmissible to a succeeding generation where it also manifests itself in physical symptoms. This interaction has also been addressed by anthropologists such as Robert Boyd,[12] environmental scientists such as Peter J. Richerson,[13] and journalists such as Christine Kenneally.[14]

A caveat, however, before proceeding: In 1986, twenty scientists from around the world examined what they regarded as the relevant data and which resulted in "The Seville Statement on Violence", and which was later adopted by UNESCO in 1989, and subsequently in the United States by the American Anthropological, Psychological, and Sociological Associations. It read, in part:

> IT IS SCIENTIFICALLY INCORRECT to say that we have inherited a tendency to make war from our animal ancestors.
> IT IS SCIENTIFICALLY INCORRECT to say that war or any other violent behavior is genetically programmed into our human nature.

> IT IS SCIENGTIFICALLY INCORRECT to say that in the course of human evolution there has been a selection for aggressive behaviour more than for other kinds of behaviour.
>
> IT IS SCIENTIFICALLY INCORRECT to say that humans have a 'violent brain'.
>
> IT IS SCIENTIFICALLY INCORRECT to say that war is caused by 'instinct' or any single motivation.
>
> (Seville, 16 May 1986; emphases in original)

Even so, however, epigeneticists have stood their ground maintaining that external factors such as environment (physical and cultural) have, over the course of the generations, affected our evolution as a species, and, ultimately, may very well impact our genetic responses, thus possibly altering in the process our genetic inheritance and DNA sequences, though this latter idea has been subject to critique and by and large rejected. Thus, the effect of a traumatization on a parent or parents (e.g., Holocaust and/or genocide survivors) verbally or physically communicating such to their offspring may result in negative physiological responses. Pioneering researcher Rachel Yehouda (b. 1959) at the James J. Peters Veterans Affairs Hospital, Bronx, NY, and her colleague Amy Lehrner, Department of Psychiatry and Neuroscience, Icahn School of Medicine, Mount Sinai Hospital, New York, NY, have argued such in their 2018 paper, "Intergenerational transmission of trauma effects: putative role of epigenetic mechanisms", examining "the influence of the offspring's early environmental exposures, including postnatal maternal care as well as in utero exposure reflecting maternal stress during pregnancy", and "epigenetic changes associated with a preconception trauma in parents that may affect the germline, and impact fetoplacental interactions".[15] Irene Lacal and Rossella Ventura, both at the Department of Physiology and Pharmacology, Spienza University, Rome, Italy, argue as well that "parents' stressful experiences can influence an offspring's vulnerability to many pathological conditions, including psychopathologies, and their effects may even endure for several generations".[16] Eric J. Nestler, also at the Icahn School of Medicine, Mount Sinai Hospital, New York, summarily suggests "the possibility that behavioral experience—in particular, exposure to stress—can be passed on to subsequent generations through inheritable epigenetic modifications" and "growing evidence supports a role for epigenetic regulation as a key mechanism underlying lifelong regulation of gene expression that mediates stress vulnerability".[17] As regards the full embrace of epigenetics, however, by both the scientific and humanistic communities, Bastiaan T. Heijmans and Jonathan Mill themselves sound something of a cautionary note regarding "the seven plagues of epigenetic epidemiology": (1) we do not really know where to look, or what to look for; (2) we have to rely on imperfect technology; (3) we may be limited by available sample sizes that are optimal for epigenetic epidemiology; (4) whatever we do, it may never be enough to fully account for epigenetic differences between tissues and cells; (5) we may be trying to detect inherently small effect sizes using these sub-optimal methods and sample cohorts; (6) we lack a framework for the analysis of genome-wide epigenetic data; (7) we have to manage high expectations.[18]

Thus, what does this field of epigenetics have to say to someone arguing for the nexus between religion and genocide? Simply this: That, negatively, the passing on of the traumatic experience of one generation's genocide extends far beyond its own immediacy, and, positively, coping mechanisms addressing these genocidal events—especially for those persons of faith who survived their genocide and attributed it (in whole or in part) to the "power" of their deity (or deities) and their own faith commitments, for example, practicing ritual and prayer behaviors and maintaining ethical standards even under duress, and communicating such to their own offspring—may very well provide a source of resiliency too little examined in the past and present.

From epigenetics to *evolutionary psychology*: (Evolutionary biology as the best fact-based descriptive understanding of how we came to be needs no further elaboration for readers of this text.) Parallelingly, the evolutionary nature of religion with the dawning of human consciousness, objective recognition of others in our initially small cluster groups later expanded, ritually addressing the deaths of persons within those same groups, and climatic phenomena attributed to entities "beyond the clouds" as it were—the subject of the next chapter "Why Geography, Climate Change, and Diseases Matters"—equally speak for themselves and are subjects about which "religions" have a great deal to say.

Evolutionary psychologists, paralleling perhaps somewhat the work of both sociobiologists, and social psychologists, argue that as much as has our physical selves changes and adapt themselves to survivalist pressures from the external environment, so, too, have our brains equally evolved due to the *sturm und drang*— "stress and strain"—of those same externalities. Thus, our "psychology", our very ways of thinking about our environment, and our coping mechanisms and strategies to greet and overcome the challenges and perceived threats to our physical survival—both individually and collectively—have changed over time as we have evolved brain adaptational mechanisms coupled with those same physical changes and up to and including changes to our environments due to enhanced technological skills (e.g., building better structures to withstand hurricanes and tornadoes). Much of our past and present behaviors may therefore be better understood as the interplay of adaptational physical and mental changes enabling us to survive. For example, our physical movement from *quadrupedalism* (walking/running on all four limbs) to *bipedalism* (walking/running on two limbs) significantly becomes instrumental in moving us from similarity to others in the animal kingdom to our *humanbeingness*.[19] Equally so, once uprightness carried with it logically our ability to "look up", and, coupled with our dawning awareness and consciousness not only of our environment and its positive and negative realities, but others of the same species and different species as well—both those well-intentioned and those harmful and threateningly intentioned—gave rise to what, for want of a better phrase, we may call the "religious impulse", that is, to "make sense" of our world and our place in it. Not full-blown initially, of course, but beginning a journey of attempting to come to grips with our circumstances as we continue to experience and transmit them from one generation to the next, and on and on into an ofttimes precarious present and an as-yet undetermined future—all thoughts, ideas, and contexts about which the religions of the world and their thinkers (theologians, philosophers, spokespersons) and leaders and valued texts have much to say.

Closely linked to evolutionary psychology is the "Dual Inheritance Theory" (DIT), what some have labeled "gene-culture co-evolution" or "biocultural evolution", again maintaining that we human beings are the (unfinished) "end product" of a dual and, most importantly, an *interactive* system of Charles Darwin's "natural selection": genetic/physical adaptive evolution and cultural/psychological adaptive evolution, both determining *who* we are as a species and *what* we are as human beings. The aforementioned notion of "human universals" across time (history), cultures, and geographic locales remains foundational to DIT. Equally so, the concept or idea of "tribalism" previously addressed as positive relationships within one's own group and extending outward to potential new members and negative relationships with those classified as non-group members with no access or rejected access to the in-group itself remains a hallmark of religious communities, and, taken to conclusion, may very well result in violence against others, up to an including legitimating and sanctioning genocide.

From evolutionary psychology, we turn to *sociobiology*, perhaps a significant revisioning and rethinking of the old "nature vs. nurture" argument of years past but adding to this conversation the latest scientific understandings as well. It goal, like so many others, is to explain human behavior as the evolutionary intermix of our physicality, our mental processes and brain functions, and the various environments in which we have found ourselves, both historically and contemporarily. Of special interest, to be sure, are discussions of so-called territorial imperatives among human beings, and whether our aggressiveness is evolutionarily innate but influenced by a constellation of environmental and social factors, including religious ones, as well as the Darwinian understanding of natural selection. Consequentially, sociobiologists argue as well that certain resultant behavioral traits are therefore heritable from one generation to the next and therefore survivalist adaptations partially determined by the environments in which we human beings have found ourselves over the course of the centuries.

While initially used by geneticist John Paul Scott (1909–2000) at Bowling Green State University, OH, at a 1948 conference, the term itself came in popular and current use by biologist E. O. Wilson (1929–2021) of Harvard University in 1975 with the publication of his book *Sociobiology: The New*

Synthesis, and his follow-up text *On Human Nature*.[20] Carried to conclusion, Wilson argues as well that these sociobiological factors continue to influence both individuals and groups. Properly understood—despite its critics (e.g., paleontologist Stephen Jay Gould [1941–2002][21])—sociobiology is a descriptive attempt to ascertain the human experience and *not* a moral or ethical review of human nature, a "was and is" not an "ought".

Then, too, there is as well the field of *social psychology*, and the influence of how "group think" affects both individuals and groups in something of a symbiotic relationship. That is, social psychologists attempt to fathom how the ideas, emotions, and behaviors of individuals are influenced by the ideas, emotions, and behaviors of others, leaders as well as followers, and, in many cases, peers. Two insights, especially, are relevant here: (1) the *desire* of individuals—Socrates' acknowledgment that we are, indeed, "social animals" and our continuing desire to belong remains primary,[22] and (2) the power of *persuasion*, not only by those in positions of leadership and power but also by those within our various social circles—family, friends, acquaintances—is primary.[23] Religious communities, for good or ill, have long existed and benefited from their ability to build upon the seeming desires of individuals—expressed, acknowledged, or even unacknowledged—to belong, and the persuasive abilities of their leaders and those in authority and power to invite them into their groups and sustain their memberships. Furthering this understanding as well is the realization that social group formation is contingent upon the seeming willingness of the individual to comply with the behavioral demands of the group to the point of obedience, again, for good or ill.

When one thus thinks of those social psychologists who have found themselves and their work/experiments most noticeably in the public arena, the two names that come most readily to mind are the late Stanley Milgram (1933–1984, obedience to authority)[24] and Philip Zimbardo (b. 1933, Stanford prison experiment).[25] Less well-known today, however, is the work of Solomon Asch (1906–1996, the power of conformity),[26] Leon Festinger (1919–1989, the ability of individuals to change truth to falsehood in favor of group conformity),[27] Muzafer Sherif (1906–1988, competition breeding hostility and aggression),[28] and Albert Bandura (1925–2021, aggression as a learned behavior through imitation).[29] Significantly relevant to their own overall understanding of "humanbeingness" was the exceptional text of Scottish poet, journalist, author, anthologist, novelist, and songwriter Charles Mackay's (1814–1889) study of crowd psychology, whose own text *Memoirs of Extraordinary Popular Delusions and the Madness of Crowds* was first published in 1841 in three volumes: *National Delusions*, *Peculiar Follies*, and *Philosophical Delusions*, addressing the powerful influence of both politics *and religion* on group thinking, citing in the latter second volume the example of the Crusades as "group mania". (His original text is available online from such sources as The Internet Archive, www.archive.org.) Rounding out this history, one should add Hans Askenasy's *Are We All Nazis?* suggesting that, given the "right set" of environment factors coupled with our innate disposition to violence and aggression, we human beings all have the potential to transform ourselves into Nazi-like villains.[30]

Further, this complicated understanding from a social psychological and sociological perspective, James Waller attributes the move to genocidal behavior to the following factors: (1) evolution of human nature, (2) cultural construction of worldview (collective values, authority orientation, social dominance), (3) psychological construction of the "other" (us-them thinking, moral disengagement, blaming the victims), and (4) social construction of cruelty (professional socialization, group identification, binding factors of the group.[31] Sociologist Christopher Powell, on the other hand, while not addressing the psychological dimensions of genocide, argues that civilization itself—our evolving collective gathering—is the result of two interconnected phenomena: the monopolizing of the military by nation-states and the so-called civilizing of our species, both of which have resulted in various symbolic activities (the primary domain of religion) and the intense competition for social dominance.[32]

Again, as noted previously, the newer field of *behavioral genetics* also examines the origins and nature of individual differences, initially focusing on the study of twins, but more broadly looking into both genetic and environmental influences on those differences. As a scientific field of inquiry, it is particularly concerned with whether there is a given gene or cluster of genes that result in specific behaviors and whether their modification or removal results in changes in behavior. Generally speaking, behavioral geneticists agree that behavioral traits, even problematic ones, are influenced or conditioned by genes; with regard to environmental influences, they tend to reveal differences even in family groupings; as we age, genetic differences tend to increase their relative importance.[33] Not without critics and subject to the abuse of the data and work of the scientists themselves,[34] Robert Plomin (b. 1948) of King's College, London, GB, and his colleagues write that "four of our top-10 findings involve the environment, discoveries that could only have been found us in genetically sensitive research designs", and thus validating their own work.[35] Thus, this interplay between our (inherited) genetics and environmental influences results not only in traumatic events being passed down from one generation to the next but the *possibility* of drawing upon parental and group validation of genocidal proclivities and actual behaviors infused by certain religious orientations (e.g., good us versus evil them, superiority versus inferiority, authoritarian commanding religious leaders drawing upon sacred texts, etc.) to murder others.

Penultimately, important to this discussion and the intersection between religion and genocide and the ongoing quest to assess/determine what we are and of what we are capable, positively and negatively, is that of demography, specifically the final loss of persons victimized by genocide and legitimized by religion. Group survival is contingent upon numbers, both the retention of those already in the group, and the constant infusion of additional numbers, whether through births within or recruitment from without. Religious groups are thus no different from other groups, be they nation-states, other civil and/or cultural organizations, social groups, and the like. Different, however, is the element of the sanctity of life itself for all religious groups. Significantly diminishing those numbers through voluntary egress including possible immigration due to disillusionment is one thing; significant losses due to murder as part of a larger overall agenda of the destruction of the group itself is another. Demographically speaking, at some point, such losses will, ultimately, result in the inability of the group to sustain itself in the morrow. Thus, genocide directed against any such group *always* has the potential to finally destroy not only the present existence of the group, but, if past history is any indicator, in some but not all cases, the memory and cultural productivity and contribution of the group (i.e., the idea of cultural genocide with which Raphael Lemkin himself was also concerned). And while war is itself an additional activity in sub-group destruction—the absurd and obscene notion of "collateral damage" (civilians)[36]—Lemkin was quick to point out that genocide remains a crime both in war *and peace*.[37] The various Geneva Conventions were themselves indirectly designed to address the fate of such potential genocide victims, though such was not their focus.

Lastly, to finally round out the necessity of attempting to understand not only human biology in relation to religion and genocide, as well as the whole notion of that of which we are destructively capable, is the Christian religious understanding of Original Sin. Given the above scientific conversations, discussions, and evidence vis-à-vis inheritability, it, therefore, makes some sense to regard Original Sin as "theological heritability" for those scriptural literalists for whom the story of Adam and Eve and their defiant behavior in the Garden of Eden is passed on to succeeding generations as a taint of human nature, and, consequentially, a certain proclivity to sin. Historically, it has evolved from the writings of Augustine of Hippo (354–430) but ironically from a mistranslation by his contemporary the elusive Ambrosiaster and thus his understanding of Paul's Letter to the Romans 5:12 ("Therefore, just as sin entered the world through one man, and death through sin, and in this way, death came to all people, because all sinned"). As it evolved in the Roman Catholic Church, due largely to the esteem with which Augustine was and is held, it would come to be affirmed by both Martin Luther (1483–1546) and John Calvin (1509–1564), but rejected by Eastern Orthodoxy, though Anglicanism, Methodism, Seventh-day Adventism, Jehovah's Witnesses all accept the heritability of Adam and Eve's sin. Both Mormonism and Quakerism, however, reject the notion of Original Sin. For all these Christian denominational communities, faith in and belief in the salvific and atoning death of Jesus Christ remains the only path to resolution, reconciliation, and eternal reward (a variation of the "us vs. them" orientation to be sure).

With what then are we left? Biology does matter. Genetics does matter. Environment does matter. In truth, we are, perhaps, no closer to a fuller understanding of what we human beings are as a species, practicing the best and worst behaviors, despite all the good work of the various academic and scientific disciplines briefly explored above and the scientists and humanists who engage in this work. Religion intersects with all these aspects of understanding of the human person, provides legitimation, and all-too-often provides cover for the genocidal excesses with which we are concerned.

There is, however, one more reality which needs to be addressed: that of geography, climate change, and disease and what religion has to say in each of these arenas and how they all contribute to genocide. That is the subject of the next chapter.

Notes

1 James C. Davies (1970), "Violence and Aggression: Innate or Not?", *The Western Political Quarterly*, 23(3): 611.
2 Ibid., 622. Davies' understanding of "needs" immediately calls to mind the late American psychologist Abraham H. Maslow (1908–1970) whose critiqued and controversial "Hierarchy of Needs" originally pyramided five (from lowest to highest—Physiological needs; Safety needs; Belongingness and love needs; Esteem needs; Self-actualization—but was later expanded to include Cognitive needs; Aesthetic needs; and, ultimately, Transcendence needs. Saul McLeod (2018), "Maslow's hierarchy of needs", https://www.simplypsychology.org/maslow.html. Accessed 2 September 2021.
3 See, for example, biologist Nicholas P. Money, *The Selfish Ape: Human Nature and Our Path to Extinction* (London: Reaktion Books, 2019). More well-known, however, is that of Konrad Lorenz, *On Aggression* (New York: Harcourt, Brace & World, 1966. Translated by Marjorie Kerr Wilson). Lorenz's work, however, is subject to its own serious critiques and criticisms of his studies of the "animal kingdom", largely due to his involvement with National Socialism (Naziism) during the period of World War II, his voluntarily joining the Nazi Party and his involvement with various Nazi governmental agencies, antisemitic writings, and questionable renunciations after the war. Peter Klopfer (1994), "Konrad Lorenz and the National Socialists: On the Politics of Ethology", *International Journal of Comparative Psychology*, 7(4): 202–208; and Boria Sax (1997), "What Is a 'Jewish Dog'? Konrad Lorenz and the Cult of Wildness", *Society and Animals*, 5(1): 3–21.
4 R. Douglas Fields (2016), *Why We Snap: Understanding the Rage Circuit in Your Brain* (New York: Dutton), 286; and "Humans Are Genetically Predisposed to Kill Each Other", www.psychologytoday.com. Accessed 27 August 2021. Fields' "nine triggers of rage" are (1) life-or-death, (2) insult, (3) family, (4) environment, (5) hate, (6) order in society, (7) resources, (8) tribe, and (9) stopped, all subsumed under the mnemonic "L.I.F.E.M.O.R.T.S".
5 Thomas Piketty, *Capitalism in the Twenty-First Century* (Cambridge and London: Harvard University Press, 2014. Translated by Arthur Goldhammer); Thomas Pikkety, *The Economics of Inequality* (Cambridge and London: Harvard University Press, 2015. Translated by Arthur Goldhammer); and Walter Scheidel, *The Great Leveler: Violence and the History of Inequality from the Stone Age to the Twenty-First Century* (Princeton and Oxford: Princeton University Press, 2017).

6 Benedict Anderson, *Imagined Communities* (London and New York: Verso, 1991); Robert Ardrey, *The Territorial Imperative: A Personal Inquiry into the Animal Origins of Property and Nations* (London: Collins, 1967); Erica Carter, James Donald, and Judith Squires, eds., *Space & Place: Theories of Identity and Location* (London: Lawrence and Wishart, 1993); Barbara E. Mann, *Space and Place in Jewish Studies* (New Brunswick and London: Rutgers University Press, 2012); and Simon Winchester, *Land: How the Hunger for Ownership Shaped the Modern World* (New York: Harper Collins, 2021).

7 Donald E. Brown, *Human Universals* (New York: McGraw-Hill, 1991).

8 Ara Norenzayan and Steven J. Heine (2005), "Psychological Universals: What They Are and How Can We Know?", *Psychological Bulletin*, 131(5): 763.

9 Steven Pinker, *The Blank Slate* (New York: Viking, 2002); *The Better Angels of Our Nature: Why Violence Has Declined* (New York: Viking, 2013). This latter text and its arguments are not themselves without serious critiques. See, for example, Philip Dwyer and Mark S. Micale, eds., *On Violence in History* (New York and Oxford: Berghahn, 2020); and Philip Dwyer and Mark S. Micale, eds., *The Darker Angels of Our Nature: Refuting the Pinker Theory of History & Violence* (London: Bloomsbury Academic, 2021).

10 https://condor.depaul.edu/~mfiddler/hyphen/humunivers.htm. Accessed 29 June 2021.

11 In his 2011 review of Steven Pinker's *The Better Angels of Our Nature,* Princeton philosopher Peter Singer (b. 1946) raises the following provocatively similar questions:

- Are human beings essentially good or bad?
- Has the past century witnessed moral progress or a moral collapse?
- Do we have grounds for being optimistic about the future?
- What do we owe to the Enlightenment?
- Is there a link between the human rights movement and the campaign for animal rights?
- Why are homicide rates higher in the southerly states of this country than in northern ones?
- Are aggressive tendencies heritable?
- Are we getting smarter?
- Is a smarter world a better world?

Peter Singer (October 6, 2011), "Is Violence History?", www.nytimes.com. Accessed 6 September 2021.

12 Robert Boyd, *A Different Kind of Animal: How Culture Transformed Our Species* (Princeton and Oxford: Princeton University Press, 2018).

13 Peter J. Richerson and Robert Boyd, *Not by Genes Alone: How Culture Transformed Human Evolution* (Chicago and London: The University of Chicago Press, 2005).

14 Christine Kenneally, *The Invisible History of the Human Race: How DNA and History Shape Our Identities and Our Futures* (New York: Viking, 2014).

15 Rachel Yehouda and Amy Lehrner (2018), "Intergenerational Transmission of Trauma Effects: Putative Role of Epigenetic Mechanisms", *World Psychiatry*, 17(3): 243.

16 Irene Lacal and Rossella Ventura (2018), "Epigenetic Inheritance: Concepts, Mechanisms, and Perspectives", *Frontiers in Molecular Neuroscience*, 11(292): 1.

17 Eric J. Nestler (2016), "Transgenerational Epigenetic Contributions to Stress Responses: Fact or Fiction?", *PLOS Biology*, 14(3): 1.

18 Bastiaan T. Heijmans and Jonathan Mill (2012), "Commentary: The Seven Plagues of Epigenetic Epidemiology", *International Journal of Epidemiology*, 41: 74–78.
19 Jeremy DeSilva, *First Steps: How Upright Walking Made Us Human* (New York: Harper Collins, 2021).
20 E. O. Wilson, *Sociobiology: The New Synthesis*, Twenty-Fifth Anniversary Edition (Cambridge: Harvard University Press, 2000); *On Human Nature* (Cambridge: Harvard University Press, 1978)—which won a Pulitzer Prize one year later.
21 Stephen Jay Gould (1978), "Sociobiology: The Art of Storytelling", *New Scientist*, 530–533; *The Mismeasure of Man* (New York: W. W. Norton & Company, 1996).
22 A personal, if perhaps somewhat humorous, example: I am a "dog person" and animal behaviorists tell me/inform us that the fact that my dogs follow me around, both inside and outside, is labeled by them as "pack behavior". The same might be said of us as well.
23 Social psychologists have readily acknowledged that persuasion's variables are five: (1) who is doing the persuasion, (2) the message itself, (3) the intended object or audience, (4) the vehicle by which the message is communicated, and (5) the context in which the act of persuasion takes place.
24 Stanley Milgram, *Obedience to Authority* (New York: Harper Perennial, 2009).
25 Philip Zimbardo, *The Lucifer Effect: Understanding How Good People Turn Evil* (New York: Random House, 2008). See, earlier, Craig Haney, Curtis Banks, and Philip Zimbardo (1973), "Interpersonal Dynamics in a Simulated Prison", *International Journal of Criminology and Penology*, 1: 69–97; Thomas Carnahan and Sam McFarland (2007), "Revisiting the Stanford Prison Experiment: Could Participant Self-Selection Have Led to the Cruelty?", *Personality and Social Psychology Bulletin*, 33: 603–614. For Carnahan and McFarland, that self-selection analysis resulted in ascertaining what they believed were five common qualities: aggression, right-wing authoritarianism; Machiavellianism; narcissism; social dominance orientation; and dispositional empathy.
26 Irvin Rock, ed., *The Legacy of Solomon Asch: Essays in Cognition and Social Psychology* (London and New York: Routledge, 2016). See, also, Solomon E. Asch (1955), "Opinions and Social Pressure", *Scientific American*, 193(5): 2–9.
27 Leon Festinger, *A Theory of Cognitive Dissonance* (Stanford: Stanford University Press, 1957).
28 Muzafer Sherif, O. J. Harvey, B. Jack White, William R. Hood, and Carolyn W. Sherif, *The Robbers Cave Experiment: Intergroup Conflict and Cooperation* (Middletown: Wesleyan University Press, 1954). See, also, Muzafer Sherif (1956), "Experiment in Group Conflict", *Scientific American*, 195(5): 54–59.
29 Albert Bandura, Dorothea Ross, and Sheila A. Ross (1981), "Transmission of Aggression through Imitation of Aggressive Models", *Journal of Abnormal and Social Psychology*, 63(3): 575–582.
30 Hans Ashkenasy, *Are We All Nazis?* (Secaucus: Lyle Stuart, 1978).
31 James Waller, *Becoming Evil: How Ordinary People Commit Genocide and Mass Killing* (New York and Oxford: Oxford University Press, 2007. Second Edition), Chapter 5 "Beyond Demonization", 137–170.
32 Christopher Powell, *Barbaric Civilization: A Critical Sociology of Genocide* (Montreal and London: McGill-Queen's University Press, 2012).
33 See, McGue M. Gottesman (2015), "Behavior Genetics", in Robin L. Cautin and Scott O. Lillienfeld, eds., *The Encyclopedia of Clinical Psychology* (New York: Wiley-Blackwell), 1–11.
34 Aaron Panofsky, *Misbehaving Science: Controversy and the Development of Behavior Genetics* (Chicago and London: The University of Chicago Press, 2014).

35 Robert Plomin, John C. DeFries, Valerie S. Knopik, and Jenae M. Neiderhiser (2016), "Top 10 Replicated [Conclusions] from Behavioral Genetics", *Perspectives on Psychological Science*, 11(1): 3–23. Those findings are:

1 All psychological traits show significant and substantial genetic influence.
2 No traits are 100% heritable.
3 Heritability is caused by many genes of small effect.
4 Phenotypic correlations [observable characteristics] between psychological traits show significant and substantial genetic mediation.
5 The heritability of intelligence increases throughout development.
6 Age-to-age stability is mainly due to genetics.
7 Most measures of the 'environment' show significant genetic influence.
8 Most associations between environmental measures and psychological traits are significantly mediated genetically.
9 Most environmental effects are not shared by children growing up in the same family.
10 Abnormal is normal.

See, also, Robert Plomin, *Blueprint: How DNA Makes Us Who We Are* (Cambridge: The MIT Press, 2019); Dalton Conley, *The Genomic Factor: What the Social Genomics Revolution Reveals about Ourselves, Our History, and the Future* (Princeton and Oxford: Princeton and Oxford University Press, 2017); and Kathryn Paige Harden, *The Genetic Lottery: Why DNA Matters for Social Equality* (Princeton and Oxford: Princeton University Press, 2021).

36 Hugo Slim, *Killing Civilians: Method, Madness, and Morality in War* (Oxford and New York: Oxford University Press, 2007); Taylor B. Seybolt, *Counting Civilian Casualties: An Introduction to Recording and Estimating Nonmilitary Deaths in Conflict* (Oxford and New York: Oxford University Press, 2013); and Diane M. Nelson, *Who Counts? The Mathematics of Death and Life after Genocide* (Durham and London: Duke University Press, 2015).

37 According to Rosa Brooks, "when the war machine breaks out of its borders, we undermine the values that keep out world from sliding toward chaos...how the collapsing barriers between war and peace threaten both America and the world". Rosa Brooks, *How Everything Became War and the Military Became Everything: Tales from the Pentagon* (New York: Simon & Schuster 2016). See, also, Kenneth Hill, *War, Humanitarian Crises, Population Displacement, and Fertility: A Review of the Evidence* (Washington: The National Academies Press, 2004. Available online at www.nap.edu); Tadeusz Kugler (2016), "The Demography of Genocide", in Charles H. Anderson and Jurgen Brauer, eds., *Economic Aspects of Genocide, Other Mass Atrocities, and Their Preventions* (Oxford and New York: Oxford University Press), 102–124; Birgit Meyer and Peter van der Meer, eds., *Refugees and Religion: Ethnographic Studies of Global Trajectories* (Oxford and New York: Oxford University Press, 2021); and Eric Kaufman, *Shall the Religious Inherit the Earth: Demography and Politics in the Twenty-First Century* (London: Profile Books, 2010).

Chapter 10

Why Geography, Climate Change, and Disease Matter

Cultural production, including religion, is contingent not only upon historical circumstances but locale as well and influenced by such realities as both climate change and diseases. Like religion itself, these three topics have been under-explored in discussions of genocide. For example, the Turks' easy access to the desert in the Armenian Genocide and the Nazis' purposeful choice of locating their various death camps (*vernichtungslagers*) near railway lines for incoming transports of prisoners. Religion, too, has much to say about geography, climate change, and diseases: pastoral positivity versus urban negativity; King David's choice of Jerusalem for his capital as a hilltop fortified location. This chapter explores the relationship between religion, geography, climate change, and diseases and Genocide.

Shades of omnicide, specicide, and terracide![1] Toward the end of his book *The Selfish Ape: Human Nature and Our Path to Extinction*, biologist Nicholas P. Money, Miami University, Oxford, OH, paints a chilling portrait of the end of humanity and our planetary existence, largely the result of our own doing:

> The decline of our own species was the natural and inevitable effect of immoderate greatness. The story of its ruin is simple and obvious; and, instead of inquiring why humanity was destroyed, we should rather be surprised that it has subsisted for so long.
>
> That we have created conditions on Earth that will hasten our decline is undeniable. Here are the circumstances: Earth is warming swiftly; seawater is acidifying and choking with plastics; industrial activity is poisoning the air; deforestation is relentless; grasslands and lakes are shrinking as deserts expand and a swarm of 10 billion humans will jostle for the remaining resources by 2050. In short order, extreme weather events will become more frequent; crops will be withered by drought; fisheries will crash; populations of the larger wild animals will continue to dwindle; insect numbers will pursue their precipitous decline; plant species will perish, and the microbial majority of life will shudder unseen. On a somewhat larger timescale, coastlines will be reshaped by rising sea

DOI: 10.4324/9781003168799-10

levels. As the Antarctic ice sheet caves and dissolves, Florida and Bangladesh will vanish beneath the waves.[2]

Even earlier—and perhaps somewhat darker—Roy Scranton (b. 1976) at the University of Notre Dame, IN, penned a 2015 text *Learning to Die in the Anthropocene: Reflections on the End of Civilization* arguing for the grim reality of the end of humanity as a result of climate change.[3] Later (2017), Alejandro R. Jadad and Murray W. Erkin wrote a provocative piece entitled "Does humanity need palliative care?" and commented:

> Our economic models are not working, our political structures are corrupted, our ability to respond and adapt to our rapidly decaying environment is wanting…
>
> The real underlying pathology is the zealous overvaluation and overprotection of our current territory, beliefs, ideologies, and way of life…What if we admitted that human extinction, within a few generations, is the most likely scenario? What if our hope in the ability of technology to solve our problems is blinding us to its power to render us irrelevant and making us unable to notice how our tools aggravate our symptoms along the way? What if we decided to leave the possibility of a rosy future behind?
>
> What if it's time to think of palliative care for our collective humanity?[4]

Whatever else religions have done over the centuries, they have inspired hope among the faithful in the direst and bleakest of moments and circumstances, and, consequently, have enabled some among them/us to survive. At the same time, however, religions—in their ongoing affirmation of the sacrality of the land—are also guilty of contributing to its expropriation and exploitation when validating nation-state and political destruction (e.g., displacement and death of others in specific locales, and rendering unfit for present and return physical habitation).

Geography[5]

There is, in all reality, no more contested land today than that of Israel/Palestine adjudged sacred and holy by both Jews and Muslims and Judaism and Islam. References to its sacrality are woven throughout both the Hebrew Bible/Old Testament and the Qur'an, and both religious traditions and their adherents regard that land as one given to them by God/Allah who, historically and contemporarily, has tasked both—rather one instead of the other—with demonstrating their good stewardship of that sacred responsibility. Instances of present-day violations occur on both sides: members of the Jewish-Israeli settler movement destroying olive trees and groves nourished by Palestinian-Arab farmers for generations; Palestinian-Arabs setting fire to forests of trees planted by the Jewish National Fund (JNF; Israel's reforestation agency), and ofttimes dedicated to the memories of Israel's patrons (e.g., Presidents Harry S. Truman [1884–1972] and John F. Kennedy [1917–1963]) or its Martyrs Forest with its six million trees in memory of those who perished in the Holocaust/Shoah.

Religio-theologically, the land of Israel (ancient Palestine, derived from the Roman Latin designation *Palestina*) remains sacred to Jews as both a Holy Land (Hebrew, *Eretz K'dosha*) and a Promised Land (Hebrew, *Eretz Havtakha*), whose ultimate source is the Hebrew Bible/Old Testament itself; specifically the God of Israel, its creator and owner, chooses to give it to its first patriarch Abraham (born Abram, the Chaldean from Ur) then his descendants, the Israelite people, as Genesis 15:18–21 would have it:

> [18] On that day the LORD made a covenant with Abram and said, "To your descendants I give this land, from the [Nile] river of Egypt to the great river, the Euphrates—
> [19] the land of the Kenites, Kenizzites, Kadmonites,
> [20] Hittites, Perizzites, Rephaites,
> [21] Amorites, Canaanites, Girgashites and Jebusites".

Land thus remains central to the Jewish religious belief system to this day, when, at the conclusion of the Passover Seder ritual, Jews the world over conclude their evening with the affirmation, "*L'shana haba'a biYerushalayim*"/"Next year in Jerusalem".[6] Then, too, some religiously devout Jews make plans to be buried upon their deaths in one of Israel's four holiest cities—Jerusalem, Hebron, Safed, or Tiberias. (If, for whatever reason, an impossibility, a small bag of "holy land soil" is placed in the coffin when burial takes place outside Israel.)

Troubling, however, even before that commitment to Abraham and the ancient Israelites is the Genesis 1:28 verse

> And God blessed them [Adam and Eve]; and God said to them: "Be fruitful and multiply, and replenish the earth, *and subdue it*, have dominion over the fish of the sea, and over the fowl of the air, and over every living thing that creeps on the earth".
>
> (emphasis added)

Thus, contemporarily, one could too easily argue opens the door to the destructive exploitation of planet earth.[7]

For Christians, in addition to incorporating the Hebrew Bible/Old Testament into their sacred canon and accepting the holiness of the land itself (although one could argue a "lesser holiness" than Jews), Jerusalem looms large as the place where the Christ/Messiah/Jesus was crucified by the Romans but resurrected as well. Its takeover by the Arab world and its Muslim majority would cause a violent backlash and attempted reconquest during the early

Middle Ages period (11th–13th centuries), a series of religio-military events we have come to know as the Crusades, and which cannot be divorced from their religio-theological moorings.

For faithful and devout Muslims, Jerusalem (Arabic, *al-Quds*) remains one of Islam's three holiest cities along with Mecca and Medina, and the site of Muhammad's (537–632) "Night Journey" to the seven stages of heaven (Arabic, *al-'Isrā' wal-Mi-rāj*), transported by the winged steed Buraq, where, according to tradition, he would meet Adam, Abraham, Joseph, Aaron, Moses, John the Baptist, and Jesus before being escorted into God's Holy Presence and returning to earth.

Thus, all three monotheistic religious traditions—Judaism, Christianity, and Islam—despite the causes and rationales of blood-letting and holy/sacred land despoliation poured upon its ground stand guilty, at least in part, and condemned by their own violations of the ideals they seemingly espouse— this despite the Hebrew Bible's/Old Testament's own prohibition of land violation in wartime in Deuteronomy 20:

> [19] When you lay siege to a city for a long time, fighting against it to capture it, do not destroy its trees by putting an ax to them, because you can eat their fruit. Do not cut them down. Are the trees people, that you should besiege them?[20] However, you may cut down trees that you know are not fruit trees and use them to build siege works until the city at war with you falls.

Going down an even somewhat darker road, addressing the idea/ideal/concept of land are the notions of *settler colonialism* so much a part of the Western civilizational enterprise not only in the so-called new worlds of the Americas (i.e., Native American genocidal exploitation, and, later, African American enslavement and dispossession), infused, at least in the United States by, for some, their understanding of *manifest destiny*, but the African continent as well. Parallelly, the Nazi concept of *lebensraum* (German, "living room") must also be addressed in this discussion and cannot, ultimately, be separated from Adolf Hitler's (1889–1945) own notion of messianic-like selection of him by God for a liberating purpose not only of the German people but also of the totality of humanity from the vice-like grip of "Jewry", as revealed in his political autobiography/testament *Mein Kampf* ("My Fight" or "My Struggle").

According to Alicia Cox, University of Californian, Irvine, settler colonialism may best be understood as

> an ongoing system of power that perpetuates the genocide of indigenous peoples and cultures. Essentially hegemonic in scope, settler colonialism normalizes the continuous settler occupation, *exploiting lands and resources to which indigenous peoples have genealogical relationships*...settler colonizers are Eurocentric and assume that European values with respect to ethnic,

and therefore moral, [to which we may add *religious*] superiority are inevitable and natural…these intersecting dimensions of settler colonialism coalesce around the dispossession of indigenous peoples' lands, resources, and cultures…colonialism is not a thing of the past because the settlers have come to stay, displacing the indigenous peoples and perpetuating systems that continue to erase native lives, cultures, and histories…settler colonizers destroy indigenous peoples and cultures in order to replace them and establish themselves as the new rightful inhabitants…settler colonizers do not merely exploit indigenous peoples and lands for labor and economic interests, they displace them through settlements.[8]

And, according to Adam Barker and Emily Battell Lowman of Global Social Theory, settler colonialism has three key features:

- First, settler colonizers "come to stay"; unlike colonial agents such as traders, soldiers, or governors, settler collectives intend to permanently occupy and assert sovereignty over indigenous lands.
- Second, settler colonial invasion is a structure, not an event; settler colonialism persists in the ongoing elimination of indigenous populations (genocide), and the assertion of state sovereignty and juridical control over their lands.
- Third, settler colonialism seeks its own ends; unlike other types of colonialism,[9] in which the goal is to maintain colonial structures and imbalances in power between colonizer and colonized, settler colonization trends toward the ending of colonial difference in the form of a supreme and unchallenged settler state and people.[10]

This so-called natural right of superior Europeans to settle and colonize finds its ultimate negative expressions in the Nazi notion of *lebensraum* but prior to it in the American notion of *manifest destiny*.

The Nazi idea of *lebensraum* ("living room") actually preceded their drive to German power and European expansionism, especially eastward (German, *Generalplan Ost*). Coined by the noted geographer Friedrich Ratzel (1844–1904), when falsely combined with notions of Darwinian species survival and competition for resources, it thus became the "natural" right of biologically "superior" peoples ("Aryans") to expand beyond their own geographic borders and carried with it the subjugation of so-called inferior and lesser peoples, including the murders of those perceived as threats to those goals. With the later initial support/sanction and encouragement of the various religious institutions and their leaders (Roman Catholic, Lutheran, Protestant), the Nazis found their agenda, which included both the dispossession and murder of resident populations as well as the destruction and takeover of already-existing nation-states, importantly Poland for the construction of the death-camp system, given validation.[11] Thus, it is not a stretch of one's imagination to see in the Nazi understanding of *lebensraum* a connection to the notion of American *manifest destiny*.

Largely expressed in the 19th century and part of the overall mindset of the rationalization for Westward expansion and the displacement and worse of Native Americans, *manifest destiny* was (and, perhaps, remains) the legitimation of American expansionist ideals based on a belief in US exceptional superiority politically, governmentally, militarily, economically, and religiously (here read white Christian Protestantism) and further expanding the European vision not only locally but globally. Its author was said to be the journalist John L. O'Sullivan (1813–1895) who first used the term "divine destiny" in 1839 to promote the annexation of Texas and the Oregon Territory but would go on to use the term "manifest destiny" in his 1845 article entitled "Annexation in the Democratic Review", the year that the United States would indeed go on to annex Texas.[12] (O'Sullivan would later go on to serve as the US Minister/Ambassador to Portugal [1853–1857].) Whether "divine" or "manifest", the term and understanding are inextricably interwoven/intertwined with the view that the (Christian?) God had favored the primarily white Protestant American people to create its nation-state and its institutions, and, in gratitude for that ability to do so, consequently, to displace and worse those who did not share in that vision. For those "outsiders" who would come to embrace that vision, however, they (*some* Native Americans, *some* African Americans, *some* immigrant Americans) were to be incorporated into that dream even if their roles remained subservient to the overall power structure as it continued to evolve. Thus, like all of the concepts/ideas explored above, it, too, cannot be divorced from ideas embedded in religious thinking, and, carried to extreme, manifesting itself/themselves, in genocidal undertakings. As Andrew C. Isenberg and Thomas Richards, Jr., write

> Manifest destiny was a partisan idea that emerged in a context of division and uncertainty intended to overawe opponents of expansion. Only in the early twentieth century, as the United States had consolidated its hold on the North American West and was extending its power into the Caribbean and Pacific, did historians begin to describe manifest destiny as something it never was in the nineteenth century: a consensus. To a significant extent, historians continue to rely on the idea to explain U.S. expansion.[13]

Climate Change

Only the most climatically recalcitrant denialists—including some scientists and academics who should know better given the staggering amount of evidences worldwide[14]—would reject the understanding that climate change is having a disastrously negative effect on plant, animal, and human species, our overall planetary environment, and bodes ill for our collective future habitation. What is less explored is the impacts that these momentous changes are shown to increasingly have on escalating human violence as competition for increasingly limited resources manifest themselves.[15] Indeed, two recent studies have shown this to be the case.

In a 2013 article, Solomon H. Hsiang, Marshall Burke, and Edward Miguel have presented evidence that

> deviations from normal precipitation and mild temperatures systematically increase the risk of conflict, often substantially…the magnitude of climate influence on modern conflict is both substantial and highly significant…*there is more agreement across studies regarding the influence of climate on human conflict than has been recognized previously.* Given the large potential changes in precipitation and temperature regimes projected for the coming decades—with locations throughout the inhabited world expected to warm by 2 to 4 SDs by 2050—amplified rates of human conflict could represent a large and critical social impact of anthropogenic climate change both in low- and high-income countries.[16]

Further, Hsiang, Kyle C. Meng, and Mark A. Cane have argued that

> the probability of new civil conflicts arising throughout the tropics doubles during El Niño years relative to La Niña years. This result, which indicates that ENSO [El Niño/Southern Oscillation] may have a role in 21% of all civil conflicts since 1950, is the first demonstration that the stability of modern societies relates strongly to the global climate.[17]

Even more forcefully, however, Robert Kiel of the Stimson Center, Washington, DC, has titled his 2019 commentary "The Looming Accelerant: The Growing Links between Climate Change, Mass Atrocities, and Genocide" and examining five cases of mass atrocities: the Central African Republic (CAR), Myanmar, Nigeria, Darfur, and Syria, and concludes that climate-related problems are present in four of the five cases and only that of Darfur is potentially climate-related.[18]

Historically and religio-theologically, while "climate drama" may very well been one of the factors that led to our ancient construction of religion—attributing to the God or gods natural phenomena we could not otherwise explain (hurricanes, tsunamis, earthquakes, tornados)—over time, one consistent theme/resolution to these seemingly inexplicable spectacles became, more and more, attributable to a sinful/errant humanity and the divine(s)' chosen or preferred forms of punishment. To take but one example—earthquakes—there are several passages in both the Hebrew Bible/Old Testament and New Testament that not only record the events but assign the cause to human sinfulness:

> **Number 16:31–35:**[31] As soon as he [Moses] finished saying all this, the ground under them split apart[32] and the earth opened its mouth

and swallowed them and their households, and all those associated with Korah, together with their possessions.[33] They went down alive into the realm of the dead, with everything they owned; the earth closed over them, and they perished and were gone from the community.[34] At their cries, all the Israelites around them fled, shouting, "The earth is going to swallow us too!"[35] And fire came out from the LORD and consumed the 250 men who were offering the incense.

2 Samuel 22:8: The earth trembled and quaked, the foundations of the heavens shook; they trembled because he [God] was angry.

Psalms 104:32: he [God] who looks at the earth, and it trembles, who touches the mountains, and they smoke.

Isaiah 24:18–20:[18] Whoever flees at the sound of terror will fall into a pit;

whoever climbs out of the pit will be caught in a snare. The floodgates of the heavens are opened, the foundations of the earth shake.[19] The earth is broken up, the earth is split asunder, the earth is violently shaken.[20] The earth reels like a drunkard, it sways like a hut in the wind; so heavy upon it is the guilt of its rebellion that it falls—never to rise again.

Jeremiah 10:10:[10] But the LORD is the true God; he is the living God, the eternal King. When he is angry, the earth trembles; the nations cannot endure his wrath.

Nahum 1:5: The mountains quake before him [God] and the hills melt away. The earth trembles at his presence, the world and all who live in it.

Habakkuk 3:6: He [God] stood, and shook the earth; he looked, and made the nations tremble. The ancient mountains crumbled, and the age-old hills collapsed—but he marches on forever.

Matthew 27:50–54:[50] And when Jesus had cried out again in a loud voice, he gave up his spirit.[51] At that moment the curtain of the temple was torn in two from top to bottom. The earth shook, the rocks split[52] and the tombs broke open. The bodies of many holy people who had died were raised to life.[53] They came out of the tombs after Jesus' resurrection and went into the holy city and appeared to many people.[54] When the centurion and those with him who were guarding Jesus saw the earthquake and all that had happened, they were terrified, and exclaimed, "Surely he was the Son of God!"

Acts 16:25–31:[25] About midnight Paul and Silas were praying and singing hymns to God, and the other prisoners were listening to them.[26] Suddenly there was such a violent earthquake that the foundations of the prison were shaken. At once all the prison doors flew open, and everyone's chains came loose.[27] The jailer woke up, and when he saw the prison doors open, he drew his sword and was about to kill himself because he thought the prisoners had escaped.[28] But Paul shouted, "Don't harm yourself! We are all here!"²⁹ The jailer called for lights, rushed in and fell trembling before Paul and Silas.³⁰ He then brought them out and asked, "Sirs, what must I do to be saved?"³¹ They replied, "Believe in the Lord Jesus, and you will be saved—you and your household".

Hebrews 12:26: At that time his [God's] voice shook the earth, but now he has promised, "Once more I will shake not only the earth but also the heavens".

Revelation 16:16–20:¹⁶ Then they gathered the kings together to the place that in Hebrew is called Armageddon [Hebrew, Har/Mount Megiddo].¹⁷ The seventh angel poured out his bowl into the air, and out of the temple came a loud voice from the throne, saying, "It is done!"¹⁸ Then there came flashes of lightning, rumblings, peals of thunder and a severe earthquake. No earthquake like it has ever occurred since mankind has been on earth, so tremendous was the quake.¹⁹ The great city split into three parts, and the cities of the nations collapsed. God remembered Babylon the Great and gave her the cup filled with the wine of the fury of his wrath.²⁰ Every island fled away, and the mountains could not be found.¹⁹

However, as humanity continues to evolve and scientific explanations interact with religio-theological ones, religionists find themselves, increasingly, having to reject their previously held explanations of punishment, and, ultimately, admit or yield to a necessarily rethought understanding of the entire creative process on the part of the divine (i.e., a perfect deity creates or organizes an imperfect creation and embeds within it these all-too-often tragic planetary physical flaws, which all-too-often result in mega-deaths). Appropriate to another context, I would contend that no religious tradition, especially the Abrahamic ones of Judaism, Christianity, and Islam, have yet to construct a truly meaning explanation of such tragedies as, for example, the Banda Aceh tsunami tragedy in Indonesia in 2004, which resulted in over 225,000 deaths, Hurricane Katrina in New Orleans, LA, in the United States in 2005, which resulted in almost 2,000 deaths, and even earlier the devastating tornado in Worchester, MA, in 1953 resulting in "only" ninety-four deaths²⁰ and far too many others both before and after these events.²¹

That we humans are progressively destroying our planetary home has recently and quite dramatically been brought home with the publication of the Intergovernmental Panel on Climate Change (IPCC) report "Climate Change 2021: The Physical Science Basis". Here are its conclusions:

- A.1. It is unequivocal that human influence has warmed the atmosphere ocean, and land. Widespread and rapid changes in the atmosphere, ocean, cryosphere, and biosphere have occurred.
- A.2. The scale of recent changes across the climate system as a whole and the present state of many aspects of the climate system are unprecedented over many centuries to many thousands of years.

- A.3. Human-induced climate change is already affecting many weather and climate extremes in every region across the globe. Evidence of observed changes in extremes such as heatwaves, heavy precipitation, droughts, and tropical cyclones, and, in particular, their attribution to human influence, has strengthened since AR5.
- A.4. Improved knowledge of climate processes, paleoclimate evidence and the response of the climate system to increasing radiative forcing gives a best estimate of equilibrium climate sensitivity of 3°C with a narrower range compared to AR5.
- B.1. Global surface temperature will continue to increase until at least the mid-century under all emissions scenarios considered. Global warming of 1.5°C and 2°C will be exceeded during the 21st century unless deep reductions in CO_2 and other greenhouse gas emissions occur in the coming decades.
- B.2. Many changes in the climate system become larger in direct relationship to increasing global warming. They include increases in the frequency and intensity of hot extremes, marine heatwaves, and heavy precipitation, agricultural and ecological droughts in some regions, and proportion of intense tropical cyclones, as well as reductions in Arctic Sea ice, snow cover, and permafrost.
- B.3. Continued global warming is projected to further intensify the global water cycle, including its variability, global monsoon precipitation and the severity of wet and dry events.
- B.4. Under scenarios with increasing CO_2 emissions, the ocean and land carbon sinks are projected to be less effective at slowing the accumulation of CO_2 in the atmosphere.
- B.5. Many changes due to past and future greenhouse gas emissions are irreversible for centuries to millennia, especially changes in the ocean, ice sheets and global sea level.
- C.1. Natural drivers and internal variability will modulate human-caused changes, especially at regional scales and in the near term, with little effect on centennial global warming. These modulations are important to consider in planning for the full range of possible changes.
- C.2. With further global warming, every region is projected to increasingly experience concurrent and multiple changes in climatic impact-drivers. Changes in several climatic impact-drivers would be more widespread at 2°C compared to 1.5°C global warming and even more widespread and/or pronounced for higher warming levels.
- C.3. Low-likelihood outcomes, such as ice sheet collapse, abrupt ocean circulation changes, some compound extreme events and warming substantially larger than the assessed *very likely* range of future warming cannot be ruled out and are part of risk assessment. [Emphasis in original.]
- D.1. From a physical science perspective, limiting human-induced global warming to a specific level requires cumulative CO_2 emissions,

reaching at least net zero CO_2 emissions, along with strong reductions in other greenhouse gas emissions. Strong, rapid and sustained reductions in CH_4 emissions would also limit the warming effect resulting from declining aerosol pollution and would improve air quality.
- D.2. Scenarios with very low or low GHG emissions lead within years to discernible effects on greenhouse gas and aerosol concentrations, and air quality, relative to high and very high GHG emissions scenarios. Under these contrasting scenarios, discernible differences in trends of global surface temperatures would begin to emerge from natural variability within around 20 years, and over longer time periods for many other climatic impact-drivers (*high confidence*).[22]

Given this rather alarming "doomsday scenario", it is no small wonder that, in 2020, on the initiative of professors Taner Akçam and Thomas Kühne of the Strassler Center for Holocaust and Genocide Studies, Clark University, Worchester, Massachusetts, published "Genocide Studies and the Climate Emergency: A Statement from Fellow Scholars" with an initial database of twenty-two signatories. Contained within is the following:

> The interrelationship thus between ecocidal and genocidal warfare, waged against peoples and planet is built into this anthropocenic turn... The tsunami of violence which must necessarily follow [the hardening of nation-state barriers] will make of our studies of atrocities to date little more than way stations en route to a universal Calvary.[23]
>
> As genocide scholars, we need to rethink what we study and why, not just with a view to the horrors of the past but the interconnections between the past and the present, and why these interconnections matter to our fate as a global society, not to say species. Above all, we need to ask why climate change, as with the pandemic [of COVID-19] is impacting 'first and worst' on the most exposed and vulnerable, on people of colour, primarily in the Global South, on the rural as well as urban poor, on subsistence, nomadic and pastoralist societies, the dispossessed and displaced from war zones but also indigenous peoples otherwise First Nations, everywhere.
>
> As the clock ticks down to planetary nemesis our historically dispassionate role and critical distance seeking out the sources and drivers of both genocidal and ecocidal mass murder at macro, meso and micro levels, requires now a rapid, clear-sighted but also *passionate* reconfiguration to scrutinizing and calling out the culpability and responsibility of immensely powerful, national and corporate polluting interests for the environmental damage and mass death they have inflicted and continue to inflict, and for which they ought to be accountable in precisely the same way of other more recognizable génocidaires.
>
> We do not need to be environmental experts to tell the truth about the peril we face as a human community, nor to flinch from acting as

role models in our efforts to educate and mobilize our students to act as if that truth were real.

Though I have reserved potential "solutions" to Chapter 11, at this juncture, suffice it to say that the religions of the world, perhaps or because of their historical complicity, have a decidedly positive role in addressing climate change and its relationship to genocide. As Lynn White noted in his classic 1967 article "The Historic Roots of our Ecological Crisis",

> What people do about their ecology depends on what they think about themselves in relation to things around them. Human ecology is deeply conditioned by beliefs about our nature and destiny—that is, by religion.[24]

Disease

Prior to the COVID-19 (Corona Virus December 2019) pandemic of 2020 and 2021, the rampant disease, which most altered the course of human history in the minds of many if not all, was the Black Death or Bubonic Plague, which infected Europe, Eurasia, and Africa between the years 1346 and 1353 and took the lives of somewhere between 75,000,000 and 200,000,000 persons. Less well-known, perhaps, was the Great Famine of 1315–1317, which, earlier changed not only the human geography of Northern Europe but the land and environment themselves and claimed 6,000,000 lives. Accompanying this earlier devastation were animal deaths of cattle and sheep due to disease (perhaps as high as 80%), rampant criminality, and even cannibalism, and infanticide. As was equally the case with the initial religious assessments as to causes, divine punishments toward an errant humanity loomed largest, but specific groups (Jews, Romani, foreigners, beggars, pilgrims, those affected with skin diseases such as lepers) found themselves the targets of violent responses as both carriers and spreaders of both plagues and famines and using satanic and other rituals toward such perverse ends. (That these same groups were themselves also afflicted, affected, and infected did little to nothing to change the mindsets of political and/or religious leaderships and their followers, the vast majority of whom were ignorant of any scientific knowledge whatsoever.) Yet, as Barbara Bramanti et al. note as well, "large epidemics of plague, which have had significant demographic, social, and economic consequences, have been recorded in Western European historical documents since the sixth century".[25] As the late University of Kansas professor and pioneer in the art of digital humanities Lynn H. Nelson (1931–2012) wrote when combining these two mega-events:

> Each caused millions of deaths, and each in its way demonstrated in dramatic fashion the existence of new vulnerabilities in Western European society. Together they subjected the population of medieval Europe to

tremendous strains, leading many people to challenge old institutions and doubt traditional values, and, by so doing, these calamities altered the path of European developments in many areas.

Specifically addressing the Black Death, he wrote:

> The effects of that plague and its successors on the men and women of medieval Europe were profound: new attitudes toward death, the value of life, and of one's self. It kindled a growth of class conflict, a loss of respect for the [Roman Catholic] Church, and the emergence of a new pietism (personal spirituality) that profoundly altered European attitudes toward religion. Still another effect, however, was to kindle a new cultural vigor in Europe, one in which the national languages, rather than Latin, were the vehicle of expression.

He concludes:

> These were natural disasters, but they were made all the worse by the inability of the directing elements of society, the princes and the clergy, to offer any leadership during these crises.[26]

Plus ça change, plus c'est la même chose/the more things change, the more they stay the same!

The three events which have been the focus of this chapter—the sacrality of the land, climate change, and epidemics—all have a decidedly religious awareness both historically and contemporarily, and not all of it positive. That negative escalations of each have the potential to, ultimately, result in violence and taken to conclusion genocide should give the human community pause to continually reassess the role, purpose, and function of religion as an aspect of human cultural production and activity. Before concluding this text, we bring together all of the various connected strands leading us both to a summary assessment and the most practical and realistic appraisal of where we go from here.

Notes

1 While not originally included in the list of "Cides", it is appropriate to introduce it here: *terracide* is the destruction of the planet, both consciously and non-consciously, by the human species.
2 Nicholas P. Money, *The Selfish Ape: Human Nature and Our Path to Extinction* (London: Reakton Books Ltd., 2019), 92.
3 Roy Scranton, *Learning to Die in the Anthropocene: Reflections on the End of Civilization* (San Francisco: City Lights Publishers, 2015). See, also: Roy Scranton, *We're Doomed: Essays on War and Climate Change* (New York: Soho Press, 2018).

4 Alejandro R. Jadad and Murray W. Erkin (2017), "Does Humanity Need Palliative Care?", *European Journal of Palliative Care*, 24(3): 102.
5 Though not directly addressing the relationship between religion, geography, and genocide, in 2009, the journal *Space and Polity*, 13(1) devoted its issue to "Geographies of Genocide", examining the sites of Democratic Kampuchea, Guatemala, and the US, and additionally addressing "Geographical Information Systems Technology for Genocide Prevention: The Case of Darfur" (Matthew Levinger, 69–76); and "Creating Geocidal Space: Geographers and the Discourse of Annihilation, 1890–1933" (Sarah K. Danielsson, 55–68), this last showcasing the work of German geographer Friedrich Ratzel (1844–1904) and his colleagues and arguing that their work on *Lebensraum* and its expansion laid an intellectual foundation for the exterminationist work of National Socialism/Nazism.
6 Reference to Jerusalem occurs 669 times in the Hebrew Bible/Old Testament; the Land of Israel 154 times.
7 According to the [Francis] *Brown*-[S. R.] *Driver*-[Charles A.] *Briggs Hebrew and English Lexicon*, published by the Clarendon Press, Oxford, in 1906, and still a standard etymological reference, the Hebrew verb *kavash* (kaf, vet, shin) means "to subdue, force, dominate, bring into bondage, tread down, beat or make a path, press, squeeze, knead, attack, assault". In further examining fifty-four English translations, "subdue" appears thirty-six times; "subjugate" once; "master" thrice; "bring it under your control" thrice; "take control" once; "be its master" thrice; "take charge" once; "rule over" once; "govern" once; "conquer" once; "make it subject" once; and, interestingly enough, "care for My creation" once [*The Voice Bible*, Ecclesia Bible Society and Thomas Nelson Publishers, 2012.], www.biblegateway.com.
8 Alicia Cox (2017), "Settler Colonialism", www.oxfordbibliographiesonline.com. Accessed 5 October 2021. See, also, Patrick Wolfe (2006), "Settler Colonialism and the Elimination of the Native", *Journal of Genocide Research*, 8(4): 387–409, which succinctly lays out the theoretical thinking undergirding this understanding; emphasis added. Important as well are the two texts by Tunisian French-Jewish writer and essayist Albert Memmi (1920–2020) *The Colonizer and the Colonized* (Boston: Beason Press, 1991), and *Decolonization and the Decolonized* (Minneapolis: University of Minnesota Press, 2006. Translated by Robert Bonnono).
9 In "A Typology of Colonialism", Nancy Shoemaker furnishes the following listing of different types of colonialism and defining each: (1) Settler Colonialism; (2) Planter Colonialism; (3) Trade Colonialism; (4) Transport Colonialism; (5) Imperial Power Colonialism; (6) Not-in-My-Backyard Colonialism; (7) Legal Colonialism; (8) Rogue Colonialism; (9) Missionary Colonialism; (10) Romantic Colonialism; (11) Postcolonial Colonialism. www.historians.org. Accessed 5 October 2021.
10 Adam Barker and Emma Battell Lowman, "Settler Colonialism", https://globalsocialtheory.org. Accessed 5 October 2021.
11 The Nazis, including Hitler himself, drew in part their inspiration from the American story of westward expansion and their concomitant dispossession of Native Americans, destruction of tribal properties especially sacred sites, forced relocations to so-called reservations (sometimes rationalized for their own and others' safety), destruction of animal life (buffaloes), and, where "appropriate", murders of men, women, and children. See, for example, Carroll P. Kakel, III, *The American West and the Nazi East: A Comparative and Interpretive Perspective* (New York: Palgrave Macmillan, 2011); and Frank Usbeck, *Fellow Tribesman: The*

Image of Native Americans, National Identity, and Nazi Ideology in Germany (New York and Oxford; Berghahn Books, 2015).
12 There he wrote,

> The right of our manifest destiny to over spread and to possess the whole of the continent which Providence [God] has given us for the development of the great experiment entrusted to us. It is right such as that of the tree to the space and air and the earth suitable for the full expansion of its principle and destiny of growth (emphasis added).
> www.let.rug.nl/essays/1801–1900/maniest-destiny/manifest-destiny--the-philosophy-that-created-a-nation.php. Accessed 5 October 2021.

13 Andrew C. Isenberg and Thomas Richards, Jr., (2017), "American Wests: Rethinking Manifest Destiny", *Pacific Historical Review*, 86(1): 4.
14 For example, examining 3,000 published papers on climate change since 2001 (out of more than 88,125 papers), Mark Lynas, Benjamin Z. Houlton, and Simon Perry concluded:

> We identify four accepted papers out of the sub-set of 3000, as evidenced by abstracts that were rated as implicitly or explicitly skeptical of human-caused global warming. In our sample, utilizing pre-identified skeptical keywords we found 28 papers that were implicitly or explicitly skeptical. We conclude with high statistical that the scientific consensus on human-caused contemporary climate change—expressed as a proportion of the total publications—exceeds 99% in the peer-reviewed scientific literature.

(2021), "Greater than 99% Consensus on Human Caused Climate Change in the Peer-Reviewed Scientific Literature", *Environmental Research Letters* 16: 114005, https://doi.org/10.1088/1748–9326/av2966. Accessed 20 October 2021.
15 In their massively over-sized volume, editors Jürgen Scheffran, Michael Brzoka, Hans Günter Brauch, Peter Michael Link, Janpeter Schilling, have addressed the intersections between humanity, climate change and conflict, *Climate Change, Human Security, and Violent Conflict* (Heidelberg, London, and New York: Springer, 2012). See, also, Alex Alvarez, *Unstable Ground: Climate Change, Conflict, and Genocide* (Lanham: Rowman and Littlefield, 2017); Christian Parenti, *Tropic of Chaos: Climate Change and the New Geography of Violence* (New York: Nation Books, 2011); and Jürgen Zimmerer, ed., *Climate Change and Genocide: Environmental Violence in the 21st Century* (London and New York: Routledge, 2015).
16 Solomon M. Hsiang, Marshall Burke, and Edward Miguel (2013), "Quantifying the Influence of Climate and Human Conflict", *Science*, 341: 1212; emphasis added.
17 Solomon M. Hsiang, Kyle C. Meng, and Mark A. Cane (2011), "Civil Conflicts Are Associated with the Global Climate", *Nature*, 476: 438.
18 Robert Kiel (2019), "The Looming Accelerant: The Growing Links between Climate Change, Mass Atrocities, and Genocide", part of their Strengthening Global Governance Project, www.stimson.org. Accessed 15 October 2021.
19 Cited by Jelle Zeilinga de Boer and Donald Theodore Sanders, *Earthquakes in Human History* (Princeton and Oxford: Princeton University Press, 2005), especially Chapter 2 "In the Holy Land: Earthquakes and the Hand of God" (22–44) and Chapter 4 "Earthquakes in England: Echoes in Religion and Literature" (65–87).
20 Peter J. Thuessen, *Tornado God: American Religion and Violent Weather* (Oxford and New York: Oxford University Press, 2020).

21 Steven Leonard Jacobs (2006), "Acts of a Vengeful God? The Flood, Hurricanes, Tsunamis, Holocaust, and Genocide", *Bulletin of the Council for the Scientific Study of Religion (CSSR)*, 35(3): 62–65.
22 IPCC. "Climate Change 2021: The Physical Science Basis—Summary for Policymakers". Working Group, I contribution to the Sixth Assessment Report of the Intergovernmental Panel on Climate Change.
23 The use of the word/term "Calvary"—the site of Christ's crucifixion—is significant and indicative of how religion and religious language and rhetoric, even metaphorically, continues to impact all manner of civil discourse.
24 Lynn White (1967), "The Historical Roots of our Ecological Crisis", *Science*, 155: 1203–1207. Throughout, he is highly critical not only of the evolving nature of Christianity—perceiving a "dualism" between humanity and its relationship to God and nature and still operative today—but our infatuation with so-called technological progress coupled with both Enlightenment and post-Enlightenment secularized thinking, including science itself.
25 Barbara Bramanti, Nils Chr. Stenseth, Lars Wallace, and Xu Lei (2016), "Plague: A Disease Which Changed the Path of Human Civilization", in Ruifu Yang and Andrey Anisimov, eds., *Yersina Pestis: Retrospective and Perspective* (Dordrecht: Springer), 1.
26 Lynn H. Nelson (n.d.), "Lectures in Medieval History: The Great Famine (1315–1317) and the Black Death (1346–1351)", http://www.vlib.us/medieval/lectures/black_death.html. Accessed 16 October 2021.

Chapter 11

Changing the Conversation
What Is to Be Done?

This chapter reviews and comments upon a plethora of practical and pragmatic suggestions presented to forestall, intervene, punish, and prevent genocides, and whether they have directly included religion or religions in their proposals. It concludes with my own very concrete suggestions on the relational nexus between religion and genocide and how to prevent the latter's reoccurrence.

What follows, then, is a rather lengthy introduction to the concerns of this chapter based on an unpublished presentation given more than a decade ago entitled "Genocide: Prevention, Intervention, Punishment—An Unholy Trinity?", revised and updated for this book. Its own conclusions, however, remain tragically and unfortunately relevant.

Before doing so, however, it is worthwhile to respond, at least initially, to the following assessments from Brudholm's and Cushman's *The Religious in Responses to Mass Atrocity*:

> The overwhelming and horrible nature of mass atrocities throws into relief the limits of language, human justice, and our moral understanding[1]...In short, religious actors often exert an independent influence on the political process of coming to terms with the past, in particular when they have a well-defined political theology of reconciliation and institutional autonomy.[2]

Thus, what is obviously recognized early on is that both religions and their leaderships—and their followerships—may very well play outsized and disproportionate roles in the aftermath of genocides, especially as advocates for reconciliation and healing because their "visions", more often than not, move us beyond the realms of the ordinary and limitations of human endeavors and thinking, but suggest moving us forward because of their own conceptions of seeming "divine mandates". Such mandates and their power should not be too readily dismissed in the arenas of international and/or nation-state conflicts because of their abilities to harness human energy positively as forces for good.

Secondly, as Cushman further argues drawing upon the innovative work of the late Polish-British sociologist Zygmunt Bauman (1925–2017) and his 1989 text *Modernity and the Holocaust*:[3]

> Modernity was not then and is not now in and of itself a guarantee of the prevention of genocide, and, in fact, might actually be facilitated by modernity...Genocide is modernity's evil twin, a doppelganger, which hangs heavily over the mythology and institutional structures of global progress.[4]

To be sure, this is not to dismiss outright Lemkin's own understanding that, whatever else genocide was and is, it is that "crime of crimes" that has been perpetrated throughout history. But, rather, that it is to recognize that modernity—in the cases of the Holocaust/Shoah, Cambodia, Bosnia, Darfur, Syria, Myanmar, and now China in the case of the Rohingya—has added a technological element so significant that modern *genocidaires* can now accomplish the end goal of the extermination/annihilation of increasingly larger minority and powerless populations with an ease never accorded them in the past.

Finally, as Brian S. Turner writes:

> To some extent, genocide represents the limits of what is comprehensible in a social science, because genocidal or degenerate war charts out an arena within which social science concepts palpably falter and fail. This sense of the inexplicable nature of mass, excessive killing has been commented on by Peter Berger in his *Rumor of Angels: Modern Society and the Rediscovery of the Supernatural* [New York: Doubleday, 1969.] who says that modern genocide appears to exist outside the boundaries of enormity for which we have no ultimately credible explanation. Can we extend sympathy to the perpetrators? In this context, both sympathy and revenge may fail as human emotions. Sympathetic acceptance is hardly possible because we cannot recognize them as fellow humans. Revenge is not adequate, and it would take place on such a scale that we would also lose our humanity by inflicting revenge.[5]

Coherent and rational explanations why some persons and some groups perpetrate genocide, at least according to Turner, do not work. The social sciences that seemingly address human behaviors and social relationships (e.g., anthropology, archaeology, economics, history, human geography, Judaic studies, linguistics, political science, psychology, religious studies) do not work. Neither sympathy for the victims nor revenge against the perpetrators seemingly do not work. How then in a real and realistic way are we to "make sense" of what has transpired in the past, is transpiring in the present, and might very well transpire in the future? What *concrete* steps can we as collective humanity take to ensure our group survival when one of our groups is threatened out of existence? And, ultimately, can religions play a decidedly preventative, interventionist, and reconciliatory role in relegating genocides to historical examples only of the very worst of human behaviors?

Context

A Vignette and a Caveat

Philip Gourevitch, in his now justly and rightly well-known book *We Wish to Inform You That Tomorrow We Will Be Killed with Our Families: Stories from Rwanda*, tells of the following encounter:

> Listening to him, I was reminded of a conversation I had with an American military intelligence officer who was having a supper of Jack Daniels and Coca-Cola at a Kigali bar.
> "I hear you're interested in genocide", the American said. "Do you know what genocide is?"
> I asked him to tell me.
> "A cheese sandwich", he said. "Write it down. Genocide is a cheese sandwich".
> I asked him how he figured that.
> "What does anyone care about a cheese sandwich?" he said. "Genocide, genocide, genocide. Cheese sandwich, cheese sandwich, cheese sandwich. Who gives a shit. Crimes against humanity. Where's humanity. You? Me? Did you see a crime committed against you? Hey, just a million Rwandans. Did you ever hear about the Genocide Convention?"
> I said that I had.
> "That convention", the American at the bar said, "makes a nice wrapping for a cheese sandwich".[6]

The tripartite issue of prevention, intervention, and punishment continues to be addressed on a regular basis in a wide variety of settings: academic conferences, governmental meetings, and United Nations forums the most obvious, as well as graphic and dramatic accounts in all media—social and other. Why, then, does it appear so incredibly difficult after the too-long denied Armenian Genocide by the Turks, the Holocaust/Shoah against the Jews by the Nazis and their allied minions, the Tutsis by the Hutus in Rwanda, the Bosnians by the Serbs, and the Darfurians by other Sudanese to seemingly get the "good people" of this planet to universally proclaim "this human tragedy is, *in truth and in fact*, an intolerable genocide, and we and our countries and our governments and our militaries will no longer allow this crime of crimes to perpetuate itself upon our species"? The late Leo Kuper (1904–2004), one of the true doyens of the field of genocide studies and professor of sociology at UCLA, wrote:

> In the modern age it is harder to locate the intention to commit genocide at the societal level because of the anonymous and amorphous structural forces that dictate the character of our world. And there can be no doubt that *the present structure of international relations facilitates the crime of genocide* by the primacy accorded to national self-interest the protection extended to offending governments, and superpower rivalry and destructive intervention in the internal affairs of divided and other vulnerable societies. But how then are we to modify and transform these anonymous and amorphous worldwide structural forces and to create a new world order in time to respond to the many genocidal emergencies?[7]

How, indeed, to turn our world into an anti-genocidal world without fomenting armed conflict, worldwide and physically destructive revolutions, and the over-turning or over-throwing of all *non-democratic regimes* presently in existence today remains the question.[8] Genocide or cheese sandwich? The problem remains.

Prevention

Task Number One: Prevention

Any discussion, no matter how creative or innovative regarding the prevention, intervention, and punishment of genocide, must begin with prevention. How to ensure that the tragedies of the past do not become the realities of the present or the foundations of the future?

Firstly, therefore, is education, both as a preventative and as a deterrent: educational planning globally must start *at all levels* with those in positions of social, economic, governmental, and military control who have the memories of the genocidal past as part of their own knowledge database when they assume decision-making positions of power. This is ideally—but not idealistically—*the first revolution*: Rethinking curricula at all levels from toddlers to graduate schools, from public to private institutions and everything in between, including seminaries, not only in history but also in all of the interdisciplinary educational modalities upon which education draws.

There are two initial concerns, however: (1) No longer, given the realistic current state of expanded genocide education, can the Holocaust/Shoah be segregated out as a separate examination, but must be reconsidered within the overall historical plural contexts of genocide. And not only within Jewish communities and state-mandated educational systems—especially in the United States—but universally. (2) In every locale where people are seriously committed to anti-genocide, this education, also, must mean a serious examination of the past—good and bad— across the board: For example, no longer examining the Holocaust/Shoah alone, but also the treatment of Native Americans (ironically, a subject with which the Nazis themselves were particularly interested) and African Americans by the larger intrusive and colonialist society of the United States. No longer limiting such examinations of those perpetrators who perform(ed) their genocidal acts directly but examining, too, all manner of society and societal influences that shared and share in the responsibility for genocide, i.e., governmental, social, political, educational, and religious actors. How to focus the light and lens of this microscope on oneself, on one's own community (however defined), on one's own nation-state, in addition to the external focus on others, becomes the challenge for the best and brightest of educators committed to anti-genocide education.

Part of this overall educational endeavor, additionally, must involve the further development and expansion of Genocidal Early Warning Systems and their translation and implementation into the very centers of governments responsible for their actualization. But, following Shakespeare "Ay, there's the rub!" Such systems are predicated on the commitment of humanity to humanity, that the destruction of one group is the potential destruction of all groups. Those who have already done the initial work of conceptualizing such systems—Jerusalem's Israel Charny,[9] Britain's Kumar Rupesinghe, and the late Franklin Littell in the United States, for example—have thus far been unsuccessful in seeing their pioneering work translated into governmental realities, despite the fact that, in 1999, more than two decades ago, then US President Bill Clinton (b. 1946) called for the establishment of a National Genocide Early Warning Center. Collective humanity thus far has not manifested, however, the collective will to demand—yes demand! —of those in power the fullest implementation of these historic strategies.

Equally, even those organizations fully committed to and concerned with human rights—Amnesty International, Human Rights Watch, Survival International, Red Cross International—have not, to this point, made such systems among their highest priorities. Hence, the call for *a second revolution*: joining in increasing numbers those organizations, and advocating, in the strongest possible manner, "upping the ante" by calling for Genocide Early Warning Systems throughout the world.

Intervention

Task Number Two: Intervention

At least in the West, but elsewhere as well, we are still globally enamored of the historic moment in 1648 at the signing of the Treaty of Westphalia which, for all intents and purposes, affirmed the sovereignty and territorial integrity of what we continue to define as the *inviolable* nation-state. Genocidal intrusions into one's neighboring state must realistically and of necessity call forth united or singular military intervention; genocidal destruction within the borders of one's own nation-state remains, seemingly, beyond the scope of military intervention, governmental sanction, or humanitarian aid.[10] To be sure, each external response is fraught with its own set of problems and difficulties. Serially addressing each:

Military intervention must make sense over and above nation-state sovereignty because the potentially violent spill-over effect is ever-present. But only *united* military action has its own potential for defusing escalating armed conflict and prevent it from descending into imperialist and territorial ambition. Saul Mendlovitz and John Fousek called for a UN "Constabulary" to address genocide.[11] John Heidenrich called for an "international legion of volunteers" already positioned throughout the world whenever a genocidal act intrudes upon the world scene.[12] The late Herbert Hirsch (1942–2019) of Virginia Commonwealth University called for a profound rethinking of our political institutions, social interactions, and, fundamentally human nature itself, coupled with an ultimate commitment to universal human rights and the building of a mass movement.[13] Already more than two decades ago, the European Union began positioning itself by setting up a military rapid reaction force, consisting of nine such troops of 1,500 soldiers to be deployed at short notice to conflicts around the world, with Britain, France, Italy, and Spain initially committed and others following suit.[14] This idea of the RRF may very well prove to be a model for the African continent, the Middle East, and other "hot spots". Our economically globally interdependent world and its leaders are slowly coming to realize, more and more, that that which affects one potentially affects all. Anti-genocide military—and other interventions—mandate collective nation-state unity (the very premise undergirded the founding of the League of Nations and its successor the United Nations) and supersede individual nation-states' sovereignties. Slowly and painfully, nation-states and their leaderships are beginning to accept this, and the well-educated anti-genocide citizenries must be there to remind all of them of it.

Vratislav Pechota makes a most astute observation about military involvement in genocide:

> The defense of superior orders poses an especially difficult question. It rests on the demands of discipline in the bureaucratic and military hierarchies of the states. A soldier's dilemma in the question of obedience (on the one hand, he may be liable to be shot by a court-martial if he disobeys an order, and, on the other hand, to be hanged by a judge and jury if he obeys it) has not been satisfactorily resolved in the Genocide Convention. Until the principle that superior orders do not free an accused of responsibility for an international crime is transformed into national law and spelled out in terms that leave no doubt of the duty to

refuse to obey an order to perform a criminal act, it may be impossible to enforce in practice the principle of strict criminal liability embraced by the Convention.[15]

Governmental interventions including such things as economic sanctions, monetary and payment freezes, and trade embargoes, equally work on the level of united actions. In the face of sovereign state genocidal behavior by one, the contra-sanctioning by the many should quickly reflect itself in economic and other downturns, which any leadership desirous of staying in power and avoiding the revolutionary displacement of a political coup will itself tend to initiate cessation of genocidal activities.

Humanitarian intervention in the face of ongoing armed conflict in the areas where genocides are actively taking place poses threats not only to the victim populations but to the relief workers as well. Mary Anderson, for example, among others, has written about the dilemmas presented by such relief efforts in Jonathan Moore's edited text *Hard Choices: Moral Dilemmas in Humanitarian Intervention*.[16]

Punishment

Task Number Three: Punishment

To be sure, the guilty must be made to pay, both at the level of leadership and followership, those who devised the plans for genocide and those who implemented those plans and perpetrated those deeds. Full commitment to the overarching sanctity of international law supersedes that of sovereign nation-state law and marks a commitment to an international community, which sets no one nation-state above that of another, *Realpolitik*, however, reveals that such has not been historically nor remains contemporarily the case. The International Criminal Court (ICC), the International Tribunal for Rwanda (ICTR), and the International Criminal Tribunal for (the former) Yugoslavia (ICTY)—especially the latter two understood by many to be the legacies of the International Military Tribunal (IMT) held at Nuremberg, Germany, at the closure of World War II (1945–1946)—all testify to this growing desire for a "new world order", one perceived, somewhat ironically by some in the United States, as directly antithetical to America's best and future long-term interests. (After all, due to the ongoing obstruction of a few US Senators, this country did sign on to the Genocide Convention, under President Ronald Regan [1911–1981] until 1988, just shy of four decades after Lemkin's death in 1959.) Writing specifically about the International Criminal Court, David Wipperman and the United States' "effect of U.S. nonparticipation", US reluctance to sign the ICC accords in Rome, and this forty-year reluctance to ratify the Genocide Convention, even after President Harry Truman's (1884–1972) endorsement of it, testify to an uncomfortable and little-spoken truth: The United States is committed to anti-genocide activities when both the perpetrators and the victims (and, perhaps, even the bystanders) are not Americans, but the aphorism that "might makes right" permits no reversal and hardens this nation's refusal to consider itself potentially guilty of any genocidal crimes in the past (e.g., African Americans or Indigenous Americans who have sought in the past to bring their concerns before the ICC), or its military or civilian constituencies potentially guilty of such crimes.[17] Ironically, too, in that the federal government declares a week-long Holocaust Remembrance and Observance that has presented no stumbling blocks whatsoever in its post-World War II relationships with Germany, but had to wait until the current Administration under President Joe Biden (b. 1942) to recognize the Armenian Genocide (March 19, 2021) because of previous concerns about US relations with Turkey and the Turks' own efforts and pressures not to do so.

The willingness of all sovereign nation-states to surrender, if only partially, their sovereignty for the greater good of a common humanity remains the agenda of concern. Unfortunately, the history of the United Nations, its bureaucratic bungling (e.g., the case of Rwanda), its favoritism, its corruption continue to reveal not the failed vision of Raphael Lemkin and others who fought so diligently to make the UN Genocide Convention a living reality, but the failed implementation of those for whom tribal politics (read and understood as nation-state sovereignty *über alles*) matters far more than living and dying human beings.

Where Do We Go from Here?

Today and Tomorrow?

After the International Commission of Inquiry on Darfur released its Report on 25 January 2005, Doug Sanders wrote an Op-Ed piece, which appeared in the Toronto *Globe and Mail* entitled "The Genocide Test—A Mass Killer's Best Friend", and concluded:

> Under the UN charter, genocide is the only permissible legal excuse, aside from the invasion of another country, for using military force to intervene in another country's affairs…Genocide is based on racist logic: Dividing the single, homogenous species of homo sapiens into arbitrary groups, and eliminating one of them. The problem is that any law designed to stop such acts must itself subscribe to this logic. Mass murder is far easier to define and does not force us into ugly moral corners. Perhaps it, and not this almost arbitrary concept, should be the crime of crimes.[18]

"Genocide", "mass murder", "ethnic cleansing": Regardless of the correct or incorrect terminologies applied, we are not talking about theoretical discussions of intellectual concepts or constructs. We are talking about the brutal behaviors inflicted upon one group of usually powerless persons to stop their own victimization by those with the power to implement their designs and achieve their goals. Creative solutions abound aplenty to prevent genocide from becoming a current or future reality, to intervene militarily, governmentally, and humanitarianly and to punish the guilty at all levels of guilt, as indicated below. What is lacking is the global will to shout, "Enough is enough! The genocide of one is the genocide of all!"

US President and World War II military hero Dwight David Eisenhower (1890–1969) is said to have remarked, "One day the people will demand of their leaders peace, and we had best step aside and let them have it". Until that same demand is made by those committed to an anti-genocide world, present and future genocides will remain the order of the day.

Practical Solutions

The place at which to appropriately begin this discussion of the practical possible solutions to the continuum of prevention, intervention, and punishment of the crime of genocide is with five United Nations documents: (1) the 1948 Universal Declaration of Human Rights (thirty articles), (2) the 1966 International Covenant on Civil and Political Rights (fifty-three articles), (3) the 1966 International Covenant on Economic, Social and Cultural Rights (thirty-one articles), (4) the 1981 Declaration on the Elimination of All Forms of Intolerance and of Discrimination Based on Religion or Belief (eight articles), and (5) 1992 Declaration on the Rights of Persons Belonging to National or Ethnic, Religious and Linguistic Minorities (nine articles).

As regards the first, two Articles are of import:

> 18: Everyone has the right to freedom of thought, conscience, and religion; this right includes freedom to change his [sic] religion or belief, and freedom either alone or in community with others and in public or private, to manifest his [sic] religion or belief in teaching, practice, worship, and observance.
>
> 27: (1): Everyone has the right freely to participate in the cultural life of the community, and to enjoy the arts and to share in scientific advancement and its benefits.
>
> (2): Everyone has the right to the protection of the moral and material interests resulting from any scientific, literary, or artistic production of which he [sic] is the author.

As regards the second, ten Articles of import:

> 2: (1): Each State Party to the present Covenant undertakes to respect and to ensure to all individuals within its territory and subject to its jurisdiction

the rights recognized in the present Covenant, without distinction of any kind, such as race, colour, sex, language, religion, political or other opinion, national or social origin, property, birth, or other status.

4: (1): In time of public emergency which threatens the life of the nation and the existence of which is officially proclaimed, the States Parties to the present Covenant may take measures derogating from their obligation under the present Covenant to the extent strictly required by the exigencies of the situation, provided that such measures are not inconsistent with their other obligations under international law and do not involve discrimination solely on the ground of race, colour, sex, language, religion or social origin.[19]

18: (1): Everyone shall have the right to freedom of thought, conscience, and religion. This right shall include freedom to have or to adopt a religion or belief of his choice, and freedom, either individually or in community with others and in public or private, to manifest his [sic] religion or belief in worship, observance, practice, and teaching.

(2): No one shall be subject to coercion which would impair his [sic] freedom to have or to adopt a religion or belief of his [sic] choice.

(3): Freedom to manifest one's religion or beliefs may be subject only to such limitations as are prescribed by law as necessary to protect public safety, order, health, or morals or the fundamental rights and freedoms of others.

(4): The States Parties to the present Covenant undertake to have respect for the liberty of parents and, where appropriate, legal guardians to ensure the religious and oral education of their children in conformity with their own convictions.

20: (2): Any advocacy of national, racial, or religious hatred that constitutes incitement to discrimination, hostility or violence shall be prohibited by law.

24: (1): Every child shall have, without any discrimination as to race, colour, sex, language, religion, national or social origin, property or birth, the right to such measures of protection as are required by his status as a minor, on the part of his family, society, and the state.

26: All persons are equal before the law and are entitled without any discrimination to the equal protection of the law. In this respect, the law shall prohibit any discrimination and guarantee to all persons equal and effective protection against discrimination on any ground such as race, colour, sex, language, religion, political or other opinion, national or social origin, property, birth, or other status.

27: In those States in which ethnic, religious or linguistic minorities exist, persons belonging to such minorities shall not be denied the right, in community with other members of their group, to enjoy their own culture, to profess and practice their own religion, or to use their own language.

As regards the third, three Articles of import:

> 2: The States Parties to the present Covenant undertake to guarantee that the rights enunciated in the present Covenant will be exercised without discrimination of any kind as to race, colour, sex, language, religion, political or other opinion, national origin, property, birth, or other status.
>
> 13: (1): They [the States Parties] further agree that education shall enable all persons to participate effectively in a free society, promote understanding, tolerance, and friendship among all nations and all racial, ethnic, or religious groups, and further the activities of the United Nations for the maintenance of peace.
>
> 15: (1): The States Parties to the present Covenant recognize the right of everyone:
> (c) to benefit from the protection of the moral and material interests resulting from any scientific, literary, or artistic production or which he [sic] is the author.

As regards the fourth, five Articles of import:

1. Every person shall have the right to freedom of thought, conscience, and religion. This right shall include freedom to have a religion or whatever belief of his choice, and freedom, either individually or in community with others and in public or private, to manifest his [sic] religion or belief in worship, observance, practice, and teaching.
2. (2): For the purpose of the present Declaration, the expression "intolerance and discrimination based on religion or belief" means any distinction, exclusion, restriction or preference based on religion or belief and having as its purpose or as its effect nullification or impairment of the recognition, enjoyment or exercise of human rights and fundamental freedoms on an equal basis.
3. Discrimination between human beings on the grounds of religion or belief constitutes an affront to human dignity and a disavowal of the principles of the Charter of the United Nations and shall be condemned as a violation of the human rights and fundamental freedoms proclaimed in the Universal Declaration of Human Rights and enunciated in detail in the International Covenants on Human Rights, and as an obstacle to friendly and peaceful relations between nations.
4. The child shall be protected from any form of discrimination on the ground of religion or belief.
5. In accordance with article 1 of the present Declaration, and subject to the provisions of article 1, paragraph 3, the right to freedom of thought, conscience, religion, or belief shall include, inter alia, the following freedoms:
    a   To worship or assemble in connection with a religion or belief, and to establish and maintain places for these purposes

b   To establish and maintain appropriate charitable or humanitarian institutions
c   To make, acquire, and use to an adequate extent the necessary articles and materials related go the rites and customs of a religion or belief
d   To write, issue and disseminate relevant publications in these areas
e   To teach a religion or belief in places suitable for these purposes
f   To solicit and receive voluntary financial and other contributions from individuals and institutions
g   To train, appoint, elect, or designate by succession appropriate leaders called for by the requirements and standards of any religion or belief
h   To observe days of rest and to celebrate holidays and ceremonies in accordance with the precepts of one's religion or belief
i   To establish and maintain communications with individuals and communities in matters of religion and belief at the national and international levels.

As regards the fifth, two Articles of import:

> 2: (1): Persons belonging to national or ethnic, religious, and linguistic (hereafter referred to as persons belonging to minorities) have the right to enjoy their own culture, to profess and practice their own religion, and to use their own language, in private and in public, freely and without interference or any form of discrimination.
>
> (5): Persons belonging to minorities have the right to establish and maintain, without any discrimination, free and personal contacts with other members of their group and with persons belonging to other minorities, as well as contacts across frontiers with citizens of other States to whom they are related by national or ethnic, religious, or ethnic ties.

The twenty-two Articles in both the Covenants and Declarations of the United Nations affirmed between 1948 and 1992—firmly establish (or *should* establish)—that religion—however defined and understood—is very much central to the evolution of the human species and, perhaps even more importantly, central to the maintenance of human communities. While positive beyond question, they, nor other UN documents, do not articulate the negative role religions have played in the legitimation and foundational underpinnings for violent behavior throughout human history. Nor do they address the role, purpose, and function of religions themselves as involved perpetrators of genocidal crimes. That primary responsibility has become the mandate of scholars, policy, and decision-makers, journalists, and popularizers in bringing that knowledge to the attention of humanity, and as noted early on, became the rationale for this text.

That having been said, these articulations also do not address the role, purpose, function of religions as "involved players" in breaking this cycle of genocidal violence as what follows attempt to do so.

Plans of Action

The United Nations 2017 Document "Plan of Action for Religious Leaders and Actors to Prevent Incitement to Violence that Could Lead to Atrocity Crimes"[20] is far and away the most significant statement to date that, if followed internationally by religious leaders world-wide (and their followers), would decidedly result in momentous changes by nation-state governmental policymakers in addressing genocide. As stated,

> The Plan of Action consists of nine groups of thematic recommendations which are organized into three main clusters:

PREVENT

1. Specific actions to prevent and counter incitement to violence (thirty eight Recommendations)
2. Prevent incitement to violent extremism (thirty Recommendations)
3. Prevent incitement to gender-based violence (ten Recommendations)

STRENGTHEN

4. Enhance education and capacity-building (twenty Recommendations)
5. Foster interfaith and intra-faith dialogue (twenty-one Recommendations)
6. Strengthen collaboration with traditions and new media (nineteen Recommendations)
7. Strengthen engagement with regional and international partners (eight Recommendations)

BUILD

8. Build peaceful, inclusive, and just societies through respecting, protecting, and promoting human rights (thirty-one Recommendations)
9. Establish networks of religious leaders (one Recommendation)

While dissecting, analyzing, and commenting upon these **178** Recommendations would prove to be a book in itself, suffice it to say they fully, if implemented, are a concrete, practical, and pragmatic set of actions for the world's religious communities to step-up and address the scourge of genocide. What is now obviously called for is a UN-hosted conference, perhaps along the lines of the World Parliament of Religions and a "push" for the world's religious communities and their leaderships to move out of their safe comfort zones and interface and interact with the governments of their own nation-states and demand that genocide be addressed fully, frontally, and publicly.[21]

Earlier, in 2005, the United Nations convened its World Summit, the outcome of which was a commitment by its member-states against the aforementioned atrocity crimes, including ethnic cleansing, and resulted in a series of documents under the rubric "Responsibility to Protect" (R2P). Three so-called Pillars continues to frame that understanding:

I The protection responsibilities of the state
II International assistance and capacity-building
III Timely and decisive collective response[22]

One example of a timely result was the 2008 document coedited by the late former US Secretary of State Madeleine K. Albright (1937–2022) and former US Secretary of Defense William S. Cohen (b. 1940) entitled "Preventing Genocide: A Blueprint for U.S. Policy Makers" with its own list of thirty-four (34) Recommendations (111–114).[23]

Academics, too, as referenced above, with the growth of the interdisciplinary field of Genocide Studies have equally weighed in on genocidally related issues of concern. In addition to those already mentioned, Neal Riemer's edited *Protection Against Genocide: Mission Impossible?* includes contributions from seven colleagues including the editor[24]; and Samuel Totten's *Last Lectures on the Prevention and Intervention of Genocide*, in addition to Totten, included thirty-nine colleagues' contributions.[25] Somewhat unique, perhaps, is that of David Hamburg, MD, whose *Preventing Geocide: Practical Steps Toward Early Detection and Effective Action* brings to the table the perspectives of one of the very few scholars schooled to the "healing arts" to examine genocide.[26] One of the earliest collaborative efforts was that of sociologist Helen Fein's (b. 1934) edited 1992 *Genocide Watch* with the inclusion of eleven colleagues including Fein herself.[27] The pioneering work of sociologist Leo Kuper (1904–1994),[28] psychologists Israel Charny (b. 1931),[29] and Erwin Staub (b. 1938)[30] must also be included in any academic bibliography.

Thus, there is no dearth whatsoever of realistic, concrete, practical, and pragmatic proposals, and recommendations to address prevention and intervention to stop genocides, and, similarly, to address punishment of those who commit genocide. What is, however, transparently lacking is the universal will of humankind—including religious communities and religious leaders and followers, *especially* religious communities and religious leaders and followers, given their numbers, public prestige, and influencing power—to raise the level of anti-genocide among the highest priorities of humanity.

Aftermath

In the aftermath of genocide, what then is to be done? In their Introduction to their edited text *Genocide's Aftermath: Responsibility and Repair*, philosophers Claudia Card, University of Wisconsin, and Armen T. Marsoobian, Southern Connecticut State University, write:

> We now see much of modern history through the lens of genocide…we believe that an understanding of how to attribute responsibility for genocide and how to repair the evils perpetrated in genocides are two of the central moral tasks of philosophers…As philosophers we are primarily concerned with a conceptual understanding of the nature of genocide and how this understanding makes moral demands upon us to respond to genocide—to respond not only in the above terms of clarifying how we attribute responsibility for genocide and how we may engender its repair but also in the more important sense of what we as individuals and as nations should do to prevent genocide.[31]

Substituting religionists for philosophers, the same affirmations and insights are equally applicable. Surveying the realities of more contemporary genocides and the roles and potential roles of religious communities—leaderships and followerships—we find the following as relevantly pertinent: (1) Gacaca Courts (Rwanda), (2) Reparations (e.g., Jews, Japanese-Americans, African Americans, Native Americans, Armenians), (3) Truth Commissions (e.g., Guatemala, South Africa), and (4) the little-discussed possibility of the power and possibility of non-violence in creating stability in post-genocidal and non-genocidal societies and nation-states (e.g., India and the United States). Coming full circle, this chapter proffers my own two strongly held suggestions presented at the International Conference on the Crime of Genocide, Athens, Greece, December 2019.

In the aftermath of the Rwandan Genocide (7 April–15 July 1994), which resulted in the deaths of more than 1,100,000 Rwandese, perpetrators, and victims alike, but certainly more so the latter (Tutsi, ~1,000,000) than the former (Hutu, ~100,000)—family, friends, and neighbors alike—continue to live together in a country where the judicial and prison systems cannot adjudicate nor house the guilty, estimated at more than 130,000, without destroying the nation-state itself and its economy. As noted earlier, among the perpetrators were priests, nuns, and pastors; houses of worship (i.e., churches) were themselves sites of mass murders and desecrations. However, religious leadership, most especially the Roman Catholic Church in Rwanda, maintains an active presence in reconciliation and rebuilding efforts.

The Gacaca Courts (*Inkiko Gacaca*), from the Kinyarwandan word for "short grass" and referencing the open-air environment where communal leaders and members have allowed the perpetrators to *publicly* state their case, admit their guilt, and ask for forgiveness—not all but many. Unfortunately, they had also been used to further legitimate the "official" narrative of the Genocide itself with only the Hutu having been found guilty and the Tutsi found totally the opposite.[32] Thus, their measure of success is mixed, but, in the interface between perpetrators and victims and the important roles of acknowledgment, forgiveness, and reconciliation—all values sanctioned and sanctified by *all* religious communities—continues to provide a potential vehicle to address genocides in the future. (One also notes that in both Europe and the United States, as well as elsewhere, some children of Nazi perpetrators have entered into dialogical and healing relationships with some children of Jewish victims.[33] Their record, too, has been mixed.)

Complicated as well, but perhaps even more so, has been the issue of Reparations vis-a-vis wronged communities of genocide victims with the best and most successful being the case of the Jews and the State of Israel (who successfully made the argument that State of Israel itself represented those Jewish victims who had no families left) and Germany in the aftermath of World War II and the Holocaust/Shoah.[34] And while Japanese-Americans have been reasonably successful in receiving reparations after their forced removal of more than 120,000 persons to Relocation Camps in Arkansas, Arizona, California, Colorado, Idaho, Utah, and Wyoming during World War II but *not* a case of genocide to be sure,[35] and Native Americans have received monetary compensation for what they and others regards as US colonial genocide (life-taking, land theft, forced relocation—e.g., the notorious "Trail of Tears"—1830–1850),[36] the ongoing tragedy of African Americans continues to languish,[37] as does the case of the Armenians whose own voices for reparations are relatively few and relatively quiet.[38] What must also be acknowledged in the context of any discussions of reparations is the political repercussions of such work as John Torpey has explored in his *Making Whole What Has Been Smashed: On Reparations Politics*.[39]

With regard to these last two instances, what appears to be lacking are the international voices of religious leaders mobilizing their own constituencies to address these genocides in the United States, Turkey, Armenia, and elsewhere to make genocidal concerns among their highest priorities.

Truth Commissions, most commonly associated with South Africa (1995) and Guatemala (1994), and sometimes also called Truth and Reconciliation Commissions, function somewhat similarly to the Gacaca Courts of Rwanda: attempting to get at the truth of what transpired, interviewing witnesses—both perpetrators, so-called "state actors" and non-state actors, and victims—and, like the Courts, having official government sanction. Less well-known Commissions were those of Argentina (1983), Australia (2018), Bolivia (1982), Canada (2006),

Chile (1990), Congo (2003), El Salvador (1992), Nepal (1990; 2014), Panama (2000), Sierra Leone (2003), and Uganda (1974).[40] Supportive and encouraging those engaged in this difficult work by religious leaders has played a significant role in legitimating these activities and remains important in the future as well.[41]

Again, as was the initial argument of religion as a participating factor in genocide, both negatively and positively, and ofttimes indirectly rather than directly, so, too, in all of these instances and examples of the difficult work of post-genocide, the involvement of religiously committed persons and groups and the traditions they represent may very well have the ongoing potential to move their societies and communities forward to healing, forgiveness, and reconciliation where possible but without diminishing or forgetting the realities of what has tragically transpired.

Under explored like so much else is educating peoples throughout the world to become an expanded global community of nonviolent and thus anti-genocide advocates is the subject of non-violence itself, and usually associated with Mahatma Gandhi (1869–1948) in India and Martin Luther King, Jr. (1929–1968) in the United States (and, ironically, both murdered by individuals who understood violent opposition as the "correct" solution to political and racial difficulties and concerns).[42]

Most associated, perhaps, with the Hindu concept of *ahimsa* and its most public advocate and practitioner Gandhi and taken to its conclusion of the Jain and Buddhist[43] religious traditions of respect for all living creatures (people, animals, insects) and refraining from life-taking, it also finds its resonance in the Hebrew/Arabic concept of *shalom/salaam* (equally understood as peace = wholeness = wellness). It has also been used someone successfully to affect political change (e.g., India, the Velvet Underground in Czechoslovakia in 1989, the United Farm Workers Movement in the United States in the 1960s, the Liberian Women's Movement for Peace in the early 2000s). What is needed first and foremost is educating the young throughout the world, most especially those in religious communities, that violence, up to and including genocide, is not the solution to humanity's problems and difficulties, that dialogue across barriers building upon respect for historical, cultural, religious, and even political and socioeconomic differences is the way forward, and that consensus agreements continue to have both present and future potential.

Finally, in a presentation at The International Conference on the Crime of Genocide, Athens, Greece, December 2019, I offered the following two strong suggestions to that audience of colleagues and interested others:

First, every society, every nation-state, remains committed to the education of its young as a path to integrated citizenship for its present and future economic prosperity, for its political stability, for the defense of its citizenry, and for the protection of its geographic boundaries. Prevention of future genocides requires—nay, demands! —of the United Nations and the various regional nation-state organizations (e.g. the European Union, the Organization of African States, etc.) that they commit themselves to the development of *a universal and international anti-genocide curriculum* at all levels, from elementary-age young people through college- and university-age young people, and that such a curriculum take as its starting point the preciousness—the sacrality—of human existence, drawing upon the work of the generations in history, literature, political science, philosophy, psychology, sociology, and religious studies. That the UN, therefore, initiate such an *Anti-Genocide Education Task Force*, initially inviting its member-states to commit themselves to sending as their representatives only those persons who, by virtue of their training, are themselves schooled in the education of the young. And that other international regional bodies be invited to do the same. And, yes, that those who come do so with the economic backing of their respective entities to pay their salaries as well as those support personnel, office and equipment needs, etc., and that they do their work away from the prying eyes of the various media, social and other, which all-too-often inhibit or obstruct such vitally important and necessary work.

I have inserted by design the word "sacrality" into my first recommendation. I did so because the very reality of the world in which we live—the planet we inhabit—is that the social-construct we call "religion" is the one identifier and signifier, which includes the largest numbers of persons, and, further, is the one entity that truly unites us even in our diversity.

Secondly, now more than one hundred twenty-five years old, the Parliament of the World's Religions has met seven times, the last meeting in Toronto (2018). Previously, the world's religious assemblages have met in 1893 in Chicago, IL, USA: in 1993 in Chicago, 8,000 persons in attendance: in 1999 in Cape Town, South Africa, 7,000 persons in attendance; in 2004 in Barcelona, Spain, 8,900 persons in attendance; in 2009 in Melbourne, Australia, 6,000 persons in attendance; and in 2015 in Salt Lake City, UT, 8,900 persons in attendance. Its purpose: to bring people of faith together to work for a more just, peaceful, and sustainable world. Leading and high-ranking clergy representing the multiplicity of the world's faiths, scholars, and practitioners, all gather together, pray together, break bread together, and unite together on issues of world concern which brings them together rather than divides them. Contemplate momentarily, if you will, the possibility of the world's religious leaders endorsing such a curriculum and using their authority, presence, and vast constituencies to support such an effort. And, because they already have in place, according to their website—www.parliamentofreligions.org--a UN Task Force, would challenge them to confront the UN Secretary-General to partner with them with the aforementioned Anti-Genocide Education Task Force.

There is an Israeli Hebrew express *Zeh maspeak bamakom/* "It is enough in this place!" This place is Planet Earth. It is high time the religious peoples of the world draw upon the combined sacred traditions they have created over the centuries, the leaderships and followerships they have, to fully and firmly reject genocide in both the present and the future.

Notes

1 As the late Secretary-General of the United Nations Kofi Annan (1938–2018) best expressed it, "For there can be no healing without peace; there can be no peace without justice; and there can be no justice without respect for human rights and the rule of law". Quoted by Thomas Cushman, "Genocidal Rupture and Performative Repair in Global Civil Society: Reconsidering the Discourse of Apology in the Face of Mass Atrocity", in Brudholm and Cushman, eds., *The Religious Response to Mass Atrocity*, 233.
2 Brudholm and Cushman, *The Religious Response to Mass Atrocity*, 4 and 14. Further, as Sara Silvestri and James Mayal note in their report "The Role of Religion in Conflict and Peace-Building", "Religion matters in contemporary international affairs in essentially four ways:

   1 It offers powerful views of cosmic order that often also generates political articulations.
   2 Religious beliefs, scriptures, rituals and symbols can easily become the foundation of ethnic or nationalist projects because they provide powerful narratives.
   3 Religious actors comprise a variegated spectrum of ordinary individuals, leaders, grassroots movements, NGOs, transnational networks, and organized institutions.
   4 Most religions are constructed around patriarchy and male leadership; this feature has not only had the effect of institutionally marginalizing women and the lesbian, gay, bisexual and transgender (LGBT) community, but has also enabled the justification or even perpetration of violence against these groups and to exaggerate masculine narratives of war and martyrdom".

   The British Academy for the Humanities and Social Sciences, 2015, www.britishacademy.ac.uk, 71.
3 Ithaca: Cornell University Press.
4 Thomas Cushman, "Genocidal Rupture and Performative Repair in Global Civil Society: Reconsidering the Discourse of Apology in the Face of Mass Atrocity", in Brudholm and Cushman, eds., *The Religious Response to Mass Atrocity*, 216.
5 Brian S. Turner (2009), "Violence, Human Rights, and Piety: Cosmopolitanism versus Virtuous Exclusions in Response to Atrocity", in Thomas Brudholm and Thomas Cushman, eds., *The Religious in Response to Mass Atrocity*, 249.
6 New York: Picardor, 1999, 170–171.
7 Leo Kuper (1992), "Reflections on the Prevention of Genocide", in Helen Fein, ed., *Genocide Watch* (New Haven: Yale University Press), 183; emphasis added.
8 I have decidedly chosen to use the phrase "non-democratic regimes" because of the pioneering work and insights of the late Rudolph J. Rummel (1932–2014), University of Hawaii, who had patiently and carefully shown through the scrupulous examination of massive amounts of data that genocide as a tangible expression of human behavior has been and is practiced far more by non-democratic regimes than democratic ones. *Death by Government* (New Brunswick: Transaction Publishers, 1999); *Statistics of Democide: Genocide and Mass Murder Since 1900* (Berlin: LIT Verlag, 2003); and *Power Kills: Democracy as a Method of Nonviolence* (New Brunswick: Transaction Publishers, 2002).
9 Israel W. Charny, ed. (1999), *Encyclopedia of Genocide* (Santa Barbara: ABC-CLIO), I: 254–272.
10 See, for example, the *International Studies Review*, 2(2), 2002, which contains seven essays addressing "Continuity and Change in the Westphalian Order", and, earlier, Gene M. Lyons and Michael Mastanduno, eds., *Beyond Westphalia:*

National Sovereignty and International Intervention (Baltimore and London: The Johns Hopkins University Press, 1995).
11 Saul Mendlovitz and John Fousek (2000), "A UN Constabulary to Enforce Law on Genocide and Crimes Against Humanity", in Neil Reimer, ed., *Protection Against Genocide: Mission Impossible* (Westport: Greenwood Publishers), 105–122.
12 John G. Heidenrich, *How to Prevent Genocide: A Guide for Policy Makers, Scholars, and the Concerned Citizen* (Westport: Praeger, 2001), 233–250.
13 Herbert Hirsch, *Anti-Genocide: Building an American Movement to Prevent Genocide* (Westport: Praeger, 2002).
14 British Broadcasting Corporation (BBC), "EU Approves Rapid Reaction Force", 23 November 2004, https://newsvote.bbc.co.uk.
15 Vratislav Pechota (1992), "Establishing Criminal Responsibility and Jurisdiction for Genocide", in Helen Fein, ed., *Genocide Watch* (New Haven and London: Yale University Press), 199–200.
16 Lanham: Rowman & Littlefield, 1998. See, also, Hans Köchler, *Humanitarian Intervention in the Context of Modern Power Politics* (Vienna: International Progress Organization, 2001).
17 David Wippman (2000), "Can an International Criminal Court Prevent and Punish Genocide?", in Neil Riemer, ed., *Protection Against Genocide: Mission Impossible?* (Westport: Praeger), 100–101. Again, see also Samantha Power, *"A Problem from Hell": America and the Age of Genocide* (New York: Basic Books, 2002).
18 Doug Sanders (5 February 2005), "The Genocide Test – A Mass Killer's Best Friend", *Globe and Mail*.
19 Paralleling the First World War, 1914–1917, the so-called Caucasus Campaign, Turkey used the threat of an Armenian-Russian alliance, including so-called fifth-column allegiance as an excuse to round up and murder Armenian men, women, and children and to use Armenians as degraded slave laborers in their military. See, for example, Harris Mylonas and Scott Radnitz, eds., *Enemies Within: The Global Politics of Fifth Columns* (Oxford and New York: Oxford University Press, 2022).
20 The 2014 UN Document "Framework of Analysis for Atrocity Crimes: A Tool for Prevention" stated that "the term 'atrocity crimes' refers to three legally defined international crimes: **genocide**, **crimes against humanity** and **war crimes**. Significantly, it went further and noted:

> In this context, the term "atrocity crimes" has been extended to include **ethnic cleansing** which, while not defined as an independent crime under international law, includes acts that are serious violations of international human rights and humanitarian law that may themselves amount to one of the recognized atrocity crimes, in particular crimes against humanity. (It further defined ethnic cleansing as "rendering an area ethnically homogeneous by using force or intimidation to remove persons of given groups from the area".)

Importantly, throughout the Document it also analyzed fourteen (14) "Risk Factors"—both "Common" (8) and "Specific" (6), all of which have the potential to result in escalating violence leading to such crimes. See also the 2006 article by David Scheffer (b. 1953), the first US Ambassador-at-Large for War Crimes Issues (1997–2001), "Genocide and Atrocity Crimes", *Genocide Studies and Prevention*, 1(3): 229–250 wherein he writes:

> There is also a critical need for a new term—"atrocity crimes"—and a new field of international law—atrocity law—to achieve a similar objective,

namely, to enable public and academic discourse to describe genocide, crimes against humanity (including ethnic cleansing), and war crimes with a single term that is easily understood by the public and accurately reflects the magnitude and character of the crimes adjudicated before international and hybrid criminal tribunals and of the law being applied by such tribunals, governments, and international organizations.

(229)

Further addressing the legal implications of atrocity crimes are Damien Rogers, *Law, Politics, and the Limits of Prosecuting Mass Atrocity* (New York: Palgrave Macmillan, 2017); and Sheri P. Rosenberg, Tibi Galis, and Alex Zucker, eds., *Reconstructing Atrocity Prevention* (Cambridge: Cambridge University Press, 2015). As to concrete and specific recommendations to address these three/four atrocity crimes, see Robert I. Rothberg, *Mass Atrocity Crimes: Preventing Future Outrages* (Washington: Brookings Institution Press, 2010).

21 The British Academy for the Humanity and Social Sciences in their 2015 Document "The Role of Religion in Conflict and Peace Building" also weighed in with their own ten (10) "Recommendations for policymakers and future research" (73–74), paralleling somewhat truncated those found in the UN Document. Additionally, the United States Holocaust Memorial Museum, Washington, DC, only recently (2021) issued its massive 180-page "Pursuing Justice for Mass Atrocities: A Handbook for Victim Groups", authored by Sarah McIntosh, and addressing such important topics as transitional justice, law and accountability, support from key actors, practical challenges, gathering and sharing information, political and public advocacy, and funding and support. (The role of religion and religious leadership is *not*, however, addressed in this comprehensive Handbook.)

22 Here again, the delayed responses to the genocide in Rwanda and Bosnia and the ongoing dickering regarding the situation in Darfur, South Sudan, continue to stain this otherwise important step forward.

23 Specifically addressing the American context but with ramifications internationally is, again, Herbert Hirsch's *Anti-Genocide: Building an American Movement to Prevent Genocide* (Westport and London: Praeger, 2002). For an extended analysis of R2P, see as well, Gareth Evans, *The Responsibility to Protect: Ending Mass Atrocity Crimes Once and For All* (Washington: Brookings Institution, 2009).

24 Westport and London: Praeger, 2000.
25 London and New York: Routledge, 2019.
26 Boulder: Paradigm Publishers, 2008.
27 New Haven and London: Yale University Press, 1992.
28 *Genocide: Its Political Use in the Twentieth Century* (New Haven and London: Yale University Press, 1983); *The Prevention of Genocide* (New Haven and London: Yale University Press, 1985); and *International Action Against Genocide* (New Haven and London: Yale University Press, 1982).
29 *Israel's Failed Response to the Armenian Genocide: Denial, State Deception, Truth versus Politization of History* (Brockton: Academic Studies Press, 2021); *How Can We Commit the Unthinkable? Genocide: The Human Cancer* (London and New York: Routledge, 2019); *Psychotherapy for a Democratic Mind: Treating Intimacy, Tragedy, Violence, and Evil* (Lanham: Lexington Books, 2018); and *The Genocide Contagion: How We Commit and Confront Holocaust and Genocide* (Lanham: Rowman & Littlefield, 2016).
30 *The Roots of Goodness and Resistance to Evil* (New York and Oxford: Oxford University Press, 2016); *The Roots of Evil: The Origins of Genocide and Other Group*

Violence (Cambridge: Cambridge University Press, 1992); and *Overcoming Evil: Genocide, Violent Conflict and Terrorism* (Oxford: Oxford University Press, 2013).
31 Claudia Card and Armen T. Marsoobian, eds., *Genocide's Aftermath: Responsibility and Repair* (Oxford: Blackwell Publishing, 2007), 1.
32 Moving beyond Rwanda, how we collectively remember these various genocides and tell and re-tell their "stories" is the subject of Karen Auerbach's *Aftermath: Genocide. Memory and History* (Victoria: Monash University, 2015).
33 Lauren Haverstock (2014), "An Analysis of the Effectiveness of the Gacaca Court System in Post-Genocide Rwanda", *Global Tides*, 8(4): 1–16; Pietro Sullo, *Beyond Genocide: Transitional Justice and Gacaca Courts in Rwanda: The Search for Truth, Justice, and Reconciliation* (New York: TMC Press/Springer, 2018).
34 As of 2005, more than €65,000,000,000 (~US$74,500,000,000) have been paid out from Germany to individual recipients and more than $14,000,000,000 to Israel as well. In 1952 (entered into force in 1953), the so-called Luxembourg Agreement (Reparations Agreement) was entered between Germany and Israel after successful negotiations, the result of efforts by the Conference on Jewish Material Claims against Germany (but not without its Jewish opponents who argued against accepting such "blood" or "guilt" monies, but, ultimately, rejected by Israel because of the economic necessities in building the new nation and absorbing its world-wide emigration of new citizens).
35 As a result of the historic US Civil Liberties Act of 1988 and Report of the Commission on Wartime Relocations and Interment established by an Act of Congress in 1980, individual survivors and their families received ~$20,000.00 each (80,000 persons equaling more than $1,600,000) and a formal apology on then-President Ronald Regan (1911–2004) who signed it into law. See, also, *Personal Justice Denied: Report of the Commission on Wartime Relocation and Interment of Civilians* (Seattle: University of Washington Press, 1997); Leslie Hatamiya, *Righting a Wrong: Japanese Americans and the Passage of the Civil Liberties Act of 1988* (Stanford: Stanford University Press, 1993); and John Tateishi, *Redress: The Inside Story of the Successful Campaign for Japanese American Reparations* (Berkeley: Heyday Publishers, 2020).
36 As of 2012, the US government, at long last, settled its suit with various Native American Tribes to the tune of $3,000,000.00, with $1,000,500,000.00 directed to individuals and $100,000,000.00 toward the purchase of some small parcels of land owned by Native Americans. Important in this context and relevant internationally as well is the 2007 UN "Declaration on the Rights of Indigenous Peoples", consisting of forty-six articles which recognize that "indigenous peoples have the right to full enjoyment, as a collective or as individuals, of all human rights and fundamental freedoms as recognized in the Charter of the United Nations, the Universal Declaration of Human Rights, and international human rights law" (Article 1). Worthy of further exploration are the genocidal consequences of (1) American Indian boarding schools, (2) the Canadian Indian residential school system—First Nations, and (3) and the "Stolen Generations" of Aboriginal and Torres Strait Islander children by the Australian government, state agencies and church missions (who also played an important and significant role in both [1] and [2]).
37 As of January 2021, US House of Representatives Sheila Jackson Lee of Texas and a number of her colleagues, again, reintroduced H.R. 40 (The bill was originally introduced by the late Democratic Representative John Conyers, Jr. [1928–2019] of Michigan and brought up annually until his retirement in 2017.):

> To address the fundamental injustice, cruelty, brutality, and inhumanity of slavery in the United States and the 13 American colonies between 1619 and

1865 and to establish a commission to study and consider a national apology and proposal for reparations for the institution of slavery, its subsequent de jure and de facto racial and economic discrimination against African Americans, and the impact of these forces on living African Americans, and to make recommendations to the Congress on appropriate remedies, and for other purposes.

In April 2021, the Judiciary Committee of the House recommended it being out of Committee for a full vote. To date (November 2021), nothing further has been reported.
Far less well-known is the historical petition presented to the United Nations in 1951 by the American Civil Rights Congress (CRC) entitled "We Charge Genocide: The Crime of the [US] Government Against the Negro People". It was, ultimately, rejected by its Human Rights Commission, then headed by Eleanor Roosevelt, widow of Franklin Delano Roosevelt, 32nd President of the US. See Steven Leonard Jacobs (2017), "'We Charge Genocide': A Historical Petition All but Forgotten and Unknown", in Scott W. Murray, ed., *Understanding Atrocities: Remembering, Representing, and Teaching Genocide* (Calgary: University of Calgary Press), 125–143. Comparing the cases of Japanese Americans and African Americans, see Rhoda Howard-Hassmann (2004), "Getting to Reparations: Japanese Americans and African Americans", *Social Forces*, 83(2): 823–840.

38 Under the chair of Professor Henry C. Theriault, Worcester College, MA, Armenian Genocide Reparations Study Group in 2015 produced its comprehensive Report, *Resolution with Justice: Reparations for the Armenian Genocide*. To date (November 2021), there appears to be no movement whatsoever publicly acknowledged regarding the Report or significant conversations between the Turkish and Armenian governments regarding reparations, the initial acknowledgment on the part of the Turks would be affirming the murders of more than 1,000,000 Armenians was, indeed and in truth, a genocide. See, also, Henry C. Theriault (2014), "Legal Avenues for Armenian Genocide Reparations", *International Criminal Law Review*, 14: 219–231; and Henry C. Theriault (2012), "From Unfair to Shared Burden: The Armenian Genocide's Outstanding Damage and the Complexities of Repair", *Armenian Review*, 53(1–4): 121–166.

39 New Brunswick and London: Rutgers University Press, 2006. See, also, Jacqueline Bhabba, Margareta Matache, and Caroline Elkins, eds., *Time for Reparations: A Global Perspective* (Philadelphia: University of Pennsylvania Press, 2021).

40 Examining many of those realities are Mark Freeman, *Truth Commissions and Procedural Fairness* (Cambridge: Cambridge University Press, 2006); Priscilla B. Hayner, *Unspeakable Truths: Transitional Justice and the Challenge3 of Truth Commissions* (London and New York: Routledge, 2010); and Robert I. Rothberg and Dennis Tompson, *Truth V. Justice: The Morality of Truth Commissions* (Princeton and Oxford: Princeton University Press, 2000).

41 Arguing as well that these various commission reports are of positive benefit to their devastated communities, see Melissa Nobles, *The Politics of Official Apologies* (Cambridge: Cambridge University Press, 2008).

42 See, for example, Sudhir Chandra, ed., *Violence and Non-Violence Across Time: History and Culture* (London and New York: Routledge, 2018); Ira Chernus (2017), "The Role of Religions in Promoting Non-Violence", *Diogenes*, 61(3–4): 46–58; Rachel M. MacNair, *Religions and Nonviolence: The Rise of Effective Advocacy for Peace* (Santa Barbra: Praeger, 2015); and William Stuart Nelson (1959), "The Tradition of Nonviolence and Its Underlying Forces", *The Journal of Religious Thought*, 1(1): 121–136.

43 Tragically, however, the case of the Buddhists in Sri Lanka is a case of genocidal violence. See the work of the late Michael Jerryson, *Buddhist Fury: Religion and Violence in Southern Thailand* (Oxford and New York: Oxford University Press, 2011); and coedited with Mark Juergensmeyer, *Buddhist Warfare* (Oxford and New York: Oxford University Press, 2010). Additionally, the ongoing violence in India between Hindus and Muslims as well as the ongoing violence between Jews and Palestinians in Israel denies the life-affirming value of shalom/salaam.

Chapter 12

Conclusion

Bringing It All Together: Religion, Violence, and Genocide

Religion, Violence, and Genocide

Bringing together these seemingly disparate threads of religion, violence, and genocide—as well as biology, geography, climate change, diseases, and other topics addressed throughout this text—this chapter posits that these threads are, in fact, *interrelated*, and, given the "right" (or wrong) set of historical and other factors and opportunities, will result in this criminal atrocity we now label genocide.

Throughout this text, the argument has been—and has been shown convincingly—that religion is a *participating factor* in (almost) all genocides all the way throughout history and contemporarily. Further and importantly, it is *not* argued that religion is the primary, secondary, or even tertiary rationale or legitimation of and for genocide, but, rather, that, in and of itself, it serves, where needed, as a significant factor in genocidal perpetration. Then, too, religion as a contributory factor in genocide has been under-explored by scholars, journalists, and popularizers, perhaps, for personal and/or professional reasons, but more importantly, because, like other academic disciplines, the academic study of religion too has developed its own set of tools and understandings with which to examine, analyze, and compare/contrast its data, but remains largely unknown outside its own fields of inquiry. One unfortunate consequence of this fact is that scholars of religion, including my own sub-field of Judaic Studies, come late if at all to the study and examination of genocide.

To further reemphasize the above: Like all human endeavors, religions are flawed social constructions despite their own self-assertions of accuracy with regard to their supposed interactions with their God or gods, their performative activities (both ritual-ceremonial and moral-ethical), and their deep valuing of their own sacred texts—arguably from their perspective—of transmission (at times through human agents) from the divine to the human. Whether in fact we are inherently "religious" persons due to our physical and/or biological/genetic nature and influenced more or less strongly by environmental factors (history, geography, climate, disease,

DOI: 10.4324/9781003168799-12

societal interactions, etc.) has also been addressed, and all of this bounded by our necessity to "make sense" of our world in order to function and survive in it. As to this last point, the position taken is that we are both "religiously-predisposed" (but not necessarily "divinely-disposed" or God/gods oriented) based on our physical selves and more strongly influenced by outside/external factors—including an innate predisposition toward violence—than, perhaps, we have been heretofore reluctant to recognize. Again, that biblical understanding of "little less than the angels" but subject to "dust and ashes". If, as the previously mentioned late Professor of Philosophy and Theology Alvin J. Reines (1926–2004), Hebrew Union College-Jewish Institute of Religion, Cincinnati, OH, argued that *all* religion is a response to *finitude*—his term—addressing the reality of our demise, then so too, can we not conclude that our violence toward others is our failing attempt to deflect/defray our own inevitable deaths by imposing it upon others, internalizing in the process the false notion/idea of our own seemingly divine invincibility and power and further committing the ultimate sin of *hubris*, to be as and to act as divines in the human sphere.

The violence of which we are capable obviously takes many forms, from the psychological, verbal, and physical directed to perceived weaker individuals and groups, to exclusion and removal from any and all spheres of influence and power of those same individuals and groups, to their ultimate removal by extermination or annihilation in horrifically creative and inventive ways made known to us throughout history. Whether our inflicting these deaths upon others is understood as a defraying/delaying tactic attempting to (falsely) stave off our own demise, done so for personal enjoyment or loyalty and commitment to our groups, or attempting to ensure the survival of the group to which we commit ourselves—not always successfully to be sure—our violent actions and reactions are all-too-often undergirded by those leaders who take great pains to spur us on to that violence—our political, military, economic, and, of course, religiously authoritative figures—who have, throughout history, promoted and encouraged that violence but not always for the noblest of motivations and/or intentions. Unlike others in positions of leadership, however, religious leaders—sometimes (more often the not?) those who see themselves as somehow "tapped" by their God or gods for that mantle of messianic-like responsibility—have, by virtue of their very charismatic personhoods, been able to accomplish so-called (mis-)perceived divine goals through human agency.

In this context, then, genocide—undergirded by religious legitimation—becomes the ultimate negative expression of the fusion of these two initially appearing seemingly different endeavors of the human species. Yet, isolating out the factors by which they are constructed and created, enumerating them early on in this text, has revealed—perhaps for the first time—that they do, indeed, share a set of factors not heretofore commonly acknowledged, and, tragically, far too easily adapted to nefarious and worse ends: the genocidal removal of a given subcommunity and its cultural productivity from the world scene, a removal which can never ultimately be overcome, as Lemkin noted more than half-a-century ago, and which, as a consequence, diminishes our human species and human community. To cite the obvious example: The plethora of the world's religions, including but not limited to the monotheisms of Judaism, Christianity, and Islam, enlarges consciousness of divine-human encounter possibilities, further expands rather than diminishes contacts and conversations among us worldwide, and opens doors to explorations previously only limitedly experienced, both by historical isolations and the tendency of numerically superior groups to discount numerically inferior ones or marginalize or exclude within themselves those persons or smaller groups whose critically negative or challenging ideas and practices are seen as threats to larger group survival and continued dominance, often with devastating results.

In Summation

We began this exploration with a rationale for this text as noted above: that religion as a *participating factor* in genocide is an under-explored arena of examination for a variety of possible reasons. For those (and other) reasons, Chapter 2 summarily presented the complexities involved in studying the topic of "religion" (e.g., the lack of definitional clarity and agreement, the various academic attempts to examine the phenomenon, etc.), and Chapter 3 further expanded that knowledge by looking at those persons and groups who *do* religion. Given the context of this examination, the segue to Chapter 4 about the relationship between religion and violence is both significant and important, and the vast and growing literature surrounding this topic serves as something of a bridge toward looking directly at the ultimate expression of group violence: genocide (Chapter 5) and those persons, individuals, and groups who *do* genocide. Broadening the base somewhat, Chapter 7 further examined the interrelated concepts of both "holy" wars and "religious" wars and their applicability to genocide. Usually not explored but equally relevant as well are the fields of biology (Chapter 8), and geography, climate change, and diseases (Chapter 9), topics not regularly associated with religion, but all of which have been and are historically and contemporarily addressed by the world's religious communities. Chapter 11 offers a series of practical and pragmatic suggestions and possibilities not only to address the cessation of genocide but also how religion itself may very well play an important role in that process. Chapter 8 moves the entire conversation in a new and different direction and opens possible doors for further examination of this nexus between hate, prejudice, stereotyping, and genocide, since both Christianity primarily and Islam to a somewhat lesser degree have both resulted in a violent animus toward Jews and Judaism and continue to do so.

Thus, the title of this text *Religion and Genocide: Changing the Conversation* is indicative of the ongoing need to enlarge the number of seats constantly and regularly at the table when examining genocides, both historically and contemporarily, as well as further emphasizing that *all* possible factors contributing to genocidal behaviors *must* be examined under the harsh glare of the microscope as the first stage of combatting this ongoing scourge of humankind.

Bibliography

Adelman, Howard, and Astri Suhrke, eds. *The Path of Genocide: The Rwanda Crisis from Uganda to Zaire*. New Brunswick and London: Transaction Publishers, 1999.

Adorno, Theodor (2020), "Education after Auschwitz", doi:10.31874/2309-1606-2019-25-2-4.

Akçam, Taner, and Thomas Kühne (2020), "Genocide Studies and the Climate Emergency: A Statement from Fellow Scholars", https://www.clark.edu.

Albanese, Catherine L. *America: Religions and Religion*. Belmont: Wadsworth, 2012. 5th Edition.

Alber, Jan, ed. *The Apocalyptic Dimensions of Climate Change*. Berlin: De Gruyter, 2021.

Alcorda, Catherine A., and Richard Sosa (2005), "Ritual, Emotion, and Sacred Symbols: The Evolution of Religion as an Adaptive Complex", *Human Nature*, 16(4): 323–359.

Alker, Hayward R., Ted Robert Gurr, and Kumar Rupesinghe, eds. *Journey through Conflict: Narratives and Lessons*. Lanham: Rowman & Littlefield, 2001.

Allhouse, Richard (2021), "Are We Genetically Predisposed to Conflict and Violence?", *The National Psychologist*, https://nationalpsychologist.com.

Alvarez, Alex. *Unstable Ground: Climate Change, Conflict, and Genocide*. Lanham: Rowman and Littlefield, 2017.

Anderson, Benedict. *Imagined Communities*. London and New York: Verso, 1991.

Anderson, Gary Clayton. *Ethnic Cleansing and the Indian: The Crime That Should Haunt America*. Norman: University of Oklahoma Press, 2014.

Anderson, Kjell. *Perpetrating Genocide: A Criminological Account*. London and New York: Routledge, 2018.

Anderson, Charles H., and Jurgen Brauer, eds. *Economic Aspects of Genocide, Other Mass Atrocities, and Their Preventions*. Oxford and New York: Oxford University Press, 2016.

Anti-Defamation League (ADL) (2002), "Islamic Anti-Semitism in Historical Perspective", https://www.adl.org.

Ardrey, Robert. *The Territorial Imperative: A Personal Inquiry into the Animal Origins of Property and Nations*. London: Collins, 1967.

Armstrong, Karen. *A History of God: The 4,000 Quest of Judaism, Christianity, and Islam*. New York: Grammercy, 2004.

Armstrong, Karen. *Fields of Blood: Religion and the History of Violence*. New York: Alfred A. Knopf, 2014.
Armstrong, Karen. *Holy Wars: The Crusades and Their Impact on Today's World*. New York: Anchor Books, 2001.
Armstrong, Karen. *The Battle for God: Fundamentalism in Judaism, Christianity, Islam*. New York: Alfred A. Knopf, 2000.
Asch, Solomon (1955), "Opinions and Social Pressure", *Scientific American*, 193(5): 2–9.
Ashkenasy, Hans. *Are We All Nazis?* New York: Lyle Stuart, 1978.
Auerbach, Karen. *Aftermath: Genocide Memory, and History*. Victoria: Monash University, 2015.
Bachman, Jeffrey S., ed. *Cultural Genocide: Law, Politics, and Global Manifestations*. Abingdon and New York: Routledge, 2019.
Bandura, Albert, Dorothea Ross, and Sheila A. Ross (1981), "Transmission of Aggression through Imitation of Aggressive Models", *Journal of Abnormal and Social Psychology*, 63(3): 575–582.
Banton, Michael, ed. *Anthropological Approaches to the Study of Religion*. London and New York: Routledge, 2004.
Barker, Adam, and Emma Battell Lowman (n.d.), "Settler Colonialism", https://globalsocialheory.org.
Barnett, Victoria. *Bystanders: Conscience and Complicity during the Holocaust*. Westport: Praeger, 2000.
Bartrop, Paul R, ed. *Modern Genocide: Analyzing the Controversies and Issues*. Santa Barbara: ABC-CLIO, 2018.
Bauman, Zygmunt. *Modernity and the Holocaust*. Ithaca: Cornell University Press, 1989.
Bellamy, Alex J. *Massacres & Morality: Mass Atrocities in an Age of Civilian Immunity*. Oxford and New York: Oxford University Press, 2012.
Bell-Fialkoff, Andrew (1993), "A Brief History of Ethnic Cleansing", *Foreign Affairs*, 72(3): 110–121.
Bell-Fialkoff, Andrew. *Ethnic Cleansing*. New York: St. Martin's Griffin, 1999.
Bergen, Doris (2001), "German Military Chaplains in World War II and the Dilemma of Legitimacy", *Church History*, 70(2): 232–247.
Berger, Peter. *Rumor of Angels: Modern Society and the Rediscovery of the Supernatural*. New York: Doubleday, 1969.
Berreby, David. *Us and Them: Understanding Your Tribal Mind*. New York: Little, Brown, and Company, 2005.
Bhabba, Jacqueline, Margareta Matache, and Caroline Elkins, eds. *Time for Reparations: A Global Perspective*. Philadelphia: University of Pennsylvania Press, 2021.
Bigabo, Felix, and Angela Jansen (2020), "From Child to Genocide Perpetrator: Narrative Identity Analysis among Genocide Prisoners Incarcerated in Muhanga Prison, Rwanda", *Psychology Research and Management*, 13: 759–774.
Bleacher, Donald W. *The Genocide Debate: Politicians, Academics, and Victims*. New York: Palgrave Macmillan, 2011.
Bloxham, Donald, and A. Dirk Moses, eds. *The Oxford Handbook of Genocide Studies*. Oxford and New York: Oxford University Press, 2010.

Boyd, Robert. *A Different Kind of Animal: How Culture Transformed Our Species*. Princeton and Oxford: Princeton University Press, 2018.

Bramanti, Barbara, Nils Chr. Stenseth, Lars Wallace, and Xu Lei (2016), "Plague: A Disease Which Changed the Path of Human Civilization", in Ruifu Yang, and Andrey Anisimov eds. *Yersina Pestis: Retrospective and Perspective* (Dordrecht: Springer), 1–26.

Breuilly, John, David Cesarani, Siniŝa Maleŝevic, Benjamin Neuberger, and Michael Mann (2006), "Debate on Michael Mann's *The Dark Side of Democracy: Explaining Ethnic Cleansing*", *Nations and Nationalism*, 12(3): 389–411.

Brooks, Rosa. *How Everything Became War and the Military Became Everything: Tales from the Pentagon*. New York: Simon and Schuster, 2016.

Brown, Donald E. *Human Universals*. New York: McGraw-Hill, 1991.

Brown, Francis, S. R. Driver, and Charles A. Briggs. *Brown-Driver-Briggs Hebrew and English Lexicon*. Oxford: Clarendon Press, 1906.

Browning, Christopher. *Ordinary Men: Reserve Police Battalion 101 and the Final Solution in Poland*. New York and London: Harper Perennial, 2017. 2nd Edition.

Brudholm, Thomas, and Thomas Cushman, eds. *The Religious Response to Mass Atrocity: Interdisciplinary Perspectives*. Cambridge: Cambridge University Press, 2009.

Bryant, Michael. *A World History of War Crimes: From Antiquity to the Present*. London and New York: Bloomsbury Academic, 2021.

Buffachi, Vittorio (2005), "Two Concepts of Violence", *Political Science Review*. 3: 193–204.

Buscher, Frank M., and Michael Phayer (1988), "German Catholic Bishops and the Holocaust, 1940–1952", *German Studies Review*, 11(3): 463–485.

Bytwerk, Randall L. (2006), "The Argument for Genocide in Nazi Propaganda", *Quarterly Journal of Speech*, 91(1): 37–61.

Calvert, John. *Sayyid Qutb and the Origins of Radical Islamism*. Oxford and New York: Oxford University Press, 2018.

Campbell, Charlie. *Scapegoat: A History of Blaming Other People*. London and New York: Duckworth Overlook, 2011.

Card, Claudia. *Confronting Evil: Terrorism, Torture, Genocide*. Cambridge: Cambridge University Press, 2010.

Card, Claudia. *The Atrocity Paradigm: A Theory of Evil*. New York and Oxford: Oxford University Press, 2002.

Carlson, John D. (2011), "Religion and Violence; Coming to Terms with Terms", in Andrew Murphy, ed., *The Blackwell Companion to Religion and Violence* (Malden and Oxford: Wiley-Blackwell), 7–22.

Carmichael, Cathy, and Richard C. Macquire, eds. *The Routledge History of Genocide*. New York and London: Routledge, 2013.

Carnahan, Thomas, and Sam McFarland (2007), "Revisiting the Stanford Prison Experiment: Could Participant Self-Selection Have Led to the Cruelty?", *Personality and Social Psychology Bulletin*, 33: 603–614.

Carruth, Cathy. *Unclaimed Experience: Trauma, Narrative, and History*. Baltimore and London: The Johns Hopkins University Press, 1996.

Carter, Erica, James Donald, and Judith Squires, eds. *Space & Place: Theories of Identity and Location*. London: Lawrence and Wishart, 1993.

Cautin, Robin L., and Scott O. Lillienfeld, eds. *The Encyclopedia of Clinical Psychology* New York: Wiley-Blackwell, 2015.

Cavanaugh, William T. *The Myth of Religious Violence: Secular Ideology and the Roots of Modern Conflict.* Oxford and New York: Oxford University Press, 2009.

Chalk, Frank (1999), "Hate Radio in Rwanda", in Howard Adelman and Astri Suhrke, eds., *The Path of Genocide: The Rwanda Crisis from Uganda to Zaire* (New Brunswick and London: Transaction Publishers), 93–110.

Chandra, Sudhir, ed. *Violence and Non-Violence across Time: History and Culture.* London and New York: Routledge, 2018.

Charny, Israel W. *A Democratic Mind: Psychiatry with Fewer Meds and More Soul.* Lanham: Rowman & Littlefield, 2016.

Charny, Israel W., ed. *Encyclopedia of Genocide.* Santa Barbara: ABC-CLIO, 1999.

Charny, Israel W. *Fascism and Democracy in the Human Mind: A Bridge between Mind and Society.* Lincoln: University of Nebraska Press, 2006.

Charny, Israel W. *How Can We Commit the Unthinkable: Genocide, the Human Cancer.* Boulder: Westview Press, 1982.

Charny, Israel W. *Israel's Failed Response to the Armenian Genocide.* Brockton: Academic Studies Press, 2021.

Charny, Israel W. *Psychotherapy for a Democratic Mind: Treating Intimacy, Tragedy, Violence, and Evil.* Lanham: Rowman & Littlefield, 2018.

Charny, Israel W. *The Genocide Contagion: How We Commit and Confront Holocaust and Genocide.* Lanham: Rowman & Littlefield, 2016.

Charny, Israel. *The Widening Circle of Genocide: A Critical Bibliographical Review.* New Brunswick and London: Transaction Publishers, 1994.

Chazen, Robert. *European Jewry and the First Crusade.* Berkeley: University of California Press, 1987.

Chazen, Robert. *God, Humanity, and History: The Hebrew First Crusade Narrative.* Berkeley: University of California Press, 2000.

Chernus, Ira (2017), "The Role of Religions in Promoting Non-Violence", *Diogenes*, 61(3–4): 46–58.

Chirot, Daniel. *Modern Tyrants.* New York: Free Press, 1994.

Clarke, Steven, Russell Powell, and Julian Savlescu, eds. *Religion, Intolerance, and Conflict: A Scientific and Conceptual Investigation.* Oxford and New York: Oxford University Press, 2013.

Claudia Card and Armen T. Marsoobian. *Genocide's Aftermath: Responsibility and Repair.* Oxford: Blackwell Publishing, 2007.

Cohen, Jeremy. *Sanctifying the Name of God: Jewish Martyrs and Jewish Memories of the First Crusade.* Philadelphia: University of Pennsylvania Press, 2004.

Comstock, W. Richard (1984), "Toward Open Definitions of Religion", *Journal of the American Academy of Religion*, 52(3): 499–517.

Conley, Dalton. *The Genomic Factor: What the Social Genomics Revolution Reveals About Ourselves, Our History, and Our Future.* Princeton and Oxford: Princeton University Press, 2017.

Cooper, Allan D. *The Geography of Genocide.* Lanham: University Press of America, 2009.

Cox, Alicia (2017), Settler Colonialism", www.oxfordbibliographiesonline.com.

Cox, Rory (2017), "Expanding the Just War: The Ethics of War in Ancient Egypt", *International Studies Quarterly*, 61: 371–384.

Critchell, Kara, Suzanne C. Knittel, Ugur Umit Ungor, and Emiliano Perra (2017), "Editors' Introduction", *Journal of Perpetrator Research*, 1(1), doi:10.21039/jpr.v1i1.51.

Crownshaw, Richard, Jane Kilby, and Anthony Rowland, eds. *The Future of Memory*. New York and Oxford: Berghahn Books, 2010.

Cubitt, Geoffrey. *History and Memory*. Manchester: Manchester University Press, 2007.

Daily, Robert. *Must There Be Scapegoats? Violence and Redemption in the Bible*. San Franciso: Harper & Row, 1978.

Danielsson, Sarah K. (2009), "Creating Genocidal Space: Geographers and the Discovery of Annihilation, 1890–1933)", *Space and Polity*, 13(1): 55–68.

Davidson, Lawrence. *Cultural Genocide*. New Brunswick and London: Rutgers University Press, 2012.

Davies, James C. (1970), "Violence and Aggression: Innate or Not?", *The Western Political Quarterly*, 23(3): 611–623.

Dawkins, Richard. *The God Delusion*. New York: Mariner Books, 2008.

de Boer, Jelle Zeilinga, and Donald Theodore Sanders. *Earthquakes in Human History*. Princeton and Oxford: Princeton University Press, 2005.

Della Costa, Mariarosa, ed. *Gynocide: Hysterectomy, Capitalist Patriarchy, and Medical Abuse of Women*. Brooklyn: Automedia, 2007.

DeSilva, Jeremy. *First Steps: How Upright Walking Made Us Human*. New York: Harper, 2021.

Dillon, Michelle, ed. *Handbook of the Sociology of Religion*. Cambridge: Cambridge University Press, 2005.

Domarus, Max. *Hitler's Speeches and Proclamations 1932–1945*. Wauconda: Boldhazy-Carducci, 1996–2004.

Douglas, Tom. *Scapegoats: Transferring Blame*. London and New York: Routledge, 1995.

Dunbar-Ortiz, Roxanne. *An Indigenous Peoples' History of the United States*. Boston: Beacon Press, 2015.

Durkheim, Emile. *The Elementary Forms of Religious Life*. New York and Oxford: Oxford University Press, 2008. Translated by Carol Cosman.

Dutton, Donald G. *The Psychology of Genocide, Massacres and Extreme Violence: Why "Normal" People Come to Commit Violence*. Westport and London: Praeger Security International, 2007.

Dworkin, Andrea. *Scapegoat: The Jews, Israel, and Women's Liberation*. New York and London: The Free Press, 2000.

Dwyer, Philip, and Mark S. Micale, eds. *On Violence in History*. New York & Oxford: Berghahn Books, 2020.

Dwyer, Philip, and Mark S. Micale, eds. *The Darker Angels of Our Nature: Refuting the Pinker Theory of History and Violence*. London: Bloomsbury Academic, 2021.

Dwyer, Phillip G., and Lyndall Ryan, eds. *Theatres of Violence: Massacres, Mass Killing, and Atrocity throughout History*. New York and Oxford: Berghahn, 2012.

Eidelberg, Shlomo, ed. & trans. *The Jews and the Crusades: The Hebrew Chronicles of the First and Second Crusades*. Hoboken: KTAV Publishing House, 1996.

Ericksen, Robert. *Theologians under Hitler*. New Haven and London: Yale University Press, 1985.
Evans, Gareth. *The Responsibility to Protect: Ending Mass Atrocity Crimes Once and For All*. Washington: Brookings Institution, 2009.
Fassin, Didier, and Richard Rechtman. *The Empire of Trauma: An Inquiry into the Condition of Victimhood*. Princton and Oxford: Princeton University Press, 2009.
Fein, Helen. *Genocide Watch*. New Haven and London: Yale University Press, 1992.
Fenech, Louis E., and W. H. McLeod. *Historical Dictionary of Sikhism*. Lanham: Rowman & Littlefield, 2014.
Festinger, Leon. *A Theory of Cognitive Dissidence*. Stanford: Stanford University Press, 1957.
Fields, R. Douglas (2016), "Humans Are Genetically Predisposed to Kill Each Other", www.psychologytoday.com.
Fields, R. Douglas. *Why We Snap: Understanding the Rage Circuits in Your Brain*. New York: Dutton, 2016.
Fitzpatrick, Sheila, ed. *Accusatory Practices: Denunciation in Modern European History*. Chicago: The University of Chicago Press, 1997.
Fox, Brian. *The Tribal Imagination: Civilization and the Savage Mind*. Cambridge and London: Harvard University Press, 2011.
Freeman, Mark. *Truth Commissions and Procedural Fairness*. Cambridge: Cambridge University Press, 2006.
Fretheim, Terrence E. (2004), "God and Violence in the Old Testament", *Word & World*, 24(1): 18–29.
Friday, Karl F. *Samurai Warfare and the State in Early Medieval Japan*. London and New York: Routledge, 2004.
Fritsche, Peter. *Germans into Nazis*. Cambridge: Harvard University Press, 1999.
Geertz, Clifford (2004), "Religion as a Cultural System", in Michael Banton, ed., *Anthropological Approaches to the Study of Religion* (London and New York: Routledge), 1–46.
Gellately, Robert. *Hitler's True Believers: How Ordinary People Became Nazis*. Oxford and New York: Oxford University Press, 2020.
"Geographies of Genocide" (2009), *Space and Polity*, 13(1): Special Issue.
Gerdmar, Anders. *Roots of Theological Anti-Semitism: German Biblical Interpretation and the Jews, from Herder and Semler to Kittel and Bultmann*. Leiden and Boston: Brill, 2009.
Gerlach, Christian. *Extremely Violent Societies: Mass Violence in the Twentieth-Century*. Cambridge: Cambridge University Press, 2010.
Girard, René. *The Scapegoat*. Baltimore and London: The Johns Hopkins University Press, 1986. Translated by Yvonne Freccero.
Gitlin, Todd, and Liel Leibovitz. *The Chosen People: America, Israel, and the Ordeals of Divine Election*. New York and London: Simon and Schuster, 2010.
Glick, Leonard (2009), "Religion and Genocide", in Steven Leonard, ed., *Confronting Genocide: Judaism, Christianity, Islam* (Lanham: Lexington Books), 95–118.
Gottesman, McGue (2015), "Behavior Genetics", in Robin L. Cautin, and Scott O. Lillienfeld, eds., *The Encyclopedia of Clinical Psychology* (New York: Wiley-Blackwell), 1–11.

Gould, Kenneth J. *They Got the Blame: The Story of Scapegoats in History.* New York: Association Press, 1944.
Gould, Stephen J. (1978), "Sociobiology: The Art of Storytelling", *New Scientist*, 16(80); 530–533.
Gould, Stephen J. *The Mismeasure of Man.* New York: W. W. Norton and Company, 1996.
Gourevitch, Philip. *We Wish to Inform You that Tomorrow We Will be Killed with Our Families: Stories from Rwanda.* New York: Picador, 1999.
Grabowski, Jan. *The Polish Police: Collaboration in the Holocaust.* Washington: United States Holocaust Memorial Museum, 2016.
Grand, Sue, and Jill Salberg, eds. *Trans-generational Trauma and the Other: Dialogues across History and Difference.* London and New York: Routledge, 2017.
Greenberg, Amy S. *Manifest Destiny and American Territorial Expansion: A Brief History with Documents.* Boston: Bedford/St. Martin's, 2012.
Greene, Joshua. *Moral Tribes: Emotion, Reason, and the Gap between Us and Them.* New York: Penguin Books, 2014.
Guiora, Amos N. *The Crime of Complicity: The Bystander in the Holocaust.* Lanham: Ankerwyke Publishing, 2017.
Guttman, Roy, David Rieff, and Anthony Dworkin, eds. *Crimes of War 2.0: What the Public Should Know.* New York and London: W. W. Norton and Company, 2007. Revised and Updated Edition.
Haas, Peter. *Morality after Auschwitz: The Radical Challenge of the Nazi Ethic.* Philadelphia: Fortress Press, 1988.
Hagen, John, and Winona Raymond-Richmond. *Darfur and the Crime of Genocide.* Cambridge: Cambridge University Press, 2008.
Haim, Sylvia (1955), "Arabic Antisemitic Literature: Some Preliminary Notes", *Jewish Social Studies*, 17(4): 307–312.
Halter, Marek. *Why the Jews? The Need to Scapegoat.* New York: Arcade Publishers, 2020. Translated by Grace McQuillan.
Hammer, Dean. *The God Gene: How Faith is Hardwired into Our Genes.* New York and London: Doubleday, 2004.
Haney, Craig, Curtis Banks, and Philip Zimbardo (1973), "Interpersonal Dynamics in a Simulated Prison", *International Journal of Criminology and Penology*, 1: 69–97.
Harden, Kathryn Paige. *The Genetic Lottery: Why DNA Matters for Social Equality.* Princeton and Oxford: Princeton University Press, 2021.
Harff, Barbara, and Ted Robert Gurr, eds. *Preventing Mass Atrocities: Policies and Practices.* London and New York: Routledge, 2019.
Harris. Sam. *The End of Faith: Religion, Terror, and the Future of Reason.* New York: W. W. Norton & Company, 2004.
Hatamiya, Leslie. *Righting a Wrong: Japanese Americans and the Passage of the Civil Liberties Act of 1988.* Stanford: Stanford University Press 1993.
Hatzfeld, Jean. *Machete Season: Killers in Rwanda Speak.* New York: Picador, 2006. Translated by Linda Coverdale.
Haverkamp, Eva (2009), "Martyrs in Rivalry: The 1096 Jewish Martyrs and the Theban Legion", *Jewish History*, 23: 319–342.
Haverstock, Lauren (2014), "Analysis of the Effectiveness of the Gacaca Court System in Post-Genocide Rwanda", *Global Tides*, 8(4): 1–16.

Hayes, Carlton J. H. *Nationalism: A Religion*. New Brunswick and London: Transaction Publishers, 2016.
Hayner, Priscilla B. *Unspeakable Truths: Transitional Justice and the Challenge of Truth Commissions*. London and New York: Routledge, 2010.
Heidenrich, John G. *How to Prevent Genocide: A Guide for Policy Makers, Scholars, and the Concerned Citizen*. Westport: Praeger, 2001.
Heijmanns, Bastiaan, and Jonathan Mill (2012), "Commentary: The Seven Plagues of Epigenetic Epidemiology", *International Journal of Epidemiology*, 41: 74–78.
Herf, Jeffrey (2005), "The 'Jewish War' Goebbels and the Antisemitic Campaign of the Nazi Propaganda Ministry", *Holocaust and Genocide Studies*, 19(1): 51–80.
Herman, Edward S., and David Peterson. *The Politics of Genocide*. New York: Monthly Review Press, 2010.
Heschel, Susannah. *The Aryan Jesus: Christian Theologians and the Bible in Nazi Germany*. Princeton and Oxford: Princeton University Press, 2008.
Hilberg, Raul. *Perpetrators, Victims, Bystanders*. New York: Harper Perennial, 1993.
Hill, Kenneth. *Humanitarian Crises, Population Displacement, and Fertility: A Review of the Evidence*. Washington: The Academic Press, 2004.
Hirsch. Herbert. *Anti-Genocide. Building an American Movement to Prevent Genocide*. Westport: Praeger, 2002.
Hitchens, Christopher. *God Is Not Great: How Religion Poisons Everything*. New York: Twelve Books, 2007.
Howard-Hassmann (2004), "Getting to Reparations: Japanese Americans and African Americans", *Social Forces*, 83(2): 823–840.
Hsiang, Solomon M., Kyle C. Meng, and Mark A. Crane (2011), Civil conflicts are associated with the global climate", *Nature*, 476: 438–441.
Hsiang, Solomon M., Marshall Burke, and Edward Miguel (2013), "Quantifying the Influence of Climate and Human Conflict", *Science*, 341(6151), doi:10.11261/science.1235367.
Hudson, Rex. *Who Becomes a Terrorist: The 1999 Government Report on Profiling Terrorists*. Lanham: The Lyons Press, 2002.
Hutchinson, William D., and Hartmut Lehmann, eds. *Many Are Chosen: Divine Election and Western Nationalism*. Harrisburg: Trinity Press International, 1994.
Inazumi, Mitsue. *Universal Jurisdiction in Modern International Law: Expansion of National Jurisdiction for Prosecuting Serious Crimes under International Law*. Cambridge: Intersentia Publishing Ltd, 2005.
IPCC [Intergovernmental Panel on Climate Change] (2021), "Climate Change 2021: The Physical Science Basis—Summary for Policymakers", Working Group I contribution to the Sixth Assessment Report of the Intergovernmental Panel on Climate Change.
Isenberg, Andrew C., and Thomas Richards, Jr. (2017), "Alternative Wests: Rethinking Manifest Destiny", *Pacific Historical Review*, 86(1): 4–17.
Jackman, Mary (2001), "License to Kill: Violence and Legitimacy in Expropriative Social Relations", in John T. Jost and Brenda Major, eds. *The Psychology of Legitimacy: Emerging Perspectives on Ideology, Justice and Intergroup Relations* (Cambridge: Cambridge University Press), 437–467.
Jacobs, Janet. *Memorializing the Holocaust: Gender, Genocide, and Collective Memory*. London and New York: I. B. Tauris, 2010.

Jacobs, Steven Leonard (2006), "Acts of a Vengeful God? The Flood, Hurricanes, Tsunamis, Holocaust, and Genocide", *Bulletin of the Council or the Scientific Study of Religion* (CSSR), 35(3): 62–65.

Jacobs, Steven Leonard. *Antisemitism: Exploring the Issues.* Santa Barbara: ABC-CLIO, 2020.

Jacobs, Steven Leonard, ed. *Confronting Genocide: Judaism, Christianity, Islam.* Lanham: Lexington Books, 2009.

Jacobs, Steven Leonard (2020), "Crusades", in Steven Leonard Jacobs, *Antisemitism: Exploring the Issues* (Santa Barbara: ABC-CLIO), 29–32.

Jacobs, Steven Leonard (2011), "Franklin H. Littell's and Israel W. Charny's Early Warning Systems", *Journal of Ecumenical Studies*, 46(4): 599–608.

Jacobs, Steven Leonard (2010), "Genocidal Religion", *Journal of Hate Studies*, 9(1): 221–235.

Jacobs, Steven Leonard (2010), "Holocaust or Genocide/Holocaust and Genocide: The Controversy Continues", in Nancy Ruprecht and Wendy Koenig, eds., *Holocaust Persecution: Responses and Consequences* (Cambridge: Cambridge Scholars Press), 213–221.

Jacobs, Steven Leonard (2021), "Holy Wars, Judaism, Violence, and Genocide: An Unholy Quadrinity", in Stephen Smith and Sara Brown, eds., *Routledge Handbook of Religion, Mass Atrocity, and Genocide* (London and New York: Routledge), 37–43.

Jacobs, Steven Leonard (2020), "Judaism", in Michael Jerryson, ed., *Religious Violence Today: Faith and Conflict in the Modern World* (Santa Barbara: ABC-CLIO), 463–546.

Jacobs, Steven Leonard (2005), "Language Death and Revival after Cultural Destruction: Reflections on a Little Discussed Aspect of Genocide", *Journal of Genocide Research*, 7(3): 423–430.

Jacobs, Steven Leonard (2017), "Review of *Fields of Blood: Religion and he History of Violence* by Karen Armstrong, and *Did God Really Commit Genocide? Coming to Grips with the Justice of God* by Paul Coppan and Matthew Flanagan", *Genocide Studies International*, 11(2): 261–266.

Jacobs, Steven Leonard (2009), "Revisiting Hateful Science: The Nazi 'Contributions of the Journey of Antisemitism", *Journal of Hate Studies*, 7(1): 47–75.

Jacobs, Steven Leonard (2005), "The Last Uncomfortable 'Religious' Question: Monotheistic Exclusivism and Textual Superiority in Judaism, Christianity, and Islam as Sources of Hate and Genocide", *Journal of Hate Studies*, 4(1): 133–143.

Jacobs, Steven Leonard (2007), "The Protocols of Hamas", *Reform Judaism*, 26–31.

Jacobs, Steven Leonard, "The Religion Genocide Nexus", in Ben Kiernan, Tracy Lemos, and Tristan Taylor, eds., *The Cambridge World History of Genocide* (Cambridge: Cambridge University Press), forthcoming; December 2022.

Jacobs, Steven Leonard (2017), "'We Charge Genocide': A Historical Petition All but Forgotten and Unknown", in Scott W. Murray, ed., *Understanding Atrocities: Remembering, Representing, and Teaching Genocide* (Calgary: Calgary University Press,), 125–143.

Jacobs, Steven, and Mark Weitzman. *Dismantling the Big Lie: The Protocols of the Elders of Zion.* Los Angeles and Jersey City: Simon Wiesenthal Center and KTAV Publishing House, 2003.

Jadad, Alexjandro R., and Murray W. Erkin (2017), "Does humanity need palliative care?", *European Journal of Palliative Care*, 24(3): 102–103.

Jensen, Olaf, and Claus-Christian W. Szewjanmann, eds. *Ordinary People as Mass Murderers: Perpetrators in Comparative Perspective*. New York: Palgrave Macmillan, 2008.

Jerryson, Michael. *Buddhist Fury: Religion and Violence in Southern Thailand*. Oxford and New York: Oxford University Press, 2011.

Jerryson, Michael (2021), "Religious Violence as Emergency Mindset", *Journal of Religious Violence*, doi:10.5840/jrv2021-4684.

Jerryson, Michael, and Mark Juegensmeyer, eds. *Buddhist Warfare*. Oxford and New York: Oxford University Press, 2010.

Jikeli, Gunther, ed. *The Return of Religious Antisemitism*. Cham: Mdpi AG, 2021.

Jost, John T., and Brenda Major, eds. *The Psychology of Legitimacy: Emerging Perspectives on Ideology, Justice and Intergroup Relations*, Cambridge: Cambridge University Press, 2001.

Kakel, Carroll P. III. *The American West and the Nazi East: A Comparative and Interpretive Perspective*. New York: Palgrave Macmillan, 2011.

Kamen, Henry. *The Spanish Inquisition: A Historical Revision*. New Haven and London: Yale University Press, 2014.

Kaplan, Thomas Pegelow, Jürgen Matthäus, and Mark W. Hornburg, eds. *Beyond 'Ordinary Men': Christopher Browning and Holocaust Historiography*. Leiden: Ferdinand Schöningh/Brill, 2019.

Kaufman, Eric. *Shall the Religious Inherit the Earth: Demography and Politics in the Twenty-First Century*. London: Profile Books, 2010.

Kay, Alex J. and David Stahel (2020), "Crimes of the Wehrmacht: A Re-evaluation", *Journal of Perpetrator Research*, 3(1): 95–127.

Kedar, Benjamin Z. (1998), "Crusade Historians and the Massacres of 1096", *Jewish History*, 12(2): 11–31.

Kellow, Christine L., and Leslie Stevens (1998), "The Role of Hate Radio in the Rwandan Genocide", *Journal of Communications*, 48(3): 107–128.

Kenneally, Christine. *The Invisible History of the Human Race: How DNA and History Shape Our Identities and Our Futures*. New York: Viking, 2014.

Kiel, Robert (2019), "The Looming Accelerant: The Growing Links between Climate Change, Mass Atrocities, and Genocide", www.stimson.org.

Kirsch, Jonathan. *The Grand Inquisitor's Manuel: A History of Terror in the Name of God*. New York: Harper One, 2008.

Klopfer, Peter (1994), "Konrad Lorenz and the National Socialists: On the Politics of Ethnology", *International Journal of Comparative Psychology*, 7(4): 202–208.

Koch, Ariel (2017), "The New Crusaders: Contemporary Extreme Right Symbolism and Rhetoric", *Perspectives on Terrorism*, 11(5): 13–24.

Köchler, Hans. *Humanitarian Intervention in the Context of Modern Power Politics*. Vienna: International Progress Organization, 2001.

Kugler, Tadeusz (2016), "The Demography of Genocide", in Charles H. Anderson, and Jurgen Brauer, eds., *Economic Aspects of Genocide, Other Mass Atrocities, and Their Preventions* (Oxford and New York: Oxford University Press), 102–124.

Kuper, Leo. *Genocide: Its Political Use in the Twentieth Century*. New Haven and London: Yale University Press, 1983.

Kuper, Leo. *International Action against Genocide*. New Haven and London: Yale University Press, 1982.

Kuper, Leo. *The Prevention of Genocide*. New Haven and London: Yale University Press, 1985.

Lacal, Irene, and Rosella Ventura (2018), "Epigenetic Inheritance: Concepts, Mechanisms, and Perspectives", *Frontiers in Molecular Neuroscience*, 11(292), doi:10.3389/Inmol.2018.00292.

Lang, Berel. *Act and Idea in the Nazi Genocide*. Syracuse: Syracuse University Press, 2003.

Lang, Berel. *Genocide: The Act as Idea*. Philadelphia: University of Pennsylvania Press, 2016.

Lemkin, Raphael (1946), "Genocide", *The American Scholar*, 15(2): 227–230.

Lemkin, Raphael. *Axis Rule in Occupied Europe: Laws of Occupation, Analysis of Government, Proposals for Redress*. Washington, DC: Carnegie Endowment for International Peace, 1944.

Lemkin, Raphael (1947), "Genocide as a Crime under International Law", *The American Journal of International Law*, 41(1): 145–151.

Levi, Primo. *The Drowned and the Saved*. New York: Simon and Schuster, 1988. Translated from the Italian by Raymond Rosenthal.

Levinger, Matthew (2009), "Geographical Information Systems Technology for Genocide Prevention: The Case of Darfur", *Space and Polity*, 13(1): 69–76.

Levy, Daniel, and Natan Sznaider. *The Holocaust and Memory in the Global Age*. Philadelphia: Temple University Press, 2016.

Lewy, Guenter. *Perpetrators: The World of the Holocaust Killers*. Oxford and New York: Oxford University Press, 2017.

Lifton, Robert Jay. *The Nazi Doctors: Medical Killing and the Psychology of Genocide*. New York: Basic Books, 1986.

Lorenz, Konrad. *On Aggression*. New York: Harcourt, Brace, & World, 1966. Translated by Marjorie Kerr Wilson.

Lower, Wendy. *Hitler's Furies: Women in the Nazi Killing Fields*. New York: Houghton Mifflin Harcourt, 2011.

Luck, Edward C. (2019), "Roots of Ambivalence: The United Nations, Genocide, and Mass Atrocity Prevention", in Barbara Harff and Ted Robert Gurr, eds., *Preventing Mass Atrocities: Policies and Practices* (London and New York: Routledge), 156–175.

Lynas, Mark, Benjamin Z. Houlton, and Simon Perry (2021), "Greater than 99% Consensus on Human Caused Climate Change in the Peer-Reviewed Scientific Literature", *Environmental Research Letters*, 16: 114005, doi:10.1088/17489326/av2966.

Lyons, Gene M., and Michael Mastanduno, eds. *Beyond Westphalia: National Sovereignty and International Intervention*. Baltimore and London: The Johns Hopkins University Press, 1995.

Maalouf, Amin. *The Crusades through Arab Eyes*. New York: Schocken Books, 1984. Translated by Jon Rothschild.

Mackay, Charles. *Memoirs of Extraordinary Popular Delusions and the Madness of Crowds*. CreateSpace, 2011. Reprint.

Macleod, Saul (2018), "Maslow's hierarchy of needs", https://www.simplypsychology.org/maslow.html.

MacNair, Rachel. *Religions and Nonviolence: The Rise of Effective Advocacy for Peace.* Santa Barbara: Praeger, 2015.

Macquire, Daniel C., and Sa'diyya Shaikh, eds. *Violence against Women in Contemporary World Religions: Roots and Cures.* Cleveland: Pilgrim Press, 2007.

Madsen, Deborah L. *American Exceptionalism.* Jackson: University Press of Mississippi, 1998.

Malkiel, David (2001), "Destruction of Conversion: Intention and Reaction, Crusaders and Jews, in 1096)", *Jewish History*, 15: 257–280.

Mann, Barbara E. *Space and Place in Jewish Studies.* New Brunswick and London: Rutgers University Press, 2012.

Mann, Michael (2000), "Were the Perpetrators of Genocide 'Ordinary Men' or 'Real Nazis'? Results from Fifteen Hundred Biographies", *Holocaust and Genocide Studies*, 14(3): 331–366.

Mann, Michael. *The Dark Side of Democracy: Explaining Ethnic Cleansing.* Cambridge: Cambridge University Press 2004.

McIntosh, Sarah. *Pursuing Justice for Mass Atrocities: A Handbook for Victim Groups.* Washington: United States Holocaust Memorial Museum, 2021.

Memmi, Albert. *Decolonialization and the Decolonized.* Minneapolis: University of Minnesota Press, 2006. Translated by Robert Bonnono.

Memmi, Albert. *The Colonizer and the Colonized.* Boston: Beacon Press, 1991.

Mendlovitz, Saul, and John Fousek (2000), "A UN Constabulary to Enforce Law on Genocide and Crimes Against Humanity", in Reimer, Neal, ed. *Protection against Genocide: Mission Impossible?* (Westport: Greenwood Press), 105–122.

Meyer, Birgit, and Peter van der Meer, eds. *Refugees and Religion: Ethnographic Studies of Global Trajectories.* Oxford and New York: Oxford University Press, 2021.

Michaels, Paula A., and Christine Twomey, eds. *Gender and Trauma since 1900.* London and New York: Bloomsbury Academic, 2021.

Milgram. Stanley. *Obedience to Authority.* New York: Harper Perennial, 2009.

Milson, Menahem (2011), "A European Plot on the Arab Stage: The Protocols of the Elders of Zion in the Arab Media", Inquiry & Analysis Series No. 690, MEMRI [Middle East Media Research Institute]; *Posen Papers in Contemporary Antisemitism*, No. 12, The Vidal Sassoon International Center for the Study of Antisemitism, The Hebrew University of Jerusalem.

Money, Nicholas P. *The Selfish Ape: Human Nature and Our Path to Extinction.* London: Reaktion Books, 2019.

Moore, Jonathan, ed. *Hard Choices: Moral Dilemmas in Humanitarian Intervention.* Lanham: Rowman & Littlefield, 1999.

Morgan, Lewis Henry. *Ancient Society.* Cambridge: Harvard University Press, 2000. Reprint.

Morsink, Johannes. *Inherent Human Rights: Philosophical Roots of the Universal Declaration of Human Rights.* Philadelphia: University of Pennsylvania Press, 2009.

Morsink, Johannes. *The Universal Declaration of Human Rights and the Challenge of Religion.* Columbia: University of Missouri Press, 2017.

Morsink, Johannes. *The Universal Declaration of Human Rights and the Holocaust.* Washington: Georgetown University Press, 2019.

Morsink, Johannes. *The Universal Declaration of Human Rights: Origins, Drafting, & Intent*. Philadelphia: University of Pennsylvania Press, 1999.
Munson, Heny (2005), "Religion and violence: Review article", *Religions*, 35(4), doi: 10.106/j.religion.2005.10.006.
Murphy, Andrew, ed. *The Blackwell Companion to Religion and Violence*. Malden and Oxford: Wiley-Blackwell, 2011.
Murray, Scott W., ed. *Understanding Atrocities: Remembering, Representing, and Teaching Genocide*. Calgary: Calgary University Press, 2017.
Mylonas, Harris, and Scott Radnitz, eds. *Enemies Within: The Global Politics of Fifth Columns*. Oxford and New York: Oxford University Press, 2022.
Naimark, Norman M. *Fires of Hatred: Ethnic Cleansing in Twentieth-Century Europe*. Cambridge and London: Harvard University Press, 2001.
Nathan, Julie (2019), "The Genocidal Propensity of Antisemitism", www.abc.net.au.
Neier, Aryeh. *War Crimes, Brutality, Genocide, Terror, and the Struggle for Justice*. New York: Random House, 1998.
Nelson, Cary (2021), "Annotated Timeline of Jewish-Christian Relations and the History of Anti-Semitism", in Cary Nelson, and Michael C. Gizzi, eds. *Peace and Faith: Christian Churches and the Israeli-Palestinian Conflict* (Philadelphia and Boston: Academic Studies Press), 491–529.
Nelson, Cary, and Michael C. Gizzi, eds. *Peace and Faith: Christian Churches and the Israeli-Palestinian Conflict*. Philadelphia and Boston: Academic Studies Press, 2021.
Nelson, Diane M. *Who Counts? The Mathematics of Death and Life after Genocide*. Durham and London: Duke University Press, 2015.
Nelson, John K. (1990), "The Anthropology of Religion: A Field Statement for the Department of Anthropology, University of California, Berkeley, CA".
Nelson, Lynn H. (n.d.), "Lectures in Medieval History: The Great Famine (1315–1317) and the Black Death (1346–1351)", https://www.vlib.us/medieval/lectures/black_death.html.
Nelson, William Stuart (1959), "The Tradition of Nonviolence and Its Underlying Forces", *The Journal of Religious Thought*, 1(1): 121–136.
Nesler, Eric J. (2016), "Transgenerational Epigenetic Contributions to Stress Response: Fact or Fiction?", *PLOS Biology*, 14(3), doi:10.1371/journal.pbio.1002426.
Nettler, Ronald L. *Past Trials and Tribulations: A Muslim Fundamentalist's View of the Jews*. London: Pergamon, 1987.
Nirenberg, David. *Anti-Judaism: The Western Tradition*. New York and London: W. W. Norton and Company, 2013.
Nobles, Melissa. *The Politics of Unofficial Apologies*. Cambridge: Cambridge University Press 2008.
Norenzayan, Ara, and Steven J. Heine (2005), "Psychological Universals: What They Are and How Can We Know?", *Psychological Bulletin*, 131(5): 763–784.
Novic, Elisa. *The Concept of Cultural Genocide: An International Law Perspective*. Oxford and New York: Oxford University Press, 2016.
Nye, Mallory. *Religion: The Basics*. London and New York: Routledge, 2008.
O'Donnel, Cian (2015), "Rewriting the Just War Tradition: Just War in Classical Greek Political Thought and Practice", *International Studies Quarterly*, 59: 1–10.

O'Sullivan, John L. (1845), "Annexation in the Democratic Review", www.let.rug.nl/essay/1801-1900/manifest-destiny/manifest-destiny-the-philosophy-thatg-created-a-nation-php.

Pals, Daniel. *Seven Theories of Religion.* Cambridge: Harvard University Press, 1996.

Panofsky, Aaron. *Misbehaving Science: Controversy and the Development of Behavior Genetics.* Chicago and London: The University of Chicago Press, 2014.

Parenti, Christian. *Tropic of Chaos: Climate Change and the New Geography of Violence.* New York: Nation Books, 2011.

Peoples, Hervey C., Pavel Duda, and Frank W. Marlowe (2016), "Hunter-Gatherers and the Origin of Religion", *Human Naure*, 27: 261–282, doi:10.1007/s12110-016-9260-0.

Perera, Sylvia Brinton. *The Scapegoat Complex: Toward a Mythology of Shadow and Guilt.* Toronto: Inner City Books, 1986.

Personal Justice Denied: Report on the Commission on Wartime Reconciliation and Interment of Civilians. Seattle: University of Washington Press, 1997.

Piketty, Thomas. *Capitalism in the Twenty-First Century.* Cambridge and London: Harvard University Press, 2014. Translated by Arthur Goldhammer.

Piketty, Thomas. *The Economics of Inequality.* Cambridge and London: Harvard University Press, 2015. Translated by Arthur Goldhammer.

Pinker, Steven. *The Better Angels of Our Nature: Why Violence Has Declined.* New York: Viking, 2013.

Pinker, Steven. *The Blank Slate.* New York: Viking, 2002.

Plomin, Robert, John C. DeFries, Valerie S. Knopnik, and Jeanae M. Neiderhiser (2016), "Top 10 Replicated [Conclusions] from Behavioral Genetics", *Perspectives on Psychological Science*, 11(1): 3–23.

Plomin, Robert. *Blueprint: How DNA Makes Us Who We Are.* Cambridge: The MIT Press, 2019.

Powell, Christopher. *Barbaric Civilization: A Critical Sociology of Genocide.* Montreal and London: McGill-Queen's University Press, 2012.

Power, Samantha. *"A Problem from Hell": America in an Age of Genocide.* New York: Basic Books, 2013.

Randall, Amy E., ed. *Genocide and Gender in the Twentieth Century: A Comparative Survey.* London and New York: Bloomsbury Academic, 2015.

Rappaport, Roy A. (1971), "The Sacred in Human Evolution", *Annual Review of Ecology and Systematics*, 2: 23–44.

Reimer, Neal, ed. *Protection against Genocide: Mission Impossible?* Westport: Greenwood Press, 2000.

Richerson, Peter J., and Robert Boyd. *Not by Genes Alone: How Culture Transformed Human Evolution.* Chicago and London: The University of Chicago Press, 2005.

Richter, Elihu, and Alex Barnea (2009), "Tehran's Genocidal Incitement against Israel", www.meforum.org/2167/irna-genocidal-incitement-israel.

Ring, Nancy C., Kathleen S. Nash, Mary N. MacDonald, Fred Glennon, and Jennifer S. Glancy. *Introduction to the Study of Religion.* Maryknoll: Orbis Books, 2012.

Robbins, Thomas (1997), "Religious Movements and Violence: A Friendly Critique: *Nova Religio: The Journal of Alternative and Emergent Religions*, 1(1): 13–29.

Rock, Irvin, ed. *The Legacy of Solomon Asch: Essays in Cognition and Social Psychology.* London and New York: Routledge, 2016.

Rogers, Damien. *Law, Politics, and the Limits of Prosecuting Mass Atrocity.* New York: Palgrave Macmillan, 2017.
Rosenberg, Sheri P., Tibi Galis, and Alex Zucker, eds. *Reconstructing Atrocity Prevention.* Cambridge: Cambridge University Press, 2015.
Roth, John K. *Sources of Holocaust Insight: Learning and Teaching About the Genocide.* Cascade: Wipf and Stock, 2020.
Roth, John K. *The Failure of Ethics: Confronting the Holocaust, Genocide and Other Mass Atrocities.* Oxford and New York: Oxford University Press, 2015.
Roth, John K., and Carol Rittner, eds. *Teaching about Rape in War and Genocide.* New York: Palgrave Macmillan, 2016.
Roth, Norman (1994), "Bishops and Jews in the Middle Ages", *The Catholic Historical Review,* LXXX (1): 1–17.
Rothberg, Robert I. *Mass Atrocity Crimes: Preventing Future Outrages.* Washington: Brookings Institution Press, 2010.
Rothberg, Robert I., and Dennis Tompson. *Truth V. Justice: The Morality of Truth Commissions.* Princeton and Oxford: Princeton University Press, 2000.
Rummel, Rudolf J. *Death by Government.* New Brunswick and London: Transaction Publishers, 1999.
Rummel, Rudolf J. *Power Kills: Democracy as a Method of Nonviolence.* New Brunswick and London: Transaction Publishers, 2002.
Rummel, Rudolf J. *Statistics of Democide: Genocide and Mass Murder Since 1900.* Berlin: LIT Verlag, 2003.
Ruprecht, Nancy, and Wendy Koenig, eds., *Holocaust Persecution: Responses and Consequences.* Cambridge: Cambridge Scholars Press, 2010.
Russell, Jeffrey Burton. *Exposing Myths about Christianity.* Downer's Grove: InterVarsity Press, 2012.
Samuels, David (2014), "Do Jews Carry Trauma in Our Genes: A Conversation with Rachel Yehuda", www.tabletmag.com.
Sanders, Doug. "*The Genocide Test – A Mass Killer's Best Friend.*" Toronto: Globe and Mail, 2005.
Sandmel, David Fox (2021), "Preface to a Timeline: A Brief History of Anti-Semitism", in Cary Nelson, and Michael C. Gizzi, eds., *Peace and Faith: Christian Churches and the Israeli-Palestinian Conflict* (Philadelphia and Boston: Academic Studies Press), 482–490.
Sandmel, David Fox (2021), "The Kairos Document: Anti-Semitism and BDS", in Cary Nelson, and Michael C. Gizzi, eds., *Peace and Faith: Christian Churches and the Israeli-Palestinian Conflict* (Philadelphia and Boston: Academic Studies Press), 277–295.
Sax, Boria (1997), "What is a 'Jewish Dog'? Konrad Lorenz and the Cult of Wildness", *Society and Animals,* 5(1): 3–21.
Scheffer, David (2006), "Genocide and Atrocity Crimes", *Genocide Studies and Prevention,* 1(3): 229–250.
Scheidel, Walter. *The Great Leveler: Violence and the History of Inequality from the Stone Age to the Twenty-First Century.* Princeton and Oxford: Princeton University Press, 2017.
Schreffran, Jürgen, Michael Brzoka, Hans Günger Brauch, Peter Michael Link, and Janpeter Schilling, eds. *Climate Change, Human Security, and Violent Conflict.* Heidelberg, London, and New York: Springer, 2012.

Scranton, Roy. *Learning to Die in the Anthropocene: Reflections on the End of Civilization*. San Francisco: City Lights Publishers, 2015.

Scranton, Roy. *We're Doomed: Essays on War and Climate Change*. New York: Soho Press, 2018.

Semelin, Jacques. *Purify and Destroy: The Political Uses of Massacre and Genocide*. New York: Columbia University Press, 2007. Translated by Cynthia Schoch.

Semple, Ellen Churchill (1908), "Geographical Location as a Factor in History", *Bulletin of the American Geographical Society*, XL (2): 65–81.

Seybolt, Taylor B. *Counting Civilian Casualties: An Introduction to Recording and Estimating Nonmilitary Deaths in Conflict*. Oxford and New York: Oxford University Press, 2013.

Sherif, Muzafer (1956), "Experiment in Group Conflict", *Scientific American*, 195(5): 54–59.

Sherif, Muzafer, O. J. Harvey, Jack White, William R. Hood, and Carolyn W. Sherif. *The Robbers Cave Experiment: Intergroup Conflict and Cooperation*. Middletown: Wesleyan University Press, 1954.

Shoemaker, Nancy (2015), "A Typology of Colonialism", www.historians.org.

Silvestri, Sara, and James Mayal (2015), "The Role of Religion in Conflict and Peace-Building", *The British Academy for the Humanities and Social Sciences*, https://www.britishacademy.ac.uk.

Singer, Peter (2011), "Is Violence History?", https://www.nytimes.com.

Slim, Hugo. *Killing Civilians: Method, Madness, and Morality in War*. Oxford and New York: Oxford University Press, 2007.

Smart, Ninian. *Dimensions of the Sacred: A History of the World's Beliefs*. Berkeley: University of California Press, 1999.

Smart, Ninian. *The Religious Experience*. New York: Pearson, 1996. 5th Edition.

Smart, Ninian. *The Religious Experience of Mankind*. New York: Charles C. Scribner's Sons, 1976. 2nd Edition.

Smeulers, Alette, Maartje Weerdesteijn, and Barbara Hola, eds. *Perpetrators of International Crimes: Theories, Methods, and Evidence*. Oxford and New York: Oxford University Press, 2008.

Smith, Anthony D. *Chosen Peoples: Sacred Sources of National Identity*. Oxford and New York: Oxford University Press, 2003.

Smith, Blake (2021), "Is Being Essentially Jewish? The Poet Benjamin Fondane [1896–1944] Sought to Hold God Accountable for a Confusing, Alienating World", *Tablet Magazine*, www.tabletmag.com/sections/argts-letters/is-being-essentially-jewish.

Smith, Jonathan Riley (2000), "Rethinking the Crusades", *First Things*, www.firstthings.com.

Smith, Jonathan Z. *Imagining Religion: From Babylon to Jonestown*. Chicago and London: The University of Chicago Press, 1982.

Snowden, Frank M. *Epidemics and Society: From the Black Death to the Present*. New Haven and London: Yale University Press, 2009.

Spoerl, Joseph S. (2020), "Parallels between Nazi and Islamist Anti-Semitism", *Jewish Political Science Review*, 31(1/2): 210–244.

Staub, Ervin. *Overcoming Evil: Genocide, Violent Conflict, and Terrorism*. Oxford and New York: Oxford University Press, 2013.

Staub, Ervin. *The Roots of Goodness and Resistance to Evil*. New York and Oxford: Oxford University Press, 2016.
Steftja, Izabela, and Jessica Trisko Darden. *Women as War Criminals: Gender, Agency, and Justice*. Stanford: Stanford University Press, 2020.
Steigmannn-Gall, Richard. *The Holy Reich: Nazi Conceptions of Christianity, 1919–1945*. Cambridge: Cambridge University Press, 2003.
Stephanson, Anders. *Manifest Destiny: American Expansion and the Empire of Right*. New York: Hill and Wang, 1995.
Stier, Baruch. *Committed to Memory: Cultural Meditations on the Holocaust*. Amherst: University of Massachusetts Press, 2003.
Stone, Dan, ed. *The Historiography of Genocide*. New York: Palgrave Macmillan, 2008.
Strange, Deryn, and Melanie K. T. Takarangi (2015), "Memory Distortion for Traumatic Events: The Role of Mental Imagery", *Frontiers in Psychiatry*, 6(27): 1–4.
Straus, Scot (2005), "Darfur and the Genocide Debate", *Foreign Affairs*, 84(1): 123–133.
Subin, Anna Della. *Accidental Gods: On Men Unwittingly Turned Divine*. New York: Metropolitan Books, 2021.
Sullo, Pietro. *Beyond Genocide: Transitional Justice and Gacaca Courts in Rwanda: The Search for Truth, Justice and Reconciliation*. New York: TMC Press/Spinger, 2018.
Swatos, William H., Jr., ed. *Encyclopedia of Religion and Society*. Walnut Creek: AltaMira Press, 1998.
Tateishi, John. *The Inside Story of the Successful Campaign for Japanese American Reparations*. Berkeley: Heyday Publications, 2020.
Teter, Magda. *Blood Libel: On the Trail of an Antisemitic Myth*. Cambridge and London: Harvard University Press, 2020.
The Voice Bible. Nashville: Ecclesia Bible Society and Thomas Nelson Publishers, 2012.
Theriault, Henry (2012), "From Unfair to Shared Burden: The Armenian Genocide's Outstanding Damage and the Complexities of Repair", *Armenian Review*, 53(1–4): 121–166.
Theriault, Henry (2014), "Legal Avenues for Armenian Genocide Reparations", *International Criminal Law Review*, 14: 219–231.
Thuessen, Peter J. *Tornado God: American Religion and Violent Weather*. Oxford and New York: Oxford University Press, 2020.
Tibi, Bassam (2010), "From Sayyid Qutb to Hamas: The Middle East Conflict and the Islamization of Antisemitism", ISGAP Working Paper, ISBN: 978-0-9819058-8-4.
Titelman, Gregory Y. *Random House Dictionary of Popular Proverbs and Sayings*. New York: Random House, 1996.
Torpey, John. *Making Whole What Has Been Smashed: On Reparations Politics*. New Brunswick and London: Rutgers University Press, 2017.
Torrey, E. Fuller. *Evolving Brains, Emerging Gods: Early Humans and the Origins of Religion*. New York: Columbia University Press, 2017.
Totten, Samuel, and Henry Theriault. *The United Nations Genocide Convention: An Introduction*. Toronto: University of Toronto Press, 2020.
Totten, Samuel, ed. *Last Lectures on the Prevention and Intervention of Genocide*. London and New York: Routledge, 2018.

Trachtenberg, Joshua. *The Devil and the Jews: The Medieval Conception of the Jew and Its Relation to Modern Anti-Semitism*. Philadelphia: The Jewish Publication Society of America, 2002. Reprint.

Tumblety, Joan, ed. *Memory and History: Understanding Memory as Source and Subject*. New York and London: Routledge, 2013.

Usbeck, Frank. *Fellow Tribesman: The Image of the Native Americans, National Identity, and Nazi Ideology in Germany*. New York and Oxford: Berghahn Books, 2015.

Valentino, Benjamin. *Final Solutions: Mass Killing and Genocide in the 20th Century*. Ithaca and London: Cornell University Press, 2004.

Wade, Nicholas. *The Faith Instinct: How Religion Evolved & Why It Endures*. New York: The Penguin Press, 2009.

Waller, James. *Becoming Evil: How Ordinary People Commit Genocide and Mass Killing*. Oxford and New York: Oxford University Press, 2007. 2nd Edition.

Warren, Mary Ann. *Gendercide: The Implications of Sex Selection*. Lanham: Rowman & Allen, 1985.

Weikart, Richard. *Hitler's Religion: The Twisted Belief That Drove the Third Reich*. Washington: Regnery History, 2015.

Weinberg, Albert K. *Manifest Destiny: A Study of Nationalist Expansionism in American History*. Chicago: Quadrangle Books, 1935.

Wellman, James K., and Kyoko Tokuno (2004), "Is Religious Violence Inevitable?", *Journal for the Scientific Study of Religion*, 43(1): 291–296.

White, Lynn (1967), "The Historic Roots of our Ecological Crisis", *Science*, 155: 1203–1207.

Whitlock, Flint. *The Beasts of Buchenwald: Karl & Ilse Koch, Human-Skin Lampshades, and the War Crimes Trial of the Century*. Brule: Cable Publishing, 2011.

Wilson, E. O. *On Human Nature*. Cambridge and London: Harvard University Press, 1978.

Wilson, E. O. *Sociobiology: The New Synthesis*. Cambridge and London: Harvard University Press, 2000. Twenty-Fifth Anniversary Edition.

Winchester, Simon. *Land: How the Hunger for Ownership Shaped the Modern World*. New York: Harper Collins, 2021.

Wolfe, Patrick (2006), "Settler Colonialism and the Elimination of the Native", *Journal of Genocide Research*, 8(4): 387–409.

Wolfe, Stefan. *Ethnic Conflict: A Global Perspective*. Oxford and New York: Oxford University Press, 2006.

Yang, Ruifu, and Andrey Anisimov eds. *Yersina pestis: Retrospective and Perspective*. Dordrecht: Springer, 2016.

Yehouda, Rachel, and Amy Lehner (2018), "Intergenerational Transmission of Trauma Effects: Putative Role of Epigenetic Mechanisms", *World Psychiatry*, 17(3): 243–257.

Zimbardo, Philip. *The Lucifer Effect: Understanding How Good People Turn Evil*. New York: Random House, 2008.

Zimmerer, Jürgen, ed. *Climate Change and Genocide: Environmental Violence in the 21st Century*. London and New York: Routledge, 2015.

Zographos, Markos (2021), "Genocidal Antisemitism: A Core Ideology of the Muslim Brotherhood", ISGAP (The Institute for the Study of Global Antisemitism and Policy), Occasional Papers No. 4.

Appendix

Convention on the Prevention and Punishment of the Crime of Genocide

Approved and proposed for signature and ratification or accession by General Assembly resolution 260 A (III) of 9 December 1948 Entry into force: 12 January 1951, in accordance with article XIII

The Contracting Parties,

Having considered the declaration made by the General Assembly of the United Nations in its resolution 96 (I) dated 11 December 1946 that genocide is a crime under international law, contrary to the spirit and aims of the United Nations and condemned by the civilized world,

Recognizing that at all periods of history genocide has inflicted great losses on humanity, and

Being convinced that, in order to liberate mankind from such an odious scourge, international co-operation is required,

Hereby agree as hereinafter provided:

Article I

The Contracting Parties confirm that genocide, whether committed in time of peace or in time of war, is a crime under international law which they undertake to prevent and to punish.

Article II

In the present Convention, genocide means any of the following acts committed with intent to destroy, in whole or in part, a national, ethnical, racial or religious group, as such:

a Killing members of the group;
b Causing serious bodily or mental harm to members of the group;
c Deliberately inflicting on the group conditions of life calculated to bring about its physical destruction in whole or in part;
d Imposing measures intended to prevent births within the group;
e Forcibly transferring children of the group to another group.

Article III

The following acts shall be punishable:

a   Genocide;
b   Conspiracy to commit genocide;
c   Direct and public incitement to commit genocide;
d   Attempt to commit genocide;
e   Complicity in genocide.

Article IV

Persons committing genocide or any of the other acts enumerated in article III shall be punished, whether they are constitutionally responsible rulers, public officials or private individuals.

Article V

The Contracting Parties undertake to enact, in accordance with their respective Constitutions, the necessary legislation to give effect to the provisions of the present Convention, and, in particular, to provide effective penalties for persons guilty of genocide or any of the other acts enumerated in article III.

Article VI

Persons charged with genocide or any of the other acts enumerated in article III shall be tried by a competent tribunal of the State in the territory of which the act was committed, or by such international penal tribunal as may have jurisdiction with respect to those Contracting Parties which shall have accepted its jurisdiction.

Article VII

Genocide and the other acts enumerated in article III shall not be considered as political crimes for the purpose of extradition.

   The Contracting Parties pledge themselves in such cases to grant extradition in accordance with their laws and treaties in force.

Article VIII

Any Contracting Party may call upon the competent organs of the United Nations to take such action under the Charter of the United Nations as they consider appropriate for the prevention and suppression of acts of genocide or any of the other acts enumerated in article III.

Article IX

Disputes between the Contracting Parties relating to the interpretation, application or fulfilment of the present Convention, including those relating to the responsibility of a State for genocide or for any of the other acts enumerated in article III, shall be submitted to the International Court of Justice at the request of any of the parties to the dispute.

Article X

The present Convention, of which the Chinese, English, French, Russian and Spanish texts are equally authentic, shall bear the date of 9 December 1948.

Article XI

The present Convention shall be open until 31 December 1949 for signature on behalf of any Member of the United Nations and of any non-member State to which an invitation to sign has been addressed by the General Assembly.

The present Convention shall be ratified, and the instruments of ratification shall be deposited with the Secretary-General of the United Nations.

After 1 January 1950, the present Convention may be acceded to on behalf of any Member of the United Nations and of any non-member State which has received an invitation as aforesaid.

Instruments of accession shall be deposited with the Secretary-General of the United Nations.

Article XII

Any Contracting Party may at any time, by notification addressed to the Secretary-General of the United Nations, extend the application of the present Convention to all or any of the territories for the conduct of whose foreign relations that Contracting Party is responsible.

Article XIII

On the day when the first twenty instruments of ratification or accession have been deposited, the Secretary-General shall draw up a procés-verbal and transmit a copy thereof to each Member of the United Nations and to each of the non-member States contemplated in article XI.

The present Convention shall come into force on the ninetieth day following the date of deposit of the twentieth instrument of ratification or accession.

Any ratification or accession effected subsequent to the latter date shall become effective on the ninetieth day following the deposit of the instrument of ratification or accession.

Article XIV

The present Convention shall remain in effect for a period of ten years as from the date of its coming into force.

It shall thereafter remain in force for successive periods of five years for such Contracting Parties as have not denounced it at least six months before the expiration of the current period.

Denunciation shall be effected by a written notification addressed to the Secretary-General of the United Nations.

Article XV

If, as a result of denunciations, the number of Parties to the present Convention should become less than sixteen, the Convention shall cease to be in force as from the date on which the last of these denunciations shall become effective.

Article XVI

A request for the revision of the present Convention may be made at any time by any Contracting Party by means of a notification in writing addressed to the Secretary-General.

The General Assembly shall decide upon the steps, if any, to be taken in respect of such request.

Article XVII

The Secretary-General of the United Nations shall notify all Members of the United Nations and the non-member States contemplated in article XI of the following:

a   Signatures, ratifications and accessions received in accordance with article XI;
b   Notifications received in accordance with article XII;
c   The date upon which the present Convention comes into force in accordance with article XIII;
d   Denunciations received in accordance with article XIV;
e   The abrogation of the Convention in accordance with article XV;
f   Notifications received in accordance with article XVI.

Article XVIII

The original of the present Convention shall be deposited in the archives of the United Nations.

A certified copy of the Convention shall be transmitted to each Member of the United Nations and to each of the non-member States contemplated in article XI.

Article XIX

The present Convention shall be registered by the Secretary-General of the United Nations on the date of its coming into force.

About the Author

Steven Leonard Jacobs returned to the Department of Religious Studies at the University of Alabama as Associate Professor and Aaron Aronov Endowed Chair of Judaic Studies on January 1, 2001, and received tenure as of August 2004. He was promoted to Full Professor in August 2017. He received his BA from Penn State University; and his BHL, MAHL, DHL, DD, and rabbinic ordination from the Hebrew Union College-Jewish Institute of Religion. A resident of Alabama for four decades, he has taught at Spring Hill College, Mobile; University of Alabama at Birmingham, Birmingham-Southern College, Samford University, Birmingham; the University of Alabama in Huntsville and Calhoun Community College, Huntsville; as well as serving congregations in Birmingham, Mobile, Huntsville, Tuscaloosa, and Dallas, Texas. In 2019, he was honored with the transition to Emeritus Aaron Aronov Endowed Chair of Judaic Studies.

Dr. Jacobs' primary research foci are in biblical studies, translation and interpretation, including the Dead Sea Scrolls; Jewish-Christian relations; and Holocaust and genocide studies.

Index

Note: Page numbers followed by "n" denote endnotes.

Aboriginal Peoples 61
Adorno, Theodor 88
African Americans 151, 154
Age of the Lone Wolf: A Study of Lone Wolf and Leaderless Terrorism 105–106
Akçam, Taner 141
al-Banna, Hassa 103, 113
al-Bashir, Omar 66
Albright, Madeleine K. 160
al-Husseini, Mohammed Amin 80–81
al kiddushat Ha-Shem (the sanctification of the Holy Name of God) 43
al-Qaeda ("The Base") 103, 106, 113
Al-Qaradawi, Yusuf 113
Althaus, Paul 80, 110
Amadinejad, Mahmoud 113
Ambroaster 126
Amnesty International 151
anthropology of religion 22–24
Anti-Genocide Education Task Force 164
antisemitism (social-cultural, political-economic, religious-theological, racial-biological, anti-Zionist/anti-Israel) 110
Armstrong, Karen 36, 40
Asch, Solomon 124
Ashkenasy, Hans 125
Axis Rule in Occupied Europe 1, 46

Baker, Alan 114
Bandura, Albert 124
Bauman, Zygmunt 148
behavioral genetics 125
Biden, Joe 154
Bin Laden, Osama 103, 113
Black Death (Bubonic Plague) 142

blood libel 112
Blut und boden 114
British Academy for the Humanity and Social Sciences 167n21
Brown, Donald E. 119–120
Bush, George W. 66

Calvin, John 126
Carlson, John D. 27n8
Cathar/Albigensian Heresy 102
Cavanaugh, William 36, 40, 41
Charny, Israel 3, 72n27, 151, 160
Chirot, Daniel 85–87
Christian Identity Movement 106
Climate Change 2021—The Physical Science Basis—A Summary for Policymakers 139–141
Cohen, William S. 160
Comstock, W. Richard 12–14
Convention on the Prevention and Punishment of the Crime of Genocide 2, 46, 57–58, 59
core elements (community, doctrines & texts, ethics, myths, relevance, rituals, sacrality, symbolization) 7–9
Cox, Alicia 134–135
Crusades 100, 134
cultural genocide 11n2, 71n11, 126

Davies, James Chowning 117–118
Dawkins, Richard 36
Declaration of the World Islamic Front against the Jews and the Crusaders 103
de Cuellar, Javier Perez 55
Demography 125–126

Draft International Convention on the Prevention and Punishment of the Crime of Anti-Semitism 114
Durkheim, David Émile 12, 15, 36, 41

Early warning systems 72n 21, 73n 22, 151
Eisenhower, Dwight David 144
epigenetics 120–122
ethnic cleansing 61
European Union 152
evolutionary psychology 122–123; Dual Inheritance Theory (DIT) 123
Extraordinary Chamber in the Courts of Cambodia (ECCC) 46, 62–63

Fein, Helen 160
Festinger, Leon 124
Feuerbach, Ludwig 16
Fields, R. Douglas 118–119
First Nations 61
Fish, Stanly 20
Fousek, John 152
Frazer, James George 16
Fretheim, Terrence E. 37
Freud, Sigmund Shlomo 19

Gacaca Courts (*Inkiko Gacaca*, Rwanda) 161–162
Gandhi, Mahatma 163
Geertz, Clifford James 15
gendercide 60
Geneva Conventions 99–100, 102, 148, 153, 154
Genocide, Abortion 59, 60
Geocide, Black 59, 60
Genocide Convention 2, 46, 49, 51, 52, 53, 54, 57, 114, 126, 153
genocide, cultural 60, 126
Genocide Studies and the Climate Emergency: A Statement from Fellow Scholars 141–142
genocide (systematic behaviors, physical destruction, destruction of cultural output, defining, state-sanctioned exercises), definition of 4, 6–7
genocide, white 59, 60
Girard, René 36, 42
Gourevitch, Philip 148
Government Report on Profiling Terrorists 105
Gratian 99
Great Famine 142

Guterres, Antonio 51
Guterres Report (Report on the Prevention of Genocide) 57–59

Hamitic Hypothesis 24
Harris, Sam 36
Heidenrich, John 152
Hirsch, Herbert 152
history of religion 24–25
Hitchens, Christopher 36
Holocaust/*Shoah* 106, 109, 133, 148, 150, 151
Holy Land (*Eretz K'dosha*) 133
homo erectus 34n3
homo genocidosus 32
homo religiosus 31
host desecration 112
Human Rights Watch 151

Inquisitions 100, 102
Institute for the Study and Eradication of Jewish Influence on German Religious Life 110
Institute on the Holocaust and Genocide 3, 74n27
International Court of Justice (ICJ) 46, 62–63
international Covenant on Civil and Political Rights 52
International Criminal Court (ICC) 10, 46, 58, 62–64, 66, 153
International Criminal Tribunal for (the former) Yugoslavia (ICTY) 10, 46, 62, 153
International Criminal Tribunal for Rwanda (ICTR) 10, 46, 62, 153
International Military Tribunal ((IMT) 10, 46, 62–64, 153
Islamic Anti-Semitism in Historical Perspective 112
Islamophobia 114

James, Paul 16
James, William 16
Jerusalem (*al-Quds*) 134
jihad 102–103
Just War Theory 96, 98, 99, 100

Kant, Immanuel 16
Khomeini, Ruhollah Musavi 113
King, Martin Luther, Jr. 163
Kisito, Maria 84
Kittel, Gerhard 82, 110

Kühne, Thomas 141
Kuper, Leo 148–149, 160

lebensraum 134–136
Lemkin, Raphael 1, 46, 52, 60, 126, 148, 153, 154, 173
Liberian Women's Movement for Peace 163
Littell, Franklin 151
Luther, Martin 126

Mackary, Charles 124
Mahabharata 98
Mandaville, Peter 16
Manifest Destiny 61, 134–136
Mann, Michael 78, 91n11
Martineau, Harriet 16
martyrdom 43
Marx, Karl Heinrich 19
Mayal, James 165n2
Memoirs of Extraordinary Popular Delusions and the Madness of Crowds 124; *National Delusions Popular Follies* 124; *Philosophical Delusions* 124
Mendlovitz, Saul 152
Milgram, Stanley 124
milkemet mitzvah/hovah (obligatory war) 96
milkemet reshut (permitted/optional war) 96
Misago, Augustin 84
Money, Nicholas P. 131–132
Morgan, Lewis Henry 24
Mukangango, Gertrude 84
Müller, Johan Heinrich Ludwig 82–83, 110
Munson, Henry 12
Munyeshyaka, Wenceslas 84
Muslim Brotherhood 103, 113

Native Americans 61, 144–145n11, 151, 154
Nawaf-Savafi, Seyyid 113
Nelson, John K. 24
Nelson, Lynn H. 142–143
Neusner, Jacob 20
non-violence (*ahimsa, shalom, salaam*) 162, 163
Ntakirutimana, Elizaphan 84–85
Nye, Mallory 21–22

Original Sin 126
O'Sullivan, John L. 13
Otto, Rudolf 16

Pals, Daniel 18, 20
Parallels between Nazi and Islamic Anti-Semitism 113
participating factors (tribalism, exclusivism, privileged access to the divine, particularistic and parochial readings of sacred texts) 4–6, 9, 11n13, 41, 51, 84, 103, 117, 171, 173
Pechota, Vratislav 152–153
phenomenology of religion 25
philosophy of religion 25
Plomin, Robert 125, 120n35
Pope Pius XII (Eugenio Pacelli) 110
Powell, Christopher 125
Powell, Colin 66
Preventing Genocide: A Blueprint for U.S. Policymakers 160
Promised Land (*Eretz Havtakha*) 133
Protocols of the Learned Elders of Zion 109, 112
psychology of religion 25–26
Pursuing Justice for Mass Atrocities: A Handbook for Victim Groups 167n21

Qutb, Sayyid 103, 113

Ratzel, Friedrich 135
Reagan, Ronald 153
Red Cross International 151
religicide 50
religion (system, communal multi-generational, set of behaviors, attempt to make meaningful sense, system of communications) definition of 4, 6; open definition 12–14
Rennie, Bryan 21
reparations (African Americans, Holocaust/*Shoah*, Japanese Americans) 162, 168n34–169n38
Resolution with Justice: Reparations for the Armenian Genocide 169n38
Responsibility to Protect (R2P) 46, 58, 62–63, 160
ritual murder 112
Robbins, Thomas 38
Ruhashyankiko, Nicodeme 51, 55
Ruhashyankiko Report (Study of the Question of the Prevention and Punishment of the Crime of Genocide) 46, 51–55
Rukundo, Emmanuel 85
Rummel, Rudolph J. 163n 8
Rupesingh, Kumar 151

sacrality 32
sacrifice 43
Saint Augustine 96, 98, 99, 126
Saint Thomas Aquinas 96
Sanders, Doug 154
Schleiermacher, Friedrich 16
Seromba, Althanase 85
settler colonialism 134–135, 144n9
Seville Statement on Violence 120–121
Sherif, Muzafer 124
Silvestri, Sara 165n2
Smart, Ninian 21
Smith, Jonathan Z. 27n12
social psychology 124–125
sociobiology 123–124
sociology of religion 26
Stackhouse, Max Lynn 16
Stanton, Gregory 66
Staub, Erwin 160
Straus, Scott 66
Survival International 151

Ten Stages of Genocide 66–68
terrorism 104–105, 108n15
Thirty Years War 102
Tillich, Paul 16
Tiso, Jozef Gašpar 83
Tokuno, Kyoko 39
Treaty of Westphalia 151–152
Truman, Harry 153
Truth (and Reconciliation) Commissions 162–163
Turner, Brian S. 148

United Farm Workers Movement 163
United Nations Commission on Human Rights 52, 54, 55
United Nations Declaration of Human Rights 155–158
United Nations Declaration on the Elimination of All Forms of Intolerance and Discrimination Based on Religion or Belief 155–158
United Nations Declaration on the Rights of Indigenous Peoples 168n 36
United Nations Declaration on the Rights of Persons Belonging to National or Ethnic, Religious and Linguistic Minorities 155–158
United Nations Framework for Analysis for Atrocity Crimes 58, 64–65, 166n20
United Nations Human Rights Council 58, 104
United Nations International Covenant on Civil and Political Rights 155–158
United Nations International Covenant on Economic Social and Cultural Rights 155–158
United Nations Office on Genocide Prevention 64
United Nations Plan of Action for Religious Leaders and Actors to Prevent Incitement to Violence that Could Lead to Atrocity Crimes 159
United Nations Special Advisor on the Prevention of Genocide 58
United Nations Sub-Committee on the Prevention of Discrimination and Protection of Minorities 55
United Nations University 56
universal anti-genocide curriculum 164
Universal Declaration of Human Rights 52, 70n8

Velvet Underground 163
Vergote, Antoine 16
violence, definitions of 37–38
von Clausewitz, Carl 43–44

Wade, Nicholas 17
Waldensian Heresy 102
Waldheim, Kurt 51
Waller, James 125
Weber, Max 43
Wellman, James K. 39
well poisoning 112
Whaling, Frank 21
When to Refer to a Situation as 'Genocide' 64
Whitaker, Benjamin C. G. 55
Whitaker Report (Revised and Updated Report on the Question of the Prevention and Punishment of the Crime of Genocide) 46, 51, 55–57
World Health Organization 38
World Parliament of Religions 160, 164

Zimbardo, Philip 124
Zionist Occupation Government (ZOG) 59, 114

Printed in the United States
by Baker & Taylor Publisher Services